Synaesthesia

Synaesthesia

Classic and Contemporary Readings

Edited by
Simon Baron-Cohen and
John E. Harrison

First published 1997

2 4 6 8 10 9 7 5 3 1

Blackwell Publishers Ltd
108 Cowley Road
Oxford OX4 1JF
UK

Blackwell Publishers Inc.
238 Main Street
Cambridge, Massachusetts 02142
USA

British Library Cataloguing in Publication Data

A CIP catalogue record for this book is available from the British Library.

Library of Congress Cataloging-in-Publication Data

Synaesthesia: classic and contemporary readings/edited by Simon Baron-Cohen and John E. Harrison.
p. cm.
Includes bibliographical references and index.
ISBN 0–631–19763–X (hardbound: alk. paper). – ISBN 0–631–19764–8 (pbk.: alk. paper)
1. Synesthesia. I. Baron-Cohen, Simon. II. Harrison, John E.
RC394.S93S96 1996
152 – dc20
96-5888
CIP

Typeset in 10.5 on 12pt Palatino
by Best-set Typesetter Ltd, Hong Kong

Printed and bound in Great Britain by Marston Lindsay Ross International Ltd, Oxfordshire

Contents

Figures

Tables

Foreword

An outstanding feature of synaesthesia is its pervasiveness in the mental life of those who have it. Equally characteristic is the synaesthete's lack of curiosity about such a familiar integral part of experience until some event draws attention to its exceptional nature. For Alison Motluk (see chapter 16) it was a discussion with her school English teacher, defending the choice of a character's name (which had to be 'strong, red') in a story, which led to her realization that her way of thinking was unusual. For me, it was attending a seminar given by Dr John Harrison to the Neuro-ophthalmology Club in Queen Square, London. I knew of Galton's piece (helpfully reproduced here together with other historically important documents) but had not explored its implications.

Almost all of the questions – and more – that subsequent introspection and thought have raised are addressed in this book: the range of phenomena, differences and similarities of perception among synaesthetes, incidence, associations of gender and orientation, the anatomical and physiological substrates, and the implications of synaesthesia for theories of consciousness and for painting, literature and music.

The rapid development of neuroscience in the past 20 years means that most of these issues can now be approached experimentally, but the complexity and the range of techniques relevant to the study of synaesthesia is such that few readers will have experience of more than one or two, and many none. Here the reader is helped by the editors through their own chapters (see chapters 1 and 7), and in their encouragement of accessible explanation of the methods used, and by ensuring that controversial ideas are discussed by authors with different points of view.

What emerges is a secure body of knowledge about the phenomenology of synaesthesia and some important insights into mechanism. Questions still abound, but it is easy to see how many should be answered with the powerful new techniques of cognitive neuroscience, including functional imaging, underpinned by the experimental investigation of neural development and its genetic control at the molecular and systems levels.

Ian McDonald PhD, FRCP
Professor of Clinical Neurology, Queen Square, London

Acknowledgements

This book would not exist if Elizabeth Stewart-Jones had not written a very brief letter to *The Psychologist* in August 1986 describing her experience of synaesthesia and offering herself as a subject of research. When one of us (SBC) decided to take this seriously and look into it further, Dr Maria Wyke enthusiastically encouraged this scientific step, and contributed invaluably to the subsequent research. Elizabeth Stewart-Jones proved to be enormously generous with her time and help over the next decade. We take this opportunity to thank both of them here. It has been a fascinating and enjoyable collaboration.

Altered states of mind, or different kinds of perception, should not be scientifically controversial, since it has long been recognized that perception can be influenced by external conditions, ranging from drugs, to context effects, to spectacles. It has also long been known that different species of animal have different kinds of perceptual experience (bats being a particularly well-studied example of this), and that genes can produce altered perception within humans (colour blindness being the paradigm case). It therefore amuses us somewhat that sections of the scientific community have been at times resistant to the genuineness of synaesthesia, and especially to the idea that altered brain-wiring might cause an individual to live in a qualitatively different perceptual world, where every sound *is* a colour. To us, synaesthesia has always been an empirical issue, and we take this opportunity to thank those scientists who have been open-minded enough to look at this phenomenon in an unprejudiced and balanced way.

We owe a special debt of gratitude to some excellent colleagues with whom we have worked over the years: Chris Frith and Steve

Williams have guided our neuroimaging research, and Patrick Bolton has guided our family genetic research in synaesthesia. Laura Goldstein and Jeffrey Gray have also contributed to our thinking on the neuropsychology of synaesthesia. We have also worked with a team of talented undergraduate students: Lucy Burt, Fiona Smith-Laittan, Hannah Loder, Shibley Rahman and Helen Weyland.

Helen Weyland also helped us launch the International Synaesthesia Association (ISA), the first such group for those with the condition. The ISA now has almost 1000 members worldwide, and we are happy to invite neuroscientists who wish to undertake research into synaesthesia to contact us to request access to this large database of subjects. All the members of the ISA are naturally keen to help further research into their condition. Research is needed for its own sake, since very few synaesthetes 'suffer' from synaesthesia in any sense, or would wish to be free of their condition. Rather, they tend to say that it is the rest of us (who lack synaesthesia) who are unfortunate! To them, our experience is so one-dimensional! We thank the members of the ISA and their families for their continued support of, and participation in, research into synaesthesia. We are particularly grateful to Julie Roxburgh, Alison Motluk, Heather Birt and Shelagh Eggo for their help in running the ISA. The ISA can be accessed on the WorldWide Web at the following address: http://nevis.stir.ac.uk/~ldg/synaesl.html.

Our research has been funded by the McDonnell-Pew Foundation, The Gatsby Trust and The Royal Society. Shibley Rahman performed the superhuman task of compiling the index to this book, for which we are indebted. Finally, we thank Bridget Lindley, Rachel McCabe-Harrison, and our families, for innumerable advice, ideas and support.

Simon Baron-Cohen
John E. Harrison
Cambridge

The following material has been previously published elsewhere:

Chapter 2, 'Synaesthesia: phenomenology and neuropsychology', by Richard E. Cytowic,

Chapter 4, 'On colored-hearing synesthesia: cross-modal translations of sensory dimensions', by Lawrence E. Marks.

Contributors

Mark E.S. Bailey
Division of Molecular Genetics, University of Glasgow, Pontecorvo Building, Anderson College, 56 Dumbarton Road, Glasgow GL11 6NU, UK.

Simon Baron-Cohen
Departments of Psychology and Psychiatry, University of Cambridge, Downing Street, Cambridge CB2 2EB, UK.

Pascal Barone
Cerveau et Vision, INSERM U.371, 69675 BRON, France.

Alexandre Batardiere
Cerveau et Vision, INSERM U.371, 69675 BRON, France.

Edmund M.R. Critchley
Department of Neurology, Preston Royal Infirmary, Sharoe Green Lane, Preston, Lancs. PR2 4HT, UK.

Richard E. Cytowic
Capitol Neurology, 1611 Connecticut Avenue, NW Suite 2, Washington, D.C., USA.

Colette Dehay
Cerveau et Vision, INSERM U.371, 69675 BRON, France.

Christopher D. Frith
Wellcome Department of Cognitive Neurology, Institute of Neurology, University of London, Queen Square, London WC1N 3BG, UK.

Jeffrey A. Gray
Department of Psychology, Institute of Psychiatry, University of London, Denmark Hill, London SE5 8AF, UK.

Peter G. Grossenbacher
National Institute of Mental Health, Bethesda, MD 20892, USA.

John E. Harrison
Section of Developmental Psychiatry, University of Cambridge, Douglas House, 18b Trumpington Road, Cambridge CB2 2AH, UK.

Keith J. Johnson
Division of Molecular Genetics, University of Glasgow, Pontecorvo Building, Anderson College, 56 Dumbarton Road, Glasgow GL11 6NU, UK.

Henry Kennedy
Cerveau et Vision, INSERM U.371, 69675 BRON, France.

Daphne Maurer
Department of Psychology, McMaster University, Hamilton, Ontario L8S 4KI, Canada.

Alison Motluk
New Scientist, *King's Reach Tower, Stamford Street, London SE1 9LS, UK.*

Julia Nunn
City University, Northampton Square, London EC1V 8LJ, UK.

Eraldo Paulesu
INB-CNR, Institute H San Raffaele, Via Olgettina 60, 20132 Milan, Italy.

Gabriel M.A. Segal
Philosophy Department, King's College, University of London, The Strand, London WC2R 2LS, UK.

Steven C.R. Williams
Department of Neurology, Institute of Psychiatry, University of London, Denmark Hill, London SE5 8AF, UK.

Part I
Background

1

Synaesthesia: an Introduction

John E. Harrison and Simon Baron-Cohen

Why a book on synaesthesia? We begin with this question because the topic of synaesthesia currently enjoys a controversial reputation, with some scientists dismissing it as an illusion or a contrivance, whilst others perceive it as a genuine natural phenomenon, in need of explanation and with important implications for cognitive neuroscience. Presumably, if you have even read this far, you are at best in the latter category, prepared to take synaesthesia seriously, in scientific terms; or at worst, prepared to be persuaded to do so. Let us try.

We have put together this book precisely because we think there is now sufficient evidence that synaesthesia is both real and amenable to scientific examination. We are sufficiently encouraged by recent developments in this field to lay out the evidence in one volume, in the hope that others may be stimulated to research further into this fascinating condition. First, what is synaesthesia?

We, along with others (Vernon 1930; Marks 1975; Cytowic 1989, 1993; Motluk 1994) define synaesthesia as occurring when stimulation of one sensory modality automatically triggers a perception in a second modality, in the absence of any direct stimulation to this second modality. So, for example, a sound might automatically and instantly trigger the perception of vivid colour; or vice versa. Many combinations of synaesthesia are reported to occur naturally, including sound giving rise to visual percepts ('coloured-hearing') and smell giving rise to tactile sensation, as in Cytowic's (1993) subject MW. Our experience suggests that coloured-hearing synaesthesia is by far the most common form and that certain combinations of synaesthesia almost never occur (for example, touch to hearing). Synaesthesia is also sometimes reported by those who have used hallucinogenic drugs, such as lysergic acid diethylamide (LSD) or mescaline. For the most part, contributors in this book focus on the naturally occurring form of synaesthesia, whilst acknowledging that there may be a connection to be found with the drug-induced form.

1.1 Historical Issues

The earliest reference we have found to synaesthesia is the account given by John Locke (1690) in his *Essay Concerning Human Understanding* in which he recounts the example of

> A studious blind man who had mightily beat his head about a visible object, and made use of the explications of his books and friends, to understand those names of light and colours, which often came his way, betrayed one day that he now understood what scarlet signified. Upon which, his friend demanded what scarlet was? The blind man answered, it was like the sound of a trumpet.

However, it was not until the closing decades of the nineteenth century that synaesthesia gained a hold in the minds of scientists and artists alike. During this period a considerable number of accounts of the condition appeared (including further accounts of blind people who claimed to be able to 'see' colours (Starr 1893), perhaps most notable amongst which was Galton's (1883) *Inquiries into Human Faculty and its Development*. Scientific interest in the condition declined with the rise of behaviourism as the dominant psychological paradigm and very little on the topic appears in the literature from the late 1920s onward. In fact, Marks (1975) reveals in his review of the topic that there were 74 publications in the 50-year period 1881–1931 as compared with a mere 16 in the 42-year period between 1932 and 1974. This was probably because behaviourism banished reference to mental states from scientific language. As synaesthesia could only be defined by self-report and reference to mental states, it was not considered amenable to scientific investigation.

Within the last few years synaesthesia has enjoyed something of a renaissance, with researchers from various disciplines within cognitive neuroscience contributing both new data and theory. Such developments have led, for the first time, to the condition being widely recognized as having a neurological reality, thereby moving it beyond 'romantic neurology' as Humphreys (1990) described it and into the realm of the scientific investigation of human experience. Why this new acceptance of the condition? Objective approaches now available are at least part of the answer.

1.2 Testing for Synaesthesia

Our own attempts at testing for the presence of the condition have relied upon gauging a subject's *consistency* at relating colour descriptions for words across two or more occasions, when the subject has no prior warning of the retest and when the length of interval between testing sessions is irrelevant (Baron-Cohen, Wyke and Binnie 1987; Baron-Cohen, Harrison, Goldstein and Wyke 1993). Using this method consistency is typically as high as 90 per cent, even when retested over years. Cytowic, in contrast, has relied upon a set of diagnostic criteria of 'clinical' symptoms (Cytowic 1989, 1993). The weakness of the latter approach is that it is entirely reliant upon the individual's subjective account of the condition. Medicine has traditionally been uncomfortable with diseases for which no objective diagnostic test exists, especially with disorders in which no physical sign exists to confirm the diagnosis.

Diagnosis on the basis of subjective symptoms rather than objective signs increases the likelihood of 'false positive' cases. This is why in our own experiments we have emphasized the need to establish independently the presence of synaesthesia. We have sought to do this using the consistency test described above, though we are aware of the possible difficulties in relying solely on this. For example, the study of subject EP reported by Baron-Cohen et al. (1987) noted that the colour percept triggered by each word seemed unpredictable on the basis of the colour correspondence for each of the component letters. In contrast, in a later study (Baron-Cohen et al. 1993) the word–colour correspondence was highly dependent upon the colour of the dominant letter within the word. For example, for subject RY the colour for the word SPEAK was found to be 'blue', due to the letter 'S' triggering a blue percept. It would in principle be possible to score 100 per cent on the consistency test by *learning to associate* a colour with each letter of the alphabet and then simply using the first letter of the word to produce the appropriate response. We say 'in principle' because in practice we suspect that this is not what goes on, since our samples include subjects whose synaesthesia is more complex than just this; and since their performance on other associative memory tasks is only ordinary.

However, the advent of neuroimaging techniques such as positron emission tomography (PET) and functional magnetic resonance imaging (fMRI) now provides an opportunity to image the brains of individuals with synaesthesia *in vivo.* Cytowic used the xenon inhalation technique to image the brain of a single subject (Cytowic and Wood 1982) and our own group has used PET (Paulesu et al. 1995; see also chapter 8) and more recently fMRI (shown in chapter 10). Some commentators (Brooks 1993) have suggested that for disease categories (such as Parkinson's disease – PD) in which positive diagnosis has proved difficult (false positive diagnosis in PD was recently reported as running at approximately 25 per cent: Hughes et al. 1992), neuroimaging may allow for more objective diagnosis. Given the marked consistency of patterns of activation in synaesthetes studied in the Paulesu et al. (1995) study, it might ultimately prove possible to determine the presence of synaesthesia objectively using functional brain imaging techniques. A discussion of the neuroimaging data can be found in chapter 8, by Frith and Paulesu.

One of the purposes of this book is to help clarify the nature of synaesthesia and to draw more satisfactory definitions of terms relating to the condition. There has been a tendency to use the term synaesthesia to describe instances in which people discuss a 'mixing of the senses'. In this vague context it seems to us that the use of the word synaesthesia covers at least five very different situations. This produces a hopeless muddle. In the following section we try to draw sharper distinctions by separately discussing the following: (a) developmental synaesthesia; (b) synaesthesia caused by neurological dysfunction; (c) synaethesia as the consequence of psychoactive drug use; (d) metaphor as pseudosynaesthesia; and finally, (e) association as pseudosynaesthesia.

1.2.1 *Developmental synaesthesia*

Use of the word 'idiopathic' in neurology is meant to imply a discrete, natural disease category for which the cause is presumed to be within the biological make-up of the patient, but is currently unknown. For instance, patients may exhibit the clinical signs and symptoms of Parkinsonism as a result of diseases such as Alzheimer's or through drug abuse, but such patients may not necessarily have Parkinson's disease. In contrast, the term idiopathic Parkinson's disease refers to the naturally occurring disease – it is primary rather than being a consequence of some other condition. We adopt the term developmental synaesthesia to refer to idiopathic cases of synaesthesia, to distinguish it from acquired synaesthesia (of which there are at least two forms) and pseudosynaesthesia.

Developmental synaesthesia in most cases has several characteristics: (a) it appears to have a childhood onset, in all cases before four years of age; (b) it is different to hallucination, delusion or other psychotic phenomena; (c) it is reported to be different to imagery arising from imagination; (d) it is not induced by drug use; (e) it is vivid; (f) it is automatic/involuntary; and (g) it is unlearnt. To reiterate, developmental synaesthesia is the target of the research in this book.

1.2.2 *Synaesthesia caused by neurological dysfunction*

A variety of neuropathological conditions have apparently given rise to acquired synaesthesias. Carnaz speculated in 1851 that synaesthesia of all forms was 'pathological and due to some optical lesion' (cited in Krohn 1893: 33) and could therefore be seen as being due to 'hyperaesthesia of the sense of colour'. A rather fuller account of the variety of acquired synaesthesia is given in chapter 7 and in Critchley's contribution (chapter 15) in this volume, but the above examples illustrate, first, that synaesthesia can be acquired, and secondly, that the resultant synaesthesic percepts should be distinguished from the more complex forms seen in developmental synaesthesia.

1.2.3 *Synaesthesia as a consequence of psychoactive drug use*

Whilst neurological factors are one cause of acquired synaesthesia, there are a number of accounts of individuals reporting synaesthesia as a consequence of neurological disorder or as a result of the use of psychoactive drugs. Cytowic (1989) usefully points to a distinction between developmental synaesthesia (that is, naturally occurring) and the forms that appear to be induced by neurological factors or by psychomimetic drug use. The mechanisms by which drug-induced synaesthesia occur are not well understood, though the use of LSD, mescaline (from the Mexican peyote cactus) and psilocin (mostly derived from the fungi of the *Psilocybe* family, but especially *Psilocybe mexicana* and *Stropharia cubensis*) are all reported to cause confusion between the sensory modalities, so that sounds are perceived as visions (Rang and Dale 1987). Neurophysiological studies reported by Aghajanian (1981) have suggested different sites of action for LSD and mescaline, with LSD seeming to work by inhibiting the serotonin-containing neurons of the raph nuclei and mescaline by acting upon the noradrenergic system. Note that drug-induced synaesthesia differs from developmental synaesthesia in several ways: (a) it is often accompanied by hallucinations and loss of reality-monitoring; (b) it is transient; (c) it usually has an onset only in adult life (or whenever the drug was used); and (d) it can produce sensory combinations which do not otherwise occur naturally.

1.2.4 *Metaphor as pseudosynaesthesia*

Almost all writers on the topic of synaesthesia have been drawn into discussion of the possibility that a number of authors, poets, artists and musicians may have had synaesthesia. A typical list of these individuals would include the composers Liszt, Rimsky-Korsakov, Messiaen and Scriabin; the poets Basho, Rimbaud and Baudelaire; the artists Kandinsky and Hockney; and, finally, the novelist Nabokov. Baudelaire's own account is reprinted in chapter 4 of this volume. We are unaware of any evidence that these individuals were tested for synaesthesia and so have no data with which to make a 'diagnosis'.

The amount of information that exists with which to *infer* that any of these individuals had synaesthesia varies substantially. In the case of the Japanese *Haiku* poetry of Basho (1644–94) we have only the interpretation made by Odin (1986) concerning the transitions made in Basho's work from one sense modality to another. For instance, he quotes as 'an intensely synaesthetic experience of nature' the following:

> As the bell tone fades,
> Blossom scents take up the ringing,
> Evening shade.

Odin suggests that 'the reverberating sound of a fading bell tone merges with the fragrant perfume of flower blossom, which in turn blends with the shadowy darkness of evening shade'. The earlier definition we provided of individuals with developmental synaesthesia stressed that auditory stimulation *at once* gives rise to the visual synaesthesic percept. The definition is based on the hundreds of identical descriptions we have collected from individuals around the world who have corresponded with us about their synaesthesia. Therefore, the gradual progression from the ringing of the bell tone to the 'ringing' of blossom scents suggests that Basho is using *metaphor* rather than actually experiencing synaesthesia. This does not necessarily mean that Basho did not have synaesthesia; simply that there is no conclusive evidence either way.

Synaesthesia became a topic of discussion in both literary and scientific circles in middle and late nineteenth-century Europe. As we have seen, Galton devoted to it part of his book *Enquiries into Human Faculty* (see chapter 3 in this volume); and in France, a congress was attended by a group of psychologists who sought to standardize the procedures and terms involved in researching the condition of *audition colorée* (Mendoza 1890). Charles Baudelaire, the poet, essayist and salon art critic, appears to have believed in the unity of sensation, as implied by his poem 'Correspondances'. However, substantial doubt exists over Baudelaire's status as a developmental synaesthete, especially given his account of hashish intoxication. Written in 1857, he suggests that 'sounds are clad in colour', an experience which he later describes as an analogy which 'assumes an unaccustomed vividness' during his use of hashish. This account echoes the French scientist Gautier (1843), who reported that he too had been able to produce artificially 'pseudo sensations of colour', in particular by the use of hashish. Another nineteenth-century French poet, Arthur Rimbaud, also made a link between sound and colour in his 'Le sonnet des voyelles' in which he attributes a colour to each of the vowels: A is black, E is white, I is red, O is blue and U is green. Huysmans, author of the decadent *fin de siècle* novel *par excellence*, imbued his hero, Duc Jean Floressas des Esseintes, with a form of taste sound synaesthesia:

> Each and every liqueur, in his opinion, corresponded in taste with the sound of a particular instrument. Dry curaçao, for instance, was like the clarinet with its piercing, velvety note; kömmel like the oboe with its sonorous, nasal timbre; crême de menthe and anisette like the flute, at once sweet and tart, soft and shrill. (Huysman 1884: 58)

Commentators such as Critchley (1994) see these accounts as evidence of the genuine nature of the authors' synaesthesia. However, Huysmans, through Des Esseintes, later describes this as an analogy, and Marks (1975: ch. 4) comments that Rimbaud later described his coloured vowels as an invention, suggesting metaphor rather than synaesthesia. It seems that, rather than describing instances of genuine synaesthesia, much of the literature cited probably reflects a form of metaphor or analogy.

The composer Alexander Scriabin and painter Wassily Kandinsky were almost certainly aware of the efforts of Rimbaud and Baudelaire to link the senses and seem to have been aware of one another's work; both were also influenced by the operatic work of Richard Wagner (1813–83). Wagner saw opera as the ideal medium for conveying his thoughts and ideas and hoped 'to touch the Christianity within us'. To this end he used a system of symbolic *leit-* or *hauptmotiven* as his 'carriers of feeling', suggesting that 'we must become knowers through feeling'. Kandinsky, in his written work *On the Spiritual in Art*, takes up Wagner's suggestion that it is possible to touch the inner spirituality through the arts. Kandinsky appears to have possessed a certain envy of music as an art form, in that music, whilst being almost totally abstract, can successfully conjure visual images (cf. Debussy's *Claire de Lune*, and Wagner's overture to *Das Rheingold*). A point of great inspiration to Kandinsky appears to have been the abstract colour visions described in the novel *Die Andere Seite* ('The Other Side') by his colleague in the *Neue Künstlervereinigung* group, Alfred Kubin (1909). Kandinsky's move towards total abstraction in his work seems to have followed from his desire to imbue his work with a synaesthesic quality. His intention was for his work to possess the quality of evoking sounds (*'klangen'*) in those who viewed his canvases. This evocation of an auditory dimension to visual representations was a move toward Kandinsky's ultimate aim of creating the *gesamtkunstwerk* ('total art work'). In seeking to create this *gesamtkunstwerk*, Kandinsky's logic was simple: the more senses that could be appealed to with a piece of work, the better the chance of touching the inner spirituality within his audience.

Kandinsky was much taken with the efforts of the Russian composer Alexander Scriabin and included in the manifesto (*Der Blau Rieter Almanac*) for his and Franz Marc's Blue Rider group an appraisal of Scriabin's 'Prometheus', or the 'Poem of Fire'. What made Scriabin's efforts so worthy in Kandinsky's view was the composer's inclusion of notation for a 'colour organ'. The keys of the *clavier à luce* when struck, rather than producing a sound, projected colours. Additionally, Myers (1915) reports that Scriabin planned to score an orchestral piece, *Mystery*, to include the same colour dimension but this time with the addition of odours. Lucie-Smith (1972) suggests that Kandinsky, like the Lithuanian artist Ciurlionis, was attempting to provide a pictorial equivalent of music. The evidence suggests that Kandinsky was trying to create a synaesthesic dimension to his work, rather than it being an expression of synaesthesia.

Evidence that Scriabin, Rimsky-Korsakov and Liszt actually had developmental synaesthesia is equally hard to find, whereas comments suggesting a contrived association are often reported. For instance, Myers recounts that for Scriabin F♯ seemed violet, whereas Rimsky-Korsakov believed it to be green, with Myers commenting that 'this deviation he attributes to an accidental association with the colour of leaves and grass arising from the frequent use of this key for pastoral music' (pp. 112–13). Myers also reports that in conversation with Scriabin during the latter's visit to England, it was stated that 'when listening to music, he has only a "feeling" of colour; only in cases where the feeling is very intense does it pass over to give an "image" of colour' (p. 113). Scriabin also concedes that Beethoven's symphonies 'are not of a kind to need colour', being 'too intellectual in character'. Such anecdotes throw further doubt on the genuineness of his synaesthesia.

More recently synaesthesia has been claimed by the author Vladimir Nabokov, the composer Olivier Messiaen (see Bernard 1986), and the artist and set designer David Hockney (see Cytowic 1989). A particularly florid description of Messiaen's colour–sound association is given in his 1947 account of 'the gentle cascade of blue-orange chords' in the piano part of the second movement of *Quator pour la fin du temps*. He is later more specific about the nature of his synaesthesia when he states that he sees 'colours which move with the music, and I sense these colours in an extremely vivid manner' (cited in Samuel 1976). The author Vladimir Nabokov interviewed in the *Listener* (1962) recounts his 'rather freakish gift of seeing letters in colour'. Interestingly he states that his wife has the gift of coloured hearing, and their son sees letters in colour and that his colours sometimes appear to be a mix of his parents' colours. For example, the letter M for Nabokov was pink and to his wife it was blue. In their son (Dimitri) they found it to be purple, which, as Nabokov suggests, is as if 'genes were painting in aquarelle'. Dimitri Nabokov described his synaesthesia in a television documentary by BBC's *Horizon* (13 December 1994).

In sum, we suggest that since metaphor is widespread in language this provides ripe conditions for confusion with developmental synaesthesia. Distinguishing the 'metaphor as pseudo-synaesthesia' from developmental synaesthesia is difficult and will rely on objective tests such as those described earlier. However, the key differences are that in metaphoric pseudo-synaesthesia (a) no percept is *necessarily* triggered; (b) the subject will often acknowledge that the description is only of an analogy; and (c) it is voluntary.

1.2.5 Association as pseudosynaesthesia

It seems possible that a second form of pseudo-synaesthesia may include individuals who have simply learnt to pair words/letters with colours. Western European culture provides a number of possible means by which colours and letters may be paired together. For example, in childhood many of us are given alphabet books in which letters are depicted in a variety of colours. Similarly, a traditional training in needlecraft involves the use of samplers. These samplers often include embroidered letters, each of which may be shown in a different colour. The example of samplers seems an unlikely explanation for developmental synaesthesia in that most synaesthetes are aware of having had colour–word/letter associations before they learned handicrafts of this sort. The example of coloured-letter books seems a more plausible route in that typically exposure to these books occurs in infancy. Nevertheless, detailed examination of the colour–letter alphabets of individuals with developmental synaesthesia often shows that successive letters have very similar colours. This is in marked to contrast to coloured alphabet books in which successive letters have markedly different colours. We suggest the term associative pseudo-synaesthesia should be retained, however, to describe those individuals who can give a good learning account of their own form of synaesthesia. Whether associative pseudo-synaesthesia has any of the features of developmental synaesthesia (such as vivid, automatic percepts, and so on) remains unknown.

1.3 Conclusions

We seem to be in need of a more specific taxonomy for dealing with investigations into synaesthesia, principally because many individuals may engage in pseudo-synaesthesic thinking (metaphor, analogy, etc.) and yet give the impression that the associations they have developed are the same 'natural' correspondences that developmental synaesthetes possess. Even amongst those cases with the developmental form of the condition, some further discrimination may be required. Elizabeth Stewart-Jones (see chapter 16 for a biographical account) appears to be different in kind to the other synaesthetes we have tested. Michael Watson, the subject of Richard Cytowic's book '*The Man who Tasted Shapes*' (1993), and discussed in the following chapter, again seems different in kind from Elizabeth.

A second issue is that of seeking to reconcile the 'subjective' experiences of people with synaesthesia with the 'objective' view of science. The problem of providing scientific explanations of subjective experience was famously and eloquently stated by the physiologist Sherrington, who traced the light from a star through the visual system. Sherrington suggested that the mechanics by which data about the star reached the visual cortex were relatively well understood, but that we had no explanation of the subjective experience (or qualia) of seeing the star: 'At this point the scheme puts its finger to its lips and is silent' (cited in Fenwick 1993). Reconciling the first- and third-person views of human cognition has proved to be a difficult enterprise, and for many years personal experience was not seen as the proper domain of science. This perspective seems to stem from Galileo's belief that the universe was made up of (a) matter, and (b) energy, the first dealing with primary qualities (velocity, weight, mass, etc.), the second with those of subjective experience (smell, vision, truth, etc.). For Galileo, only the former was properly the domain of science. Descartes possessed a similar view, suggesting that only the physical world (*res extensor*), and not the mental world (*res cogitans*), was the domain accessible to science.

As a result of Einstein's reconciliation of mass and energy, we are left with a one-stuff universe, thereby allowing, at least potentially, for scientific explanations of Descartes's *res cogitans*. In this century psychological thought has swung from concern with inner mental life to placing a premium on observable behaviour, and back again. In this context synaesthesia makes an interesting topic of investigation in that the subject matter is necessarily an internal, mental state whose existence we can only infer from the findings of behavioural testing. Cytowic has tended to rely almost entirely upon the subjective self-reports given him by his subjects with synaesthesia. We have sought to rely primarily upon objective quantification of data according to the traditional methods of experimental psychology (Baron-Cohen et al. 1987, 1993), but have allowed room to include what synaesthetes tell us about their experience in the form of questionnaire data.

1.4 An Anecdote from Studies of Functional Imaging

The study conducted by our group in collaboration with Paulesu et al. used the neuro-imaging technique of positron emission tomography (PET). This technique has allowed us to look at brain activity in individuals with synaesthesia and compare it with that of non-synaesthetes. A fascinating account from this experiment relates to the experience of a subject with synaesthesia (MT). Synaesthesic subjects were selected for this experiment on the basis that they saw colours in response to hearing words, but not in response to hearing non-speech sounds (full details are reported in chapter 6). In the debrief session, MT revealed that the tone stimulation she had received had in fact given her a very faint, light grey, visual percept. MT's blood flow map for the six scans in which she was stimulated with tones when compared to the averaged blood flow maps for controls showed a pattern of activation similar to those seen in synaesthetes listening to words.

This remarkable finding demonstrated that for this subject the blood flow maps obtained using PET reflected her personal experience.

1.5 Is Synaesthesia Heritable?

Two further issues arise from the work conducted thus far. Since Galton's assertion in 1883 that there seemed to be a strong hereditary contribution to the condition, most researchers in the field have suggested that hereditary factors appear to play a role. Cytowic, in his 1989 book, reports this fact, and our recent work strongly suggests the possibility that synaesthesia runs in successive generations. Chapter 11 by Bailey and Johnson discusses the possibility that the condition may be a genetically inherited trait.

1.6 What Are the Mechanisms Underlying Synaesthesia?

The second issue, dealing with possible mechanisms by which synaesthesia may be inherited, is discussed by Daphne Maurer (chapter 13 in this volume). She considers the possibility that synaesthesia may be a stage of normal infancy. Henry Kennedy and colleagues, in chapter 14, pursue this theme in considering the research which has been carried out into the changes that maturation brings in the perception of neonates.

Other chapters in the book explore the implications that synaesthesia may have for functional and structural theories of the brain and its activity. Neurobiological perspectives are considered by Frith and Paulesu (chapter 8), whilst Gabriel Segal discusses the possible implications for modularity of mind in chapter 12. Jeffrey Gray and colleagues pursue the idea that synaesthesia has important implications for the understanding of consciousness in chapter 10, and Grossenbacher considers the implications for models of perception in chapter 9. If this book sparks debate and new research at any or all of these levels, it will have done its job.

References

Aghajanian, G.K. 1981: In R. Hoffmeister and G. Stille (eds), *Handbook of Experimental Pharmacology*, 55(2), 89–110.

Baron-Cohen, S., Wyke, M. and Binnie, C. 1987: Hearing words and seeing colours: an experimental investigation of synaesthesia. *Perception*, 16, 761–7.

Baron-Cohen, S., Harrison, J.E., Goldstein, L.H. and Wyke, M. 1993: Coloured speech perception: is synaesthesia what happens when modularity breaks down? *Perception*, 22, 419–26.

Baudelaire, C. 1860: *Les Paradis artificiels*. Paris: Gallimard.

Bender, M.B., Rudolph, S. and Stacey, C. 1982: The neurology of visual and oculomotor systems. In *Clinical Neurology*, Hagerstown: Harper & Row.

Bernard, J. 1986: Messiaen's synaesthesia: the correspondence between colour and sound structure in his music. *Music Perception* 4(1), 41–68.

Brooks, D.J. 1993: PET studies on the early and differential diagnosis of Parkinson's disease. *Neurology*, 43 (Supplement 6), S6–S16.

Critchley, E.M.R. 1994: Synaesthesia. In *The Neurological Boundaries of Reality*, London: Farrand Press.

Cytowic, R.E. 1989: *Synaesthesia: a union of the senses*. New York: Springer-Verlag.

Cytowic, R.E. 1993: *The Man who Tasted Shapes*. London: Abacus.

Cytowic, R.E. and Wood, F.B. 1982: Synaesthesia II: psychophysical relationships in the synesthesia of geometrically shaped taste and colored hearing. *Brain and Cognition*, 1, 36–49.

Galton, F. 1883: *Inquiries into Human Faculty and its Development*. London: Dent.

Gautier, Th. 1843: Le Club des Hachichins. *La Presse* (Paris), 10 July.

Hughes, A.J., Daniel, S.E., Kilford, L. and Lees, A.J. 1992: Accuracy of clinical diagnosis of idiopathic Parkinson's disease: a clinico-pathological study of 100 cases. *Journal of Neurology, Neurosurgery and Psychiatry*, 55, 181–4.

Humphreys, G. 1990: Higher sight. *Nature*, 343, 30.

Huysman, J.K. 1884: *Against Nature*. Paris, Cres; Penguin books trans. Robert Baldick, London: Penguin, 1959.

Kandinsky, W. and Marc, F. 1915: *De Blau Rieter Almanac*.

Krohn, W.O. 1893: Pseudo-chromesthesia, or the association of colors with words, letters and sounds. *American Journal of Psychology*, 5, 20–39.

Kubin, A. 1909: *Die Andere Siete*.

Locke, J. 1690: *An Essay Concerning Human Understanding: Book 3*. London, Basset; reprinted Oxford: Clarendon Press, 1984.

Lucie-Smith, E. 1972: *Symbolist Art*. London: Thames & Hudson.

Marks, L. 1975: On colored-hearing synaesthesia: cross-modal translations of sensory dimensions. *Psychological Bulletin*, 82(3), 303–31.

Motluk, A. 1994: The sweet smell of purple. *New Scientist*, 143, 32–7.

Myers, C.S. 1915: Two cases of synaesthesia. *British Journal of Psychology*, 7, 112–17.

Nabokov, V. 1966: *Speak, Memory*. London: Penguin.

Odin, S. 1986: Blossom scents take up the ringing: synaesthesia in Japanese and Western aesthetics. *Soundings*, 69, 256–81.

Paulesu, E., Harrison, J., Baron-Cohen, S., Watson, J., Goldstein, L., Heather, J., Frackowiak, R. and Frith, C. 1995: The physiology of coloured hearing. *Brain*, 118, 671–6.

Rang, H.P. and Dale, M.M. 1987: *Pharmacology*. Edinburgh: Churchill Livingstone.

Samuel, C. 1976: Conversations with Oliver Messiaen.

Sherrington, C.F. cited in P. Fenwick, Alterations in consciousness awareness. In E.M.R. Critchley (ed.), *The Neurological Boundaries of Reality*, London: Farrand Press.

Starr, F. 1893: Note on color-hearing. *American Journal of Psychology*, 51: 416–18.

Suarez de Mendoza, F. 1890: *L'Audition coloré*. Paris: Doin.

Vernon, P.E. 1930: Synaesthesia in music. *Psyche*. 10, 22–40.

2

*Synaesthesia: Phenomenology and Neuropsychology – a Review of Current Knowledge**

Richard E. Cytowic

2.1 Introduction

Although medicine has known about synaesthesia for three centuries, it keeps forgetting that it knows. After decades of neglect, a revival of inquiry is under way. As in earlier times, today's interest is multidisciplinary. Neuroscience is particularly curious this time – or at least it should be – because of what synaesthesia might tell us about consciousness, the nature of reality, and the relationship between reason and emotion.

The word synaesthesia, meaning 'joined sensation', shares a root with anaesthesia, meaning 'no sensation'. It denotes the rare capacity to hear colours, taste shapes or experience other equally startling sensory blendings whose quality seems difficult for most of us to imagine. A synaesthete might describe the colour, shape and flavour of someone's voice, or music whose sound *looks like* 'shards of glass', a scintillation of jagged, coloured triangles moving in the visual field. Or, seeing the colour red, a synaesthete might detect the 'scent' of red as well. The experience is frequently projected outside the individual, rather than being an image in the mind's eye. I currently estimate that one in 25,000 individuals is born to a world where one sensation *involuntarily* conjures up others, sometimes all five clashing together (Cytowic 1989, 1993). I suspect that this figure is far too low.

It is an aphorism that nature reveals herself by her exceptions. Since our intellectual baggage includes deeply ingrained historical ideas about normative concepts of mind, synaesthesia not only flouts con-

*Reprinted from *Psyche* (1996).

ventional laws of neuroanatomy and psychology, it even seems to grate against common sense. Yet it should also be an aphorism (though never contemporaneously evident) that concepts which some now think of as clear, coherent and final are unlikely to appear to posterity as having any of those attributes.

Since I have previously addressed synaesthesia at book-length, and since my current task is to summarize rather than to persuade, I have tried not to clutter up this review with references. Readers wanting further background or wishing to pursue a specific point should consult Cytowic (1989, 1993). Initialed examples in this review (such as JM or MW) refer to my subjects in the 1989 text.

2.2 General Features

No matter what senses are joined in a given synaesthete, it is striking how similar the histories of all synaesthetes are. One after another, they declare that their lifelong intersensory associations remain stable. (That is, if the word 'hammer' is red with white speckles, it is always thus perceived.) Synaesthetes are surprised to discover that others do not perceive words, numbers, sounds, taste and so forth as they do. Though they recall having always had their idiosyncratic perceptions as far back as they can remember, any mention of them at an early age characteristically prompted ridicule and disbelief. Despite keeping the experience private and hidden, it remained vivid and irrepressible, beyond any willed control.

We presently know the following:

1 Synaesthesia runs in families in a pattern consistent with either autosomal or x-linked dominant transmission. (A parent of either sex can pass the trait to a child of either sex, affected individuals appear in more than one generation of a pedigree, and multiple affected siblings can occur in the same generation. So far, I have encountered no male-to-male transmission.) To give some flavour of the pedigrees I have encountered, one family has one synaesthete in each of four generations, while another family has four synaesthetes out of five siblings in the same generation.
2 Perhaps the most famous family case is that of the Russian novelist Vladimir Nabokov. When, as a toddler, he complained to his mother that the letter colours on his wooden alphabet blocks were 'all wrong', she understood the conflict he experienced between the colour of the painted letters and his lexically induced synaesthetic colours.[1] In addition to perceiving letters and words in colour, as her son did, Mrs Nabokov was also affected by music. (Parenthet-

ically, Nabokov's son Dimitri is synaesthetic. Unequivocal passing of the trait from father to son would eliminate the possibility of x-linked dominant heritability. Unfortunately, Nabokov's wife was also synaesthetic, and it is not possible to determine from which parent Dimitri inherited the trait.)

3 Female synaesthetes predominate. In the US I found a ratio of 3:1 (Cytowic 1989), while in the UK Baron-Cohen et al. (1993) found a female ratio of 8:1.

4 Synaesthetes are preponderantly non-right-handed. Additional features (see below) are consistent with anomalous cerebral dominance.

5 Synaesthetes are normal in the conventional sense. They appear bright, and come from all walks of life. The impression that they are inherently 'artistic' seems to me a sampling bias, given that famous synaesthetes such as Vladimir Nabokov, Olivier Messiaen, David Hockney and Alexander Scriabin are well known because of their art rather than their synaesthesia. Clinically, synaesthetes seem mentally balanced. Their MMPIs are unremarkable except for non-stereotypical male–female scales. Standard neurological examinations are also normal.

6 Not only do most synaesthetes contend that their memories are excellent, but cite their parallel sensations as the cause, saying for example, 'I know it's two because it's white.' Conversation, prose passages, movie dialogue and verbal instructions are typical subjects of detailed recall. The spatial location of objects is also strikingly remembered, such as the precise location of kitchen utensils, furniture arrangements and floor plans, books on shelves, or text blocks in a specific book. Perhaps related to this observation is a tendency to prefer order, symmetry and balance. Work cannot commence until the desk is arranged just so, or everything in the kitchen is put away in its proper place. Synaesthetes perform in the superior range of the Wechsler Memory Scale.

7 Within their overall high intelligence, synaesthetes have uneven cognitive skills. While a minority are frankly dyscalculic, the majority may have subtle mathematical deficiencies (such as lexical-to-digit transcoding). Right–left confusion (allochiria), and a poor sense of direction for vector rather than network maps are common.[2] A first-degree family history of dyslexia, autism and attention deficit is present in about 15 per cent. Very rarely, the sensual experience is so intense as to interfere with rational thinking (e.g. writing a speech, memorizing formulae). I have encountered no one whose synaesthesia was so markedly disruptive to rational thought as it was in Luria's famous male subject, S.

8 As a group, synaesthetes seem more prone to 'unusual experiences' than one might expect (17 per cent in my 1989 study, though if anyone knows what the general-population baseline for unusual experiences is, I should like to know). Qualitatively, one thinks of the personality constellation said to be typical of temporal-limbic epileptics. *Déjà vu*, clairvoyance, precognitive dreams, a sense of portentousness, and the feeling of a presence are encountered often enough. Singular instances in my experience include empathic healing, and an explanans of psychokinesis for what was probably an explanandum of episodic metamorphopsia. Unparalleled among my collection of other-worldly experiences is that of a woman who claimed to have been abducted by aliens and to have enjoyed sexual congress aboard their space craft. Having experienced aliens, she confided, human males could no longer satisfy her. (My thanks to Larry Marks for this gem.)

From these factors, it seems that for most people synaesthesia is ineffable: by definition it cannot be imparted to others or adequately put into words. It might seem impossible at first for science to scrutinize a phenomenon whose 'quality' must be experienced at first hand.

2.3 History of Synaesthesia

Surprisingly, synaesthesia has been known to medicine for almost 300 years. After interest peaked between 1860 and 1930, it was forgotten, remaining unexplained not for lack of trying, but simply because psychology and neurology were premature sciences. Psychological theory was jam-packed with associations, and concepts of nervous tissue were paltry. Just as concepts became recognizably modern, behaviourism appeared with such draconian restrictions that even acknowledging the existence of an inner life was taboo for a long time. Subjective experience such as synaesthesia was deemed not a proper subject for scientific study.

Synaesthesia's history is intrinsically interesting but also important if we are to understand its neurological basis, because the word was used to describe diverse phenomena in different eras. Central to my initial approach in 1980 was a sharp demarcation of synaesthesia as a sensual perception, as distinct from a mental object like cross-modal associations in non-synaesthetes, metaphoric language or even artistic aspirations to sensory fusion. By contrast, the perceptual phenomenon is unheard of in literary and linguistic circles, where the term 'synaesthesia' is understood to mean rhetorical tropes (i.e. figures of speech) or sound symbolism (*à la* Humboldt and Saussure). Whether such a demarcation remains warranted is considered below (section 2.10).

Synesthesia attracted serious attention in art, music, literature, linguistics, natural philosophy and theosophy (see chapter 1). Two books were published: *L'Audition coloré* by Suarez de Mendoza in 1890, and *Das Farbenhren und der synsthetische Faktor der Wahrnehmung* by Argelander in 1927. Most accounts emphasized coloured hearing, the most common form of synaesthesia.

This disproportion in the types of synaesthesia is itself intriguing. The five senses can have ten possible synaesthetic pairings. Synaesthetic relationships are usually unidirectional, however, meaning that for a particular synaesthete sight may induce touch, but touch does not induce visual perceptions. This one-way street, therefore, increases the permutations to 20 (or 30 if you include the perception of movement as a sixth element), yet some senses, such as sight and sound, are involved much more often than others. To persons endowed with coloured hearing, for example, speech and music are not only heard but are also a visual melange of coloured shapes, movement and scintillation.

It is rare for smell and taste to be either the trigger or the synaesthetic response. Aside from my case VE, I have found no other in which sight evokes smell; and other than my index case MW, in which taste and smell evoked widespread tactile experience, I have found none in which smell itself is the trigger. In addition to MW, I am aware of only one other synaesthete in whom taste induces a secondary sense, in this instance an experience of colour.

Aside from MW's own geometric taste, perhaps the strangest synaesthesia is 'audiomotor', in which an adolescent positioned his body in different postures according to the sounds of different words. Both English and nonsense sounds had certain physical movements, the boy claimed, which he could demonstrate by striking various poses. By way of convincing himself of this sound-to-movement association, the physician who described it planned to re-test the boy later on without warning. When the doctor read the same word list aloud ten years later, the boy assumed, without hesitation, the identical postures of a decade earlier.

By the mid-nineteenth century synaesthesia had intrigued an art movement that sought sensory fusion, and a union of the senses appeared more and more frequently *as an idea*. Multimodal concerts of music and light (*son et lumière*), sometimes including odour, were popular and often featured colour organs, keyboards that controlled coloured lights as well as musical notes. It is imperative to understand that such deliberate contrivances are qualitatively different from the involuntary experiences that I am calling synaesthesia in this review.

The Russian composer Alexander Scriabin (1872–1915) specifically sought to express his own synaesthesia in his 1910 symphony *Prometheus, the Poem of Fire*, for orchestra, piano, organ and choir. It also included a mute keyboard, a *clavier à lumières*, which controlled the play of coloured light in the form of beams, clouds and other shapes, flooding the concert hall and culminating in a white light so strong as to be 'painful to the eyes'.

Vasilly Kandinsky (1866–1944) had perhaps the deepest sympathy for sensory fusion, both synaesthetic and as an artistic idea. He explored harmonious relationship between sound and colour and used musical terms to describe his paintings, calling them 'compositions' and 'improvisations'. His own 1912 opera, *Der Gelbe Klang* ('The Yellow Sound'), specified a compound mixture of colour, light, dance and sound typical of the *Gesamtkunstwerk*.

I note that Kandinsky yearned to push aside analytic explanations and move himself and his audience closer to the quality of direct experience that synaesthesia typifies. There is an important clue in his famous dictum, 'stop thinking!', that relates to one of synaesthesia's implications in reversing the roles of reason and emotion. Kandinsky grasped that creativity is an experience, not an abstract idea, and that a mind that incessantly analyses what is there impedes that experience. (Kandinsky's 1910 adjuration was: 'lend your ears to music, open your eyes to painting, and . . . stop thinking! Just ask yourself whether the work has enabled you to "walk about" into a hitherto unknown world. If the answer is yes, what more do you want?')

In such a climate, people were intrigued with the notion that synaesthesia seemed to have a direct link to the unconscious. With time, however, attention turned to 'objective' behaviour that could be quantified or measured by machines. Humans became 'subjects', the individual was abandoned, and the mind temporarily became a black box.

Mechanistic explanations have been plentiful throughout synaesthesia's history. The notion of crossed wires turns up repeatedly. As early as 1704, Sir Isaac Newton struggled to devise mathematical formulae to equate the vibration of sound waves to a corresponding wavelength of light. Goethe noted colour correspondences in his 1810 work, *Zur Farbenlehre*. The nineteenth century saw an alchemical zeal in the search for universal correspondences and a presumed algorithm for translating one sense into another. This mechanistic approach was consistent with the then-common view of a clockwork universe based on Newton's uniform laws of motion.

2.4 Clinical Diagnosis

The abundant confusion in synaesthesia's history requires a clinical definition to distinguish it from superficially similar, but otherwise distinct, phenomena. Since the term 'diagnosis' literally means 'through knowledge', the criteria are wholly historical. (Some may find this a refreshing change from our reflexive and often unthinking use of technology.) Five diagnostic features are:

1 Synaesthesia is involuntary but elicited. It is a passive experience that happens to someone. It is unsupressable, but elicited by a stimulus that is usually identified without difficulty. It cannot be conjured up or dismissed at will, although circumstances of attention and distraction may make the experience seem more or less vivid.

2 Synaesthesia is projected. It is perceived externally in peri-personal space, the limb-axis space immediately surrounding the body, never at a distance as in the spatial teloreception of vision or audition. My subject DS, for example, is a college teacher who, on hearing music, also see objects – falling gold balls, shooting lines, metallic waves like oscilloscope tracings – that float on a 'screen' six inches from her nose. Her favourite music, she explains, 'makes the lines move upward'.

3 Distinguishing the experience of perception as 'near' (e.g. chemosensation, touch, proprioception, body schema, the orientation of one's body within Euclidean space) or 'distant' (e.g. seeing, hearing) is concordant with concepts of classical neurology and neuroanatomy. This idea was most clearly articulated by Paul Yakovlev (1894–1983), who mapped 'three spheres of motility' on to three anatomical divisions of the neuraxis (Yakovlev 1948, 1970).

4 Synaesthetic perceptions are durable and generic, never pictorial or elaborated. 'Durable' means that the cross-sensory associations do not change over time. This has been shown many times by test–retest sessions given decades apart without warning. 'Generic' means that while you or I might *imagine* a pastoral landscape while listening to Beethoven, what synaesthetes experience is unelaborated: they see blobs, lines, spirals and lattice shapes; feel smooth or rough textures; taste agreeable or disagreeable tastes such as salty, sweet or metallic.

5 Though synaesthetes are often carelessly dismissed as being just poetic, it is we who must be cautious about unjustifiably interpreting their comments. For example, my index case MW described the shape of mint as 'cool glass columns'. On analysis, this turned out to be his shorthand way of trying to convey the quality of the tactile experience – 'what is it like'. When pressed to elaborate the sensations he felt, he said:

> I can reach my hand out and rub it along the back side of a curve. I can't feel where the top and bottom end: so it's like a column. It's cool to the touch, as if it were made of stone or glass. What is so wonderful about it, though, is its absolute smoothness. Perfectly smooth. I can't feel any pits or indentations in the surface, so it must not be made of granite or stone. Therefore, it must be made of glass.

So MW tells us that the sensory attributes of *curved + cool + smooth* 'are like' rubbing a cool glass column. This is a third-person verbal description of a first-person sensory experience.

Seizure discharges in the hippocampus of the limbic system produce synaesthesia in persons who are not otherwise synaesthetic. An example is the sensation of flashing lights, a taste, a feeling of heat rising, and a high-pitched whine. Synaesthesia is experienced in 4 per cent of limbic seizures. Those that remain confined to the hippocampus produce an elementary experience – a taste, for example, is described as bitter, metallic or merely unpleasant. Only when seizures spread to the *cortex of the temporal lobe* does the perception become more specific and elaborated – 'rusty iron', 'oysters' or 'an artichoke'.

I believe that this distinction between elementary and elaborated experience is crucial if we are to craft a coherent neurological explanation of synaesthesia.

Synaesthesia is memorable. At first, we are impressed by synaesthetes' excellent figurative memory and taken with their anecdotes of how the 'extra bits' help them to remember telephone numbers, appointments and the like. It was Luria's *The Mind of a Mnemonist* (1968) that first suggested to me a link between synaesthesia and hypermnesis. The apparently limitless memory of his subject, S, seemed due to the synaesthesia that accompanied his every experience. During recall, S described a replay of somatic feelings and 'an overall sensation' during which 'the thing remembers itself'. By this, S meant that 'he' exerted no effort to retrieve the desired information. He was merely a passive observer as the reminiscence unfolded itself.

On a closer look, however, we note that what is even more memorable is the synaesthetic perception itself: 'She had a green name – I forget, it was either Ethel or Vivian.' In this example, it is the synaesthetic greenness and not the semantic label that is recalled. In other words, if Ethel is a green blob, the next time you see her you don't say: 'It's Ethel', you say: 'It's the green blob: therefore, it is Ethel.' (It would take us too far afield to explore in this review the paradox regarding how the synaesthesiae, which themselves are perceptually meaningful yet semantically vacuous, actually aid in recall. The mental gymnastics through which synaesthetes go seem counterintuitively to contradict their claims that synaesthesiae are 'simple' and 'natural' memory aids.)

That an experience rather than a thought is primary is illustrated by my subject JM, a Swiss polyglot in whom the spelling determines the perceived colour of letters, words and speech in any language. 'You know how they have that electric band with the news in Times Square?' she asks. 'That's how it is in my head. The colour flows through me, and then I think of the thing. Somebody says to me, "*wie ist Ihr Hund*?" First I have the colour, and *then* I think of my dog.'

Most of us have had a memory awakened by the smell of baked bread, flowers or some other provocative fragrance. Yet while the context vividly returns to mind, few if any non-synaesthetes assert that they can remember an actual odour or other episodic sensation, something that synaesthetes routinely claim. My index case MW accidentally brought his synaesthesia to my attention by apologizing for the delay in seating his dinner guests at table with the comment: 'There aren't enough points on the chicken.' Many years later, MW and I were again dining on roast chicken. I pointed out the irony and misquoted him by saying something about 'unwinding the curliques'. He corrected me, noting that 'I remember the *shape*, not the anecdote (unlike me, who recalled the anecdote but not the sensual details). I was remembering that it was indeed uniformly round and it needed more points.'

Synaesthesia is emotional. The experience is accompanied by a sense of certitude (the 'this is it' feeling) and a conviction that what synaesthetes perceive is real and valid. This accompaniment brings to mind that transitory change in self-awareness known as ecstasy. Ecstasy is any passion by which the thoughts are absorbed and in which the mind is for a time lost. In 1902, in *the Varieties of Religious Experience*, William James spoke of ecstasy's four qualities of ineffability, passivity, noesis and transience. These same qualities are shared by synaesthesia.

'Noetic' is a rarely used word that comes from the Greek *nous* meaning intellect or understanding. It gives us our world 'knowledge', and means knowledge that is experienced directly, an illumination that is accompanied by a feeling of certitude. James spoke of a 'noetic sense of truth' and the sense of authority that these states impart. Although so similar to states of feeling, mystical states seem to those who experience them to be also states of knowledge. They are states of insight into depths of truth unplumbed by the discursive intellect. They are illuminations, revelations, full of significance and importance, all inarticulate though they remain; and as a rule they carry with them a curious sense of authority for after-time.[3]

2.5 Lack of Obvious Agreement

Its phenomenology makes clear that synaesthesia is not an idea, but an *experience*. How does science approach this distinction between a first-person understanding of some experience and a third-person one that is supposedly objective? A lack of obvious agreement among synaesthetes compounds the apparent difficulty. In fact, this rather glaring problem – that two individuals with the same sensory pairings do not report identical, or even similar, synaesthetic responses – has sometimes been taken as 'proof' that synaesthesia is not 'real'.

Scriabin and Rimsky-Korsakov, for example, disagreed on the colour of given notes and musical keys. 'Researchers' from earlier centuries did little more than make lists of stimuli and synaesthetic responses, followed by dismay that a pattern of correspondence was not obvious. I suspect that similarity was not apparent because they were looking at the terminal stage of a conscious perception itself, instead of some earlier neural process that led to that perception.[4]

We often think of the flow of neural impulses as linear, and emphasize its terminal locus – i.e. we classically think of perception, an action or an utterance as the terminal stage of some process whose locus is somewhere in the cortex. We think of perception as a one-way street, travelling from the outside world inwards, dispatching a linear stream of neural impulses from one relay to ever more complex ones, so that the process is metaphorically like a conveyor belt running through stations in a factory, until a perception rolls off the end as the 'finished product'.

Instead of fixating on the terminal event, suppose we turn our attention to some earlier stage of neural transformation? When looking for relationships on any family tree, we find that members closer to the trunk resemble each other much more than members out on distal branches do. This is why family resemblances are more apparent in offspring when they are young children than when they are grown-up. For example, apes and humans are alike, although they hardly look it. Much of their anatomy is alike, their brains are very similar, and of course their DNA differs by only a few percent. But we need not go all the way back to DNA to see this similarity. Even in the case of different species, a human infant and a chimp infant look strikingly alike while the adult members call attention to their disparity (see Cytowic 1993: 60 for an illustration). Regarding synaesthesia, we conclude that all intervening transformations between the eye and the visual cortex are possible candidates for processest that are closer to the trunk of perception than a completed (and presumably cortically situated) visual image is.

By analogy, the consensual image we see on the screen when watching television is the terminal stage of the broadcast. Someone able to intercept the transmission anywhere between the studio camera and the TV screen would be like a synaesthete, sampling the transmission before it reached the screen fully elaborated. Presumably, their experience would be different from those of us viewing the screen. We can similarly propose and test the concept of synaesthesia as the premature display of a normal cognitive process. This implies that we are all synaesthetic, and that only a handful of people are consciously aware of the holistic nature of perception.

2.6 Neural Basis

Based initially on an analysis of phenomenology, and reasoning by analogy to more common phenomena that were qualitatively similar to the experience of synaesthesia, I concluded that synaesthesia was not a higher cortical function in the conventional sense. Momentarily disregarding what the *nature* of the link between a stimulating sensation and the synaesthetically perceived one might be, I further proposed that the *level* of this unknown link occupied a low to intermediate level of the neuraxis, rather than a higher level involving more mental mediation (Cytowic and Wood 1982a, 1982b).

Experimental results were consistent with these suppositions. The five major probes were:

1 an examination of range and context effects during psychophysical sensory matching tasks between synesthetes and non-synesthetic controls;
2 the failure of Osgood's semantic differential to expose any linguistically meaningful similarity between stimuli and synaesthetic responses (Osgood et al. 1957);
3 the manipulation of synaesthetic perception by drugs that either stimulate or depress the cortex;

4 the comparison of regional brain metabolism, via the radioactive xenon method, during synaesthetic, non-synaesthetic, and adjuvant-enhanced states; and
5 the ability to induce perceptions that were qualitatively identical to the subject's idiopathic synaesthesia during cerebral angiography, presumably by reducing oxygen substrate in the left hemisphere during both carotid and vertebral injections.

The detailed evidence and arguments appear elsewhere (Cytowic 1989, 1993). In summary, synaesthesia depends only on the left-brain hemisphere and is accompanied by large metabolic shifts away from the neocortex that result in relatively enhanced limbic expression. The hippocampus is an important and probably obligate node in whatever neural structures generate the synesthetic experience.

No matter what technology we use to make so-called 'functional pictures' of the brain at work, we expect some cortical area(s) to 'light up'. We never expect a decline. It surprises many people – especially those waiting for a machine test before casting their vote whether synaesthesia is real or imaginary – to learn that cortical metabolism plummets during synaesthesia. MW's mean hemispheric flows are low and not homogeneous to begin with, yet drop a further 18 per cent on average in the left hemisphere during synaesthesia. Such a decrease is impossible to obtain in a normal person with, for example, a drug. Even during an 'activation' trial with amyl nitrate, which subjectively intensifies the synaesthetic experience, MW's regional blood flows are *decreased* compared to baseline. Normally, any physical or mental task, or any activation procedure (e.g. drug administration, carbon dioxide or oxygen inhalation), *increases* blood flow by 5–10 per cent.

MW's cortical metabolism dropped so low during synaesthesia that he should have been blind, paralysed or shown some other conventional sign of a lesion. (Left hemispheric flows were nearly three standard deviations below our lab's acceptable limits of normal.) Yet his thinking and neurological examination were unimpaired. Such a depression of cortical metabolism during a distinct behavioural state disturbs traditionalists, who regard the more recently evolved cortex as the seat of higher analysis and reason, while assigning the limbic system (the sub-cortical ring of tissue that encircles the brainstem and is much older in evolutionary terms) to handle the more 'primitive' functions of emotion, memory and attention.

I cannot enumerate here all the supporting reasons why I single out the hippocampus as being especially – but not solely – important for synaesthetic experience. The hippocampus is also necessary for experiencing other altered states of consciousness that are qualitatively similar to synaesthesia. For example, the perceptions during LSD-induced synaesthesia, sensory deprivation, limbic epilepsy, release hallucinations, and the experiential responses during electrical stimulation of the brain, all possess a generic, elemental quality – just as they do in synaesthesia (Cytowic 1989: 91–146). This observation leads us to the topic of form constants, the enduring idea that elemental perceptual qualities exist.

2.7 Form Constants

The indescribable nature of subjective experience is not unique to synaesthesia. Heinrich Kluver faced the same difficulty when he tried, starting around 1930, to understand the experience of hallucinations. He was frustrated by the vagueness with which subjects described their experience, their eagerness to yield uncritically to cosmic or religious explanations, to 'interpret' or poetically embroider the experience in lieu of straightforward but concrete description, and their tendency to be overwhelmed and awed by the 'indescribableness' of their visions.

In explicating MW's description of mint (see p. 24), I distinguished between his factual description of curved, smooth and cool tactile attributes and his analogical explanation of the taste as 'cool glass columns'. Similarly, once Kluver got his subjects past elaborating or, even worse, 'explaining' what they saw, he identified four types of basic hallucinatory constants: (a) gratings and honeycombs; (b) cobwebs; (c) tunnels and cones; and (d) spirals. Kluver's work has been replicated and extended by others.

Variations in colour, brightness, movement, perspective, symmetry and replication provide finer gradation of the subjective experience. These are not just visual phenomena but sensory form constants that are apparent in any spatially extended sense. Initially, we thought these spatial configurations reflected some anatomic structure; then we tried mapping it to some prototypical function. Now, neuroscience is not sure what their physical correlates are, but many people do suspect that the form constants point to some deep, fundamental aspect of perception.

For example, few people claim to like explosions, yet everyone likes fireworks. Millions of pounds of entertaining explosives go up all over the world, with millions turning out to watch them. What are they, these coloured lights, flashes and bangs? They are not real things in nature, representations of anything else, and they don't remind us of anything at an intellectual level. They are as abstract as Piet Mondrian or Jackson Pollock – and yet they provoke a strong emotional reaction, inducing millions to watch and then walk away, highly satisfied, saying, 'That was wonderful', without anyone being able to say exactly what 'that' was. No other form of abstract visual expression is as popular.

The pulsation, flicker, drift, rotation and perspective of fireworks of course remind us of the form constants. When we see fireworks, do we not get a feeling of salience, as if we recognize something? Isn't the 'that' of 'that was great,' an ineffable experience of recognition? I do not think it out of line to suggest that the satisfying appeal of something as unnatural as a fireworks display lies in its astonishing similarity to an externalized catalogue of form constants.

2.8 The Implications of Synaesthesia Regarding the Primacy of Emotion

Possibly because we have historically held a dichotomy between reason and emotion, we have misunderstood and even minimized the role that emotion plays in our thinking and actions. I want to make clear that the following comments are not a direct cause-and-effect of synaesthesia, but an implication resulting from its physiologic basis. The two-fold key to this implication is: (a) appreciating the major role that the limbic brain plays in synaesthesia; and (b) considering newer non-hierarchical models of brain organization.

The word 'multiplex' is usually applied to contemporary concepts of brain organization that take into account volume transmission, distributed systems, non-linear dynamics, and the thermodynamic energy costs of any given biologic neural process. Such newer models remain largely unknown, a surprising unfamiliarity given their implications – for example, that we are irrational creatures by design, and that emotion, not reason, may play the decisive role both in how we think and act. Additionally, our brains are not passive receivers of energy flux, but dynamic explorers that actively seek out the stimuli that interest them and determine their own contexts for perception. Ommaya (in press) has elegantly articulated a number of powerful contradictions in conventional models of brain organization that led to his re-evaluation of the role of emotion in cognition and behaviour. Indeed, he describes consciousness as 'a type of emotion', and one of emotion's roles as a 'cognitive homeostat'.

The conventional hierarchical model implied that the limbic system was left behind as the neocortex burgeoned during evolution. If so, then human emotions are comparatively primitive, no more sophisticated than those of other mammals. Below the level of mammals, the limbic system is not seen in its developed form, but once we reach the mammalian line it undergoes robust elaboration. This development, however, occurs in tandem with that of the neocortex. Some mammals emerge higher in one dimension than another: rabbits, for example, have well-developed limbic brains compared to their neocortical development, whereas monkeys show the opposite trend. Humans are unique among mammals in being well-developed in both limbic and neocortical dimensions. In humans, the relationship between cortex and sub-cortical brain is not one of dominance and hierarchy, therefore, but of multiplex reciprocity and interdependence.

Anatomically, the number of human limbic fibre tracts is greater both in relative size and absolute number compared to all other fibre systems. Thanks to new techniques, we have only recently realized that there are more projections from the limbic system to the neocortex than the other way around. In other words, we have had the primary direction of flow backwards all these years. While we think that the cortex contains our representations (or models) of reality – what exists outside ourselves – it is the limbic brain that determines the salience of that information. Therefore, I join Ommaya in arguing that it is an emotional evaluation, not a reasoned one, that ultimately informs our behaviour.

I am hardly rejecting either reason or the role of the neocortex in objective assessment or assigning meaning. Though we quickly speak of reason dominating emotion, the reverse is actually true: the limbic brain easily overwhelms thinking. Let me give two clinical examples. Limbic structures have a low threshold for seizures that produce both psychic and motor manifestations without spilling over to other brain regions. Most characteristic is a *qualitative alteration of consciousness*. Well co-ordinated involuntary actions, called automatisms, seem rational and purposeful to an uninformed observer, yet the patient has no awareness or recollection of them. Limbic seizures also cause compulsive thinking, psychosis and episodes in which one cannot distinguish dreaming from waking reality. The overlap between limbic seizures and psychiatric disorders is a striking 50 per cent compared to only 10 per cent in all other kinds of epilepsy. The second example concerns the emergence from coma. In recovering from coma, patients first manifest automatisms, then voluntary movements and speech that is childlike and emotionally childish. Behaviour becomes more rational and adult-like if recovery continues. In other words, intellect cannot be reclaimed unless emotion recovers first.

Emotion did not get left behind in evolution. Reason and emotion evolved together and their neural substrates are densely interconnected. Yet each concerns itself with a different task. The word 'salience', which means to 'leap up' or 'stick out', describes how the limbic brain alerts us to what is meaningful. We might say that the emotional brain deals with *qualitatively significant information.*

The limbic brain's use of common structures for different functions such as memory, emotion and attention may partly explain why humans excel at making decisions based on incomplete information: 'acting on our hunches'. We know more than we think we know. And yet are we not always surprised at our insights, inspirations and creativity? And do we not just as often reject our direct experience in favour of 'objective facts' instead?

2.9 The Rejection of Direct Experience

My usual response to those who ask if synaesthesia is 'real' is: 'Real to whom? To you, or to those who experience it?' Questioning its reality without first having some technological confirmation shows how ready we are to reject any first-hand experience. We are addicted to the external and the rational. Our insistence on a third-person, 'objective' understanding of the world has just about swept aside all other forms of knowledge.

In the course of studying MW, for example, we came to a point of using invasive and rather sophisticated technology when he became frightened, not that we might uncover some medical abnormality, but because a machine might prove that his synaesthesia wasn't real. MW was ready to accept the judgement of a machine over his lifetime of first-hand experience. This is a remarkable commentary.

When we think of our brains, we usually think of a computer, a reasoning machine in our heads that runs things. This is consistent with the hierarchical model. But emotion – which I use to include irrational, a-rational and non-verbal knowledge and cognition – is what actually directs our thoughts and actions. Like the Wizard of Oz, it is our a-rational inner life that pulls the levers behind the curtain. Our inner knowledge behind the curtain is largely inaccessible to introspective language, which means that what we feel about something is more valid than what we think or say about that something.

Reason is just the endless paperwork of the mind. The heart of our creativity is our direct experience and the salience that our limbic brain gives it. Allowing it to be that does not stop us from overlaying rational considerations on it – after which we can talk, recount, explain, interpret and analyse to our hearts' content.

2.10 Future Issues for Research

A number of tantalizing observations need to be systematically followed up, and other issues remain to be clarified, all of which can help address the overarching question of whether my sharp demarcation between synaesthesia and other cross-modal associations remains justified. In addition to neuropsychologists, other professionals who can bring their expertise to synaesthesia include anatomists, geneticists, linguists and developmentalists.

Synaesthesia embraces an unexpected constellation of features. Traits in which non-right-handers predominate customarily feature an excess of males. Yet synaesthetes are predominantly female, and in commenting on synaesthesia's heritability, Baron-Cohen (in Baron-Cohen et al. 1993) notes that a preponderance of relatives who share the trait are also female. (Is this a sampling bias or not? Of my seven females who have a synaesthetic relative, five of the relatives are themselves female.) While mathematical and spatial (navigational) skills are said to be somewhat poorer in women than men in general, in synaesthetes we find a strong tendency towards frank abnormality.

In the US, female synaesthetes are 2.5 times more common than male synaesthetes, while the ratio is much higher in the UK, a disparity that needs an explanation. (Baron-Cohen reported a ratio of 4:1 in 1987, based on two independent samples). Some of the inequality may relate to the kind and number of synaesthetes in our respective collections. While both of our subject populations are self-selected, mine (Cytowic 1989) is smaller ($N = 42$) and contains polymodal synaesthetes whose experience is projected (i.e. experienced as outside of themselves).

Harrison and Baron-Cohen have received enquiries from several hundred possible synaesthetes, nearly all of whom manifest only coloured letters and words (as in Vladimir Nabokov). Might this be a possible *forme fruste*? Or might it mark a realm where projected cross-modal experience merges into commonplace mental imagery? It is doubtful that transatlantic genetic differences contribute to this disparity.

Related to the above is the issue of synaesthesia's incidence. Based on newly encountered cases since *Synesthesia: a union of the senses* (1989), and especially since *The Man Who Tasted Shapes* (1993), which was written for a general audience, I have revised my initial approximation from one in 100,000 to one in 25,000. In the process of discerning its true frequency, we should also determine the relative incidence of different sensory combinations. Are smell and taste really less common than sight and sound, and if so, why?

Further revisions are also possible in response to potential cases received via the Internet, either direct enquiries or those engendered by subscriber-based services such as Prodigy and CompuServe. The even-sex ratio that I have ascertained in self-selected cases submitted electronically is likely because more men than women use computers with modems that are connected to on-line services.

Turning to the purely physical realm for a moment, I performed detailed Goldmann perimetric visual field testing in only two subjects (MW and LH). However, both showed a left monocular temporal field defect consistent with an abnormality in the left hemisphere optic radiation. Nowadays in clinical practice, such a lesion is rarely noticed because scanning has replaced careful but time-consuming hands-on examination. (Not only do patients usually fail to notice such small field cuts, but clinicians must deliberately hunt for them.) While I suggest that perimetry be systematically done on prospective synaesthetes, I caution that it must be performed manually (not with automated octopus-type equipment), and with attention to colour and motion defects.

Although my ascertainment is incomplete, at least 10 per cent of synaesthetes are gay or lesbian, meaning that the actual incidence of homosexual synaesthetes could be higher. Current research indicates that some part of human sexual orientation may be immutable, and that genes and other biological components play a significant role. The co-occurrence of a homosexual orientation and synaesthesia (including its distinct cognitive profile and gender distribution) would be most interesting, and broadly in agreement with Geschwind's controversial proposal that anomalous cerebral dominance underlies atypical cognitive talents and behaviour (Geschwind and Galaburda 1987; LeVay 1993). This is obviously an early conjecture. Accordingly, detailed systematic sexual histories of synaesthetes could prove or disprove what I have only surmised.

Learning disabilities seem more common in synaesthetes and their first-degree relatives. What is the actual incidence of autism, dyslexia and attention deficit disorder (ADD) among synaesthetes? Do synaesthetes themselves so afflicted differ from other synaesthetes?

A young adult male recently phoned in to a radio programme on which I appeared and recounted a typical story of coloured hearing. He also had ADD (attention deficit disorder), and mentioned being placed on Ritalin (methylphenidate) as a teenager. Instead of telling me that the stimulant attenuated his synaesthesiae, as I fully expected, he related how it intensified the experience. This effect is the reverse of that demonstrated by my earlier drug experiments as well as anecdotal reports of synaesthetes who have taken stimulants recreationally. Since individuals with ADD have a paradoxical response to stimulants, perhaps it is not surprising for that paradoxical response to carry over to those who have synaesthesia as well.

Much can be learned from scrutinizing the effects of commonly prescribed drugs on synaesthesia. Because their psychopharmacology is usually known in depth, antidepressants, anti-migraine and anti-epileptic medications come quickly to mind. For example, subject GG noted that her synaesthesia was not as intense during the interval that she took Ludiomil (maprotiline, a norepinephrine re-uptake blocker). One wonders about the effect of popular serotonin uptake inhibitors such as Prozac (fluoxetine), Zoloft (sertraline) and Paxil (paroxetine).

Whereas there are individuals with hippocampal epileptogenic foci who experience synaesthesia during a seizure but are otherwise not synaesthetic, there also exist synaesthetes who are additionally epileptic and in whom the two phenomena are independent. A lifelong synaesthete who developed temporal lobe seizures as an adolescent notes that the anti-epileptic Tegretol (carbamezapine) made her synaesthesia less vivid (Cytowic 1989: 174).

Clinical skill and astute listening are mandatory if such experience is to be extracted from patients. Epileptics are frightened of a great many things, mostly irrational, and about which they *never* speak unless asked directly, without judgement and with compassion. It surprises many physicians to learn that epileptics are terrified foremost of dying during a seizure. If such an unfounded worry preoccupies their thoughts, it is not hard to suppose that synaesthetic experience might make them think that they are losing their minds.

Fourteen years ago, I conjectured that synaesthesia was an all-or-nothing trait that did not disappear once it was manifest in childhood. Though aware of research showing that even newborns can make cross-modal associations (Meltzoff and Borton 1979), or that cross-modal similarities in non-synaesthetic children are stronger perceptually than verbally (Marks et al. 1987), I had found no clinical evidence to support the hypothesis that synaesthesia might be more common in children, as authors from earlier eras claimed. Only this year three individuals have remarked – with some amazement and in the context of my public appearance – that they vividly recall coloured words, shapes, number forms and the like as children but no longer experienced these things as teenagers. 'I haven't thought of this since I was a child', or 'since my bar mitzvah', they typically volunteered. So, do some children lose their synaesthesia, and, if so, when? Do the hormonal storms of puberty play a role via modulation of cerebral organization? If some individuals indeed lose their conscious experience of synaesthesia, do they retain any other common synaesthetic features?

Related to this line of inquiry looms the disentanglement of phonemic from lexical stimuli, as well as issues centred on learning in those synaesthetes who experience coloured letters, numbers and words. If the letter M is red, for example, there is something about its 'M-ness' that makes it red, so some learning must be involved despite synaesthesia being a relatively low-level higher function. But how much learning, when, and of what nature? Moreover, why do some synaesthetes respond to the sound of a word while others are influenced by the spelling? Is there, as some developmentalists propose, a critical period of conceptual reorganization when children switch from speaking to reading? Could the details of such a switch explain the presumed retention of phonemic stimuli in some synaesthetes and the progression to lexical triggers in others? Given synaesthesia's heritability, one could possibly, though with effort, identify synaesthetic offspring with coloured hearing and see if the stimuli in fact do change after the acquisition of reading. Linguists no doubt could pose more sophisticated and probing experiments.

Stroop-type tests, and comparisons of homonyms, synonyms and the like are additional probes that may answer some questions and raise others. For example, a woman and her father both taste words. 'Your name, Richard, tastes like a chocolate bar', she writes, 'warm and melting on my tongue.' 'Some words are a complete "experience" in that they have flavor, texture, temperature, and are sensed in a certain place in my mouth, i.e., back of throat, tip of tongue, etc. Often, the spelling affects the taste. "Lori" tastes like a pencil eraser, but "Laurie" tastes lemony. Go figure.' In such a case, one might first verify whether the spelling or meaning determines the synaesthesia. Another concern is that there are innumerably more words than smells, so what eventually happens? (A similar case holds for those in whom sound rather than spelling determines colours.) Do tastes occur only for nouns, or concrete nouns? What about verbs, adjectives and grammatical functors? What does the word 'eraser' taste like? The questions go on.

Lastly, I did not mention cognitivists who might help to further clarify the brain basis of synaesthesia. I generally take the view that clinical observation must drive theory rather than the reverse. I think this position is even more necessary with phenomena such as synaesthesia that are largely experiential.

Just as I argued that our passion for a detached and 'objective' point of view has diminished other kinds of knowing, so too I see that the experimental emphasis on deficits is gradually smothering the clinical method of symptom analysis. And herein lies the friction between cognitive scientists, who think abstractly and in terms of computation, and those scientists who think clinically and in terms of biology. The experimental approach favoured by cognitive science takes individuals with brain damage and focuses on deficits (what is missing) to infer the existence of underlying entities that are presumably linked into a computational network. The models of this abstract approach boil down to hypothetical components in box diagrams. In contrast, the clinical approach examines symptoms, positive errors rather than negative deficits. Because it focuses on how symptoms change over time rather than being interested in how network components interact at the same time at any given moment, clinical models are predominantly procedural and contextual.

Perhaps some distrust of symptom-based accounts lies in their aura of being more hermeneutic than scientific. That is, their validation is largely aesthetic, a theory's proof residing in the harmony of its elements, its coherence of ideas and its explanatory power. Many scientists spurn this whiff of mysticism. None the less, local cognitive models strike me as overly self-contained, the inevitable isolation of a model's elements artificially reifying them into real entities without an effort to say how everything comes together. Even then, 'all together' doesn't mean how it relates to personality or the big picture, but only to other local models. Cognitive science can make a local model of anything, though the fact that it could make a model of synaesthesia without needing a model of perception strikes me as odd. Being able to see the big picture requires an enormous understanding of myriad details.

If you think that the mind is some disembodied, abstract programme that can be instantiated on any hardware capable of running it, then you can ignore the biological complexities of neural tissue. For those who think theoretically, this is both convenient and lazy. Cognitivists envisage their negative deficits in terms of lesioning one or more theoretically assumed modules in the 'system' underlying some behaviour. Independent of any clinical evidence, computational models eagerly presume the existence of logically plausible but wholly abstract sub-systems. Yet they seem to be able to say little about positive symptoms. At best, it can suggest that synaesthesia represents a breakdown of modularity (Baron-Cohen et al. 1993). While this may seem to illuminate a single case report, no strategy exists for collapsing across cases, or different *kinds* of synaesthesia.

I concur that the brain is representational, yet remain unsure (and unswayed) about its being computational. Our sensory input is digital, but our experience is analogue. Yet hypothetical modules presently drive experiment instead of theory being driven by phenomenology.

The Brodmann areas have conceptually metamorphosed into chips that serve distinct mental functions – grammar, syntax, colour, contrast or whatever. Behaviour and perception are reduced to the inputs and outputs of a presumed central processor – a concept that divorces human experience from context, history and environment. (This sounds like behaviourism revisited, although I grant that the behaviourists didn't care whether humans had a brain, let alone a cognitive architecture.) Having said all this, let me ask you to cogitate whether microgenesis, for example, can explain synaesthesia more satisfactorily than cognitive science can (Brown 1988; Hanlon 1991).

Do the elemental qualities of synaesthesia, as partially represented by the form constants, represent 'building blocks' or 'modules' of cognitive science in which a perception is assembled, like modelling a statue from bits of clay? Or is perception holistic, constrained by sensation as it unfolds from within? If so, then perception is like sculpting from a block of marble, exposing the statue within it by removing extraneous bits. In this view, synaesthesia is the conscious awareness of a normally holistic process of perception that is prematurely displayed. That is, it is awareness before the terminal target, before the final stage of neural transformation and mental mediation. If this is correct, then we are all unknowingly synaesthetic.

Notes

1 See also the index under 'color competition' in Cytowic (1989) for further examples of colour conflict both in synaesthesia and eidetic memory.
2 See Cytowic (1995: ch. 12) for the difference and for a discussion of geographical knowledge as a cognitive skill.
3 James ([1901], 1990: 343).
4 Parenthetically, I have also approached the issue of non-universal responses via the well-known topics of colour constancy and coloured shadows.

References

Argelander, A. 1927: *Das Farbenhoeren und der synaesthetische Faktor der Wahrnehmung*. Jena: Fischer.

Baron-Cohen, S., Harrison, J., Goldstein, L.H. and Wyke, M. 1993: Coloured speech perception: is synaesthesia what happens when modularity breaks down? *Perception*, 22, 419–26.

Brown, J.W. 1988: *The Life of the Mind*. Hillsdale, N.J.: Lawrence Erlbaum.
Cytowic, R.E. 1989: *Synesthesia: a union of the senses*. New York: Springer Verlag.
Cytowic, R.E. 1993: *The Man Who Tasted Shapes: a bizarre medical mystery offers revolutionary insights into reasoning, emotion, and consciousness*. New York: Putnam.
Cytowic, R.E. 1995: *The Neurological Side of Neuropsychology*. Cambridge, Mass.: MIT Press.
Cytowic, R.E. and Wood, F.B. 1982a: Synesthesia I: a review of major theories and their brain basis. *Brain and Cognition*, 1, 23–35.
Cytowic, R.E. and Wood, F.B. 1982b: Synesthesia II: psychophysical relationships in the synesthesia of geometrically shaped taste and colored hearing. *Brain and Cognition*, 1, 36–49.
Geschwind, N. and Galaburda, A.M. 1987: *Cerebral Lateralization: biological mechanisms, associations, and pathology*. Cambridge, Mass.: MIT Press.
Goethe, J.W. von 1810: *Zur Farbenlahre*, trans. C.L. Eastlake as *Theory of Colors*, London: Frank Cass, 1967.
Hanlon, R.E. (ed.) 1991: *Cognitive Microgenesis: a neuropsychological perspective*. New York: Springer Verlag.
James, W. [1901], 1990: *The Varieties of Religious Experience*. New York: Vintage Books.
Kandinsky, V. 1910: Über das Geistige. In *Der Kunst, Inbesondere in der Malerei*. Munich: Piper.
LeVay, S. 1993: *The Sexual Brain*. Cambridge, Mass.: MIT Press.
Luria, A.R. 1968: *The Mind of a Mnemonist*. New York: Basic Books.
Marks, L.E., Hammeal, R.J. and Bornstein, M.H. 1987: Perceiving similarity and comprehending metaphor. *Monographs of the Society for Research in Child Development*, 52(1), 1–102.
Meltzoff, A.N. and Borton, R.W. 1979: Intermodal matching by human neonates. *Nature*, 282, 403–4.
Newton, I. [1730], 1952: *Optiks*, 4th edn. New York: Dover Publications.
Ommaya, A.K. (in press) Neurobiology of emotion and the evolution of mind. *Journal of the American Academy of Psychoanalysis*.
Osgood, C.E., Suci, G.J. and Tannenbaum, P.H. 1957: *The Measurement of Meaning*. Chicago: University of Illinois Press.
Suarez de Mendoza, F. 1980: *L'Audition colorée*. Paris: Octave Donin.
Yakovlev, P.I. 1948: Motility, behavior and the brain: stereodynamic organization and neural co-ordinates of behavior. *Journal of Nervous and Mental Diseases*, 107(4), 313–35.
Yakovlev, P.I. 1970: The structural and functional 'trinity' of the body, brain and behavior. In H.T. Wycis (ed.), *Current Research in Neurosciences: topical problems in psychiatry and neurology*, New York: Karger, 10, 197–208.

Part II
Classic Papers

3

Colour Associations*

Sir Francis Galton

Numerals are occasionally seen in Arabic or other figures, not disposed in any particular form, but coloured. An instance of this is represented in Figure 69† towards the middle part of the column [the plate comprising figures is not reproduced here], but as I shall have shortly to enter at length into the colour associations of the author, I will pass over this portion of them, and will quote in preference from the letter of another correspondent.

Baron von Osten Sacken, of whom I have already spoken, writes.

> The localisation of numerals, peculiar to certain persons, is foreign to me. In my mind's eye the figures appear *in front* of me, within a limited space. My peculiarity, however, consists in the fact that the numberals from 1 to 9 are differently coloured; (1) black, (2) yellow, (3) pale brick red, (4) brown, (5) blackish gray, (6) reddish brown, (7) green, (8) bluish, (9) reddish brown somewhat like 6. These colours appear very distinctly when I think of these figures separately; in compound figures they become less apparent. But the most remarkable manifestation of these colours appears in my recollections of chronology. When I think of the events of a given century they invariably appear to me on a background coloured like the principal figure in the dates of that century; thus events of the eighteenth century invariably appear to me on a greenish ground, from the colour of the figure 7. This habit clings to me most tenaciously, and the only hypothesis I can form about its origin is the following: – My tutor, when I was ten to twelve years old, taught me chronology by means of a diagram on which the centuries were represented by squares, subdivided in 100 smaller squares; the squares representing

*Reprinted from *Inquiries into Human Faculty*. London: Dent, 1883.
†The reader is directed to the original text for the figures.

> centuries had *narrow coloured borders*; it may be that in this way the recollection of certain figures became associated with certain colours. I venture this explanation without attaching too much importance to it, because it seems to me that if it was true, my *direct* recollection of those coloured borders would have been stronger than it is; still, the strong association of my chronology with colour seems to plead in favour of that explanation.

Figures 66, 67. These two are selected out of a large collection of coloured Forms in which the months of the year are visualised. They will illustrate the gorgeousness of the mental imagery of some favoured persons. Of these Figure 66 is by the wife of an able London physician, and Figure 67 is by Mrs Kempe Welch, whose sister, Miss Bevington, a well-known and thoughtful writer, also sees coloured imagery in connection with dates. This Figure 67 was one of my test cases, repeated after the lapse of two years, and quite satisfactorily. The first communication was a descriptive account, partly in writing, partly by word of mouth; the second, on my asking for it, was a picture which agreed perfectly with the description, and explained much that I had not understood at the time. The small size of the Figure in the Plate makes it impossible to do justice to the picture, which is elaborate and on a large scale, with a perspective of similar hills stretching away to the far distance, and each standing for a separate year. She writes:

> It is rather difficult to give it fully without making it too definite; on each side there is a total blank.

The instantaneous association of colour with sound characterises a small percentage of adults, and it appears to be rather common, though in an ill-developed degree, among children. I can here appeal not only to my own collection of facts, but to those of others, for the subject has latterly excited some interest in Germany. The first widely known case was that of the brothers Nussbaumer, published in 1873 by Professor Bruhl of Vienna, of which the English reader will find an account in the last volume of Lewis's *Problems of Life and Mind* (p. 280). Since then many occasional notices of similar associations have appeared. A pamphlet containing numerous cases was published in Leipzig in 1881 by two Swiss investigators, Messrs Bleuler and Lehmann.[1] One of the authors had the faculty very strongly, and the other had not; so they worked conjointly with advantage. They carefully tabulated the particulars of sixty-two cases. As my present object is to subordinate details to the general impression that I wish to convey of the peculiarities of different minds, I will simply remark – First, that the persistence of the colour association with sounds is fully as remarkable as that of the Number–Form with numbers. Secondly, that the vowel sounds chiefly evoke them. Thirdly, that the seers are invariably most minute in their description of the precise tint and hue of the colour. They are never satisfied, for instance, with saying 'blue', but will take a great deal of trouble to express or to match the particular blue they mean. Fourthly, that no two people agree, or hardly ever do so, as to the colour they associate with the same sound. Lastly, that the tendency is very hereditary. The publications just mentioned absolve me from the necessity of giving many extracts from the numerous letters I have received, but I am particularly anxious to bring the brilliancy of these colour associations more vividly before the reader than is possible by mere description. I have therefore given the elaborately-coloured diagrams in Plate IV., which were copied by the artist directly from the original drawings, and which have been printed by the superimposed impressions of different colours from different lithographic stones. They have been, on the whole, very faithfully executed, and will serve as samples of the most striking cases. Usually the sense of colour is much too vague to enable the seer to reproduce the various tints so definitely as those in this Plate. But this is by no means universally the case.

Figure 68 is an excellent example of the occasional association of colours with letters. It is by Miss Stones, the head teacher in a high school for girls, who, as I have already mentioned, obtained useful information for me, and has contributed several suggestive remarks of her own. She says:

> The vowels of the English language always appear to me, when I think of them, as possessing certain colours, of which I enclose a diagram. Consonants, when thought of by themselves, are of a purplish black; but when I think of a whole word, the colour of the consonants tends towards the colour of the vowels. For example, in the word 'Tuesday,' when I think of each letter separately, the consonants are purplish-black, *u* is a light dove colour, *e* is a pale emerald green, and *a* is yellow; but when I think of the whole word together, the first part is a light gray-green, and the latter part yellow. Each word is a distinct whole. I have always associated the same colours with the same letters, and no effort will change the colour of one letter, transferring it to another. Thus the word 'red' assumes a light-green tint, while the word 'yellow' is light-green at the beginning and red at the end. Occasionally, when uncertain how a word should be spelt, I have considered what colour it ought to be, and have decided in that way. I believe this has often been a great help to me in spelling, both in English and foreign languages. The colour of the letters is never smeared or blurred in any way. I cannot recall to

> mind anything that should have first caused me to associate colours with letters, nor can my mother remember any alphabet or reading-book coloured in the way I have described, which I might have used as a child. I do not associate any idea of colour with musical notes at all, nor with any of the other senses.

She adds:

> Perhaps you may be interested in the following account from my sister of her visual peculiarities: 'When I think of Wednesday I see a kind of oval flat wash of yellow emerald green; for Tuesday, a gray sky colour; for Thursday, a brown-red irregular polygon; and a dull yellow smudge for Friday.'

The latter quotation is a sample of many that I have; I give it merely as another instance of hereditary tendency.

I will insert just one description of other coloured letters than those represented in the Plate. It is from Mrs H., the married sister of a well-known man of science, who writes:

> I do not know how it is with others, but to me the colours of vowels are so strongly marked that I hardly understand their appearing of a different colour, or, what is nearly as bad, colour-less to any one. To me they are and always have been, as long as I have known them, of the following tints:
>
> A, pure white, and like china in texture.
> E, red, not transparent; vermilion, with china-white would represent it.
> I, light bright yellow; gamboge.
> O, black, but transparent; the colour of deep water seen through thick clear ice.
> U, purple.
> Y, a dingier colour than I.
>
> The shorter sounds of the vowels are less vivid and pure in colour. Consonants are almost or quite colourless to me, though there is some blackness about M.
>
> Some association with U in the words blue and purple may account for that colour, and possibly the E in red may have to do with that also; but I feel as if they were independent of suggestions of the kind.
>
> My first impulse is to say that the association lies solely in the sound of the vowels, in which connection I certainly feel it the most strongly; but then the thought of the distinct redness of such a [printed or written] word as '*great*', shows me that the relation must be visual as well as aural. The meaning of words is so unavoidably associated with the sight of them, that I think this association rather overrides the primitive

> impression of the colour of the vowels, and the word *'violet'* reminds me of its proper colour until I look at the word as a mere collection of letters.
>
> Of my two daughters, one sees the colours quite differently from this (A, blue; E, white; I, black; O, whity-brownish; U, opaque brown). The other is only heterodox on the A and O; A being with her black, and O white. My sister and I never agreed about these colours, and I doubt whether my two brothers feel the chromatic force of the vowels at all.

I give this instance partly on account of the hereditary interest. I could add cases from at least three different families in which the heredity is quite as strongly marked.

Figure 69 fills the whole of the middle column of Plate IV and contains specimens from a large series of coloured illustrations, accompanied by many pages of explanation from a correspondent, Dr James Key of Montagu, Cape Colony. The pictures will tell their own tale sufficiently well. I need only string together a few brief extracts from his letters, as follows:

> I confess my inability to understand visualised numerals; it is otherwise, however, with regard to colour associations with letters. Ever since childhood these have been distinct and unchanging in my consciousness; sometimes, although very seldom, I have mentioned them, to the amazement of my teachers and the scorn of my comrades. A is brown. I say it most dogmatically, and nothing will ever have the effect, I am convinced, of making it appear otherwise! I can imagine no explanation of this association. [He goes into much detail as to conceivable reasons connected with his childish life to show that none of these would do.] Shades of brown accompany to my mind the various degrees of openness in pronouncing A. I have never been destitute in all my conscious existence of a conviction that E is a clear, cold, light-gray blue. I remember daubing in colours, when quite a little child, the picture of a jockey, whose shirt received a large share of E, as I said to myself while daubing it with grey. [He thinks that the letter I may possibly be associated with black because it contains no open space, and O with white because it does.] The colour of R has been invariable of a copper colour, in which a swarthy blackness seems to intervene, visually corresponding to the trilled pronunciation of R. This same appearance exists also in J, X, and Z.

The upper row of Figure 69 shows the various shades of brown, associated with different pronunciations of the letter A, as in 'fame', 'can', 'charm', and 'all' respectively. The second, third and fourth rows similarly refer to the various pronunciations of the other vowels. Then follow the letters of the alphabet, grouped according to the character of the appearance they suggest. After these come the numerals. Then I give three lines of words such as they appear to him. The first is my own name, the second is 'London', and the third is 'Visualisation'. Proceeding conversely, Dr Key collected scraps of various patterns of wall paper, and sent them together with the word that the colour of the several patterns suggested to him. Specimens of these are shown in the three bottom lines of the figure. I have gone through the whole of them with care, together with his descriptions and reasons, and can quite understand his meaning, and how exceedingly complex and refined these associations are. The patterns are to him like words in poetry, which call up associations that any substituted word of a like dictionary meaning would fail to do. It would not, for example, be possible to print words by the use of counters coloured like those in Figure 69, because the tint of each influences that of its neighbours. It must be understood that my remarks, though based on Dr Key's diagrams and statements as on a text, do not depend, by any means, wholly upon them, but on numerous other letters from various quarters to the same effect. At the same time I should say that Dr Key's elaborate drawings and ample explanations, to which I am totally unable to do justice in a moderate space, are the most full and striking of any I have received. His illustrations are on a large scale, and are ingeniously arranged so as to express his meaning.

Persons who have colour associations are unsparingly critical. To ordinary individuals one of these accounts seems just as wild and lunatic as another, but when the account of one seer is submitted to another seer, who is sure to see the colours in a different way, the latter is scandalised and almost angry at the heresy of the former. I submitted this very account of Dr Key to a lady, the wife of an ex-governor of one of the most important British possessions, who has vivid colour associations of her own, and who, I had some reason to think, might have personal acquaintance with the locality where Dr Key lives. She could not comprehend his account at all, his colours were so entirely different to those that she herself saw.

Note

1 E. Bleuler and K. Lehmann, *Zwangmässige Lichtempfindungen durch Schall und verwandte Erscheinungen*. Leipzig: Fues' Verlag (R. Reisland), 1881.

4

On Colored-hearing Synesthesia: Cross-modal Translations of Sensory Dimensions*

Lawrence E. Marks

One of the most curious and intriguing phenomena of the human mind is synesthesia – the translation of attributes of sensation from one sensory domain to another. Among the most commonplace of synesthetic perceptions are the well-known connections between color and thermal sensations: Yellow, orange, and red are frequently perceived and described as 'warm ' colors, blue and green as 'cool' colors. A scheme of warm and cool colors was described a century ago (Sully 1879).

Much more dramatic examples of synesthesia are the strong, often apparently idiosyncratic, associations reported in the literature on colored hearing and colored taste. One may read of a synesthete for whom violin music is represented as a dance of sparkling white and yellow stripes, or of another for whom the taste of vinegar conjures up bright greenness.

It is easy to dismiss synesthetic experiences as peculiar, rare, and idiosyncratic phenomena that seem to have little bearing on the operation of the 'normal' mind. What, after all, is one to do with a report like that of Luria's subject S, the mnemonist cum synesthete:

> Presented with a tone pitched at 50 cycles per second and an amplitude of 100 decibels, S saw a brown strip against a dark background that had red, tongue-like edges. The sense of taste he experienced was like that of sweet and sour borscht, a sensation that gripped his entire tongue. . . .
>
> Presented with a tone pitched at 2,000 cycles per second and having an amplitude of 113 decibels, S said: 'It looks something like fireworks tinged with a pink-red hue. The strip of color feels rough and unpleas-

*Reprinted from *Psychological Bulletin*, 82(3), 303–31.

ant, and it has an ugly taste – rather like that of a briny pickle' (Luria 1968: 45–6)

There is no doubt that many synesthetic perceptions are peculiar and idiosyncratic. But many others are not. In particular, as I hope to demonstrate, the associations between color and sound are often regular, systematic, and consistent from one person to another. Rather than displaying merely some odd, fortuitous associations, these universal synesthetic experiences reflect important cognitive properties that in several respects are common to normal people as well as to synesthetes.

Colored Hearing

An attempt to review here the entire literature on synesthesia is impossible. Prior to the turn of the twentieth century, there had already been published several books and more than a hundred papers on the topic. The richest vein of material comprises the literature on *colored hearing*: Suarez de Mendoza's review, published in 1890, contains 59 references: Krohn's (1892), contains 85; Clavière's (1898), 131; Argelander's (1927), 466; and Mahling's (1926), 533.

By the end of the nineteenth century, colored hearing was such a popular topic that a committee of seven prominent psychologists was organized at the 1890 International Congress of Physiological Psychology; its purpose was to standardize the terminology of synesthesia and to advance scientific understanding. The members included the Swiss psychologist Flournoy (who, together with Claparède, compiled data on colored vowels) and the Rumanian Gruber. Gruber (1893), like Claparède and Flournoy, attempted a largescale survey on colored hearing by means of a questionnaire; but alas, whereas Flournoy (1892) was able to obtain reports on color responses to vowels from over 200 synesthetes, Gruber obtained responses from only 23 (see Marinesco 1912).

Reports on synesthesia, especially of colored hearing, began to mount during the mid-nineteenth century. For extensive reviews of early knowledge and opinion, the interested reader is referred to Krohn (1892), Clavière (1898), Argelander (1927), and Mahling (1926).[1] Several of the nineteenth-century accounts of synesthesia appeared in medical journals (e.g. Baratoux 1887; Colman 1894; Grafé 1897; Hilbert 1895; Pedrono 1882; Quincke 1890); to some scientists of the period, colored hearing seemed a medical oddity, if not a symptom of physiological abnormality (cf. Clavière 1898). Indeed, it is of historical interest that the first scientific reference to synesthesia appears to be medical, namely, that of the turn-of-the-eighteenth-century English ophthalmologist T. Woolhouse (see Castel 1735).

During the nineteenth century, evidence began to mount that implied colored hearing is less likely a physiological perversity than a somewhat uncommon, but nonetheless interesting and important, psychological phenomenon. Galton's (1883) report on various forms of synesthesia, including colored hearing, helped to make the topic somewhat more 'respectable'; and Fechner's (1876) and Bleuler and Lehmann's (1881) studies, by providing some quantification of the frequencies of occurrence of synesthetic perceptions, demonstrated the regular nature of cross-modal analogies. The last two studies noted in particular the potency of vowel sounds in the evocation of colors, although it is readily apparent even to the examination of the literature before 1876 that vowels are an especially powerful source for the production of secondary visual 'sensations'.

Colored vowels

The fundamental question of concern here is: Do synesthetic experiences reflect some intrinsic sensory correspondences? With respect to colored hearing and particularly colored vowels, the question becomes: Is there an intrinsic relation between sound (vowel quality) and associated visual sensations (colors)? The evidence at hand suggests that there is a relation, and the theoretical position taken here is that the synesthetic relations between color and sound (vowel) quality are at least as intimate as is the well-studied relation between brightness and loudness in nonsynesthetic subjects. When people are asked to match brightness of lights to loudness of sounds, they align increasing luminances with increasing sound pressures in a systematic manner that is similar from person to person (Marks and Stevens 1966; Stevens and Marks 1965). Basically, then, the proposal set forth here is that synesthesia provides a form of systematic cross-modality matching.

Table 4.1 is a summary of reports and observations on colored hearing. One of the most interesting of the early statements is Arthur Rimbaud's ([1871] 1937) poem 'Le Sonnet des voyelles', in which the poet expressed the presumed colors of the cardinal vowels: 'A noir, E blanc, I rouge, U vert, O bleu: voyelles, Je dirai quelque jour vos naissances latentes' (p. 93).

Later, Rimbaud ([1873] 1937: 285) remarked that the colors of vowels were his *invention*:

> J'inventais la couleur des voyelles! – A noir, E blanc, I rouge, O bleu, U vert. – Je réglai la forme et le mouvement de chaque consonne, et, avec des rhythmes instinctifs, je me flattai d'inventer un verbe poétique accessible, un jour ou l'autre, à tous les sens. Je réservais la traduction.

Table 4.1 Chronological summary of literature on visual–auditory synesthesia

Source	*Date*[a]	*Description*
Pythagoras	6th cent. BC	'Music of the spheres'
Aristotle	4th cent. BC (1931)	Harmony of colors like harmony of sounds
Arcimboldo[b]	16th cent.	Devised color music
Locke	1690	Blind man apprehends scarlet by sound of a trumpet
Leibniz	1704 (1896)	Blind man apprehends scarlet by sound of a trumpet
Newton	1704	Parallel between colors of spectrum and notes of musical scale
Woolhouse[c]	*c.*1710	Synesthesia in a blind man
Castel	1725, 1735	Parallel between colors and musical notes; built color organ
Herder	1772	Natural connection of color and sound via feeling
L. Hoffmann[d]	1786	Report of colored music
E. Darwin	1790	Parallel between colors and musical notes
E.T.A. Hoffmann	1810 (1899)	*Kreisleriana*: colored music
Sachs[d]	1812	Report of colored vowels
Tieck	1828	*Schriften*: colored music
Gautier	1843, 1846	Description of colored hearing induced by hashish
Baudelaire	1857	'Correspondances'
Ludlow	1857	Description of colored hearing induced by hashish
Baudelaire	1860 (1923)	Description of colored hearing induced by hashish
Nahlowsky	1862	Description of colored hearing: pitch-brightness
Perroud[d]	1863	Report of colored vowels: physiological theory
Rimbaud	1871 (1937)	'Le Sonnet des Voyelles'
Wundt	1874	Equivalence of pitch and brightness is by analogy
Fechner	1876	Report of colored vowels

Bleuler & Lehmann	1881	Review of colored hearing and report of colored vowels: *law of brightness*, pitch–size, loudness–size
Mayerhaeusen[d]	1882	Report of colored vowels
Pedrono	1882	Report of colored music: pitch–brightness, loudness–brightness, physiological theory
Galton	1883	Report of colored vowels: synesthesia frequent in children
Hall	1883	Colored hearing frequent in children
de Rochas	1885	Report of colored vowels: pitch–brightness
Giradeau	1885	Report of colored hearing: pitch–brightness
Lauret[d]	1885, 1886	Report of colored vowels and music
Baratoux	1887	Report of colored vowels: pitch–brightness
Ghil	1887 (1938)	*Traité du Verbe*: system of colored vowels
Lauret & Duchaussoy	1887	Report of colored vowels
Albertoni	1889	Description of colored music: *auditory daltonism*
Raymond[d]	1889	Report of colored vowels
Klinckowström	1890	Report of colored vowels
Quincke	1890	Report of colored vowels
Suarez de Mendoza	1890	Review and report of colored vowels and music
Beaunis & Binet	1892	Report of colored vowels
Binet	1892	Report of colored vowels
Binet & Philippe	1892	Report of colored vowels
Flournoy	1892	Report of colored vowels
Krohn	1892	Review of colored hearing
Binet	1893	Colored hearing has associative basis
Calkins	1893	Report of colored vowels and music: associative theory
Flournoy	1893	Review of colored hearing and vowels: *law of brightness*
Gruber	1893	Questionnaire on colored hearing
Philippe	1893a	Report of colored hearing in the blind: pitch–brightness

Table 4.1 Continued

Source	*Date*[a]	*Description*
Philippe	1893b	Report of colored vowels
Starr	1893	Report of colored music: pitch–brightness
Colman	1894	Report of colored vowels: associative theory
Calkins	1895	Report of colored hearing: often pleasurable
Grafé	1897, 1898	Report of colored vowels
Clavière	1898	Review of colored hearing
Laignel-Lavastine	1901	Report of colored vowels: associative theory
Claparède	1903	Report of colored vowels: colored hearing stable over time
Dresslar	1903	Colored hearing stable over time: associative theory
Stelzner	1903, 1904	Report of colored vowels
Ulrich	1903	Report of colored vowels
Lemaitre	1904	Report of colored vowels
Lomer	1905	Report of colored vowels and music
Rossigneux	1905	Review of colored vowels from poetry
Smith	1905	Report of colored hearing: pitch–brightness
Harris	1908	Colored hearing has associative basis, hereditary tendency
Raines	1909	Report of colored music
Rose	1909	Report of colored hearing and vowels
Myers	1911	Report of colored music: pitch–brightness
Scriabin	1911	*Prometheus*: composition for sound and light
Hug-Hellmuth	1912	Report of colored vowels: psychoanalytic theory
Kandinsky	1912	Description of colored music
Marinesco	1912	Report of colored vowels and music
Schultze	1912	Report of colored vowels
Coriat	1913	Report of colored hearing and vowels

Langenbeck	1913	Report of colored vowels: associative theory
Wehofer	1913	Review of colored hearing and vowels: pitch–brightness is of vowel formants
Langfeld	1914	Report of colored music: stable over time, pitch–brightness physiological theory
Mudge	1920	Report of colored music: pitch–brightness
Wheeler	1920	Report of colored hearing: pitch–brightness, loudness–brightness
English	1923	Report of colored music: associative theory
Ginsberg	1923	Report of colored vowels and music: pitch–brightness
Henning	1923	Report of colored vowels: relations based on phonetic structure
Révész	1923	Report of colored hearing: frequent in children
Anschütz	1925	Report of colored music: pitch–brightness, pitch–size
Anschütz	1926	Report of colored vowels and music
Mahling	1926	Review of colored hearing
Argelander	1927	Review of colored hearing, report of colored vowels
Beringer[e]	1927	Report of colored hearing induced by mescaline: pitch–brightness
Collins	1929	Report of colored vowels
Voss	1929	Report of colored hearing: pitch–brightness, pitch–size, loudness–size
Vernon	1930	Report of colored music: pitch–brightness, pitch–size
Zigler	1930	Pitch–brightness, pitch–size
Hornbostel	1931	Brightness is universal attribute of sensation: pitch–brightness in nonsynesthetes
Ortmann	1933	Report and review of colored hearing: pitch–brightness
Kelly	1934	Attempt to teach colored hearing
Riggs & Karwoski	1934	Report of colored hearing: synesthesia is alignment of dimensions, pitch-brightness, pitch-size

Table 4.1 Continued

Source	*Date*[a]	*Description*
Dudycha & Dudycha	1935	Report of colored music: pitch–brightness, pitch–size
Karwoski & Odbert	1938	Report of colored music: pitch–brightness, pitch–size
Leuba	1940	Report of conditioned sensation
Ellson	1941	Report of conditioned sensation
Aiken	1942	'Music'
Karwoski, Odbert, & Osgood	1942	Report of colored music
Odbert, Karwoski, & Eckerson	1942	Report of colored music
Howells	1944	Attempt to teach colored hearing
Reichart, Jakobson, & Werth	1949	Report of colored vowels: cross-linguistic similarity
Delay, Gérard, & Racamier	1951	Report of colored hearing induced by mescaline
Masson	1952	Report of colored vowels and music: brightness is function of formant spacing
Simpson, Quinn, & Ausubel	1956	Report of pitch–hue correspondences in non-synesthetic children
Ulich	1957	Survey of synesthesia: colored music
Wicker	1968	Report of pitch–brightness correspondences in non-synesthetes
Marks	1974	Report of pitch–brightness and loudness–brightness in non-synesthetes

This summary includes reports, descriptions, and surveys, including general principles and explanations.

[a] Dates in parentheses indicate date in reference list.

[b] Cited in Eastlake (1840).

[c] Cited in Castel (1735).

[d] Cited in Suarez de Mendoza (1890).

[e] Cited in Werner (1940).

As we shall soon see, there is general agreement on the part of synesthetes as to the colors of vowels, at least when these are reported in the scientific literature. Thus, we shall be able to decide how well the poet Rimbaud's invention agrees with more generally obtained results.

Most likely under the influence of Rimbaud, the poet René Ghil ([1887] 1938) attempted to build a scientific-literary system on the presumed colors of sounds. Ghil's system of vowel colors gave *a* as black, *e* as white, *i* as blue, *o* as red, and *u* as yellow. Note that the first two pairs are the same as those given by Rimbaud. In related vein, Rossigneux (1905), on the basis of an analysis of the sounds and images of poetry, also came to derive colors of vowels. His list gave *a* as white, *e* as green and blue, *o* as red, and *u* as black. As we can see, there is absolutely no overlap between Rossigneux's and Rimbaud's schemes and only small overlap between Rossigneux's and Ghil's. Note, however, that Rossigneux meant to limit the application of his scheme to sound–color relations in poetry.

That there exist some reliable correlations between sound composition and color is evident from Table 4.1. Reports by Nahlowsky (1862), Wundt (1874), de Rochas (1885), Giradeau (1885), Baratoux (1887), Philippe (1893a), Starr (1893), Smith (1905), Myers (1911), Langfeld (1914), Mudge (1920), Wheeler (1920), Ginsberg (1923), Anschütz (1925), Voss (1929), Vernon (1930), Zigler (1930), Ortmann (1933), Riggs and Karwoski (1934), Dudycha and Dudycha (1935), Karwoski and Odbert (1938), Wicker (1968), and Marks (1974) all include the observation of a correlation between auditory pitch and visual brightness. The higher the pitch (the higher the frequency) of a sound, the greater tends to be the brightness of the photism; as Suarez de Mendoza (1890: 140) wrote, 'Thus, they appear darker when they are struck on lower notes; but so much more clear and brilliant when they are formed of higher notes.'

The importance of this observation lies not only in its content (i.e. in the particular correlation between hearing and vision) but also in the fact that it manifests an association between *dimensions* of auditory and visual experiences, not just associations between individual sensations. Synesthesia (colored hearing) consists not of random associations between isolated phenomena or qualities on two sensory domains, but rather expresses correlated dimensions or attributes. To the best of my knowledge, the first clear enunciation of this principle was made by Riggs and Karwoski (1934).

Mention should be made that high-pitched sounds, or more properly high-frequency sounds, are often described by non-synesthetic subjects as *bright*. Hornbostel (1925, 1931) argued fervently for the universality of brightness as a dimension of all sensory experience. Colored hearing appears to be one embodiment of Hornbostel's principle: Bright sounds elicit bright photisms. This is discussed more fully later.

Analysis of vowel colors Are there any other pairs of dimensions besides brightness and pitch that correlate in colored hearing? At this point, it becomes valuable to examine in detail the colors associated with various vowels. Even cursory examination of the literature shows that from one report to another, the same colors tend to be aroused by the same vowels. Consistency is nowhere near complete; nevertheless, it is strong and impressive.

In order to examine in as great detail as possible the colors ascribed to vowels, I have gathered together as many of the reports on vowel color as I could obtain. In addition to the large-scale studies of Fechner (1876), Bleuler and Lehmann (1881), and Claparède (reported by Flournoy, 1892, 1893), I tabulated results reported by Sachs, Perroud, Mayerhausen, Lauret, and Raymond (as compiled by Suarez de Mendoza, 1890) and by Galton (1883), de Rochas (1885), Baratoux (1887), Lauret and Duchaussoy (1887), Klinckowströn (1890), Quincke (1890), Beaunis and Binet (1892), Binet and Philippe (1892), Philippe (1893b), Grafé (1898), Laignel-Lavastine (1901), Claparède (1903), Stelzner (1903, 1904), Ulrich (1903), Lemaitre (1904), Lomer (1905), Gruber (reported by Marinesco, 1912), Schultze (1912), Hug-Hellmuth (1912), Langenbeck (1913), Ginsberg (1923), Henning (1923), Anschütz (1926), Argelander (1927), Collins (1929), Reichard, Jakobson, and Werth (1949), and Masson (1952).

The classification of colors used to evaluate the synesthetic responses was: yellow, red, green, blue, violet, white, gray, brown, and black; that is, all colors were classified in terms of one or more of these categories. Occasional reports of other colors were sub-divided appropriately among the nine color categories. For instance, each report of orange was divided up as .5 yellow, .5 red.

The similarities among the results are remarkable. In every set of data (those of Fechner, of Bleuler and Lehmann, of Flournoy, and of the 35 small studies), the vowel *a* predominately aroused the colors red and blue, *e* and *i* tended to be yellow and white, *o* tended to be red and black, *u* was usually blue, brown, or black, and *ou* (in French) was brown.[2] (Specific phonetic representations of the vowels are taken up below.) As Mudge (1920: 345) noted, 'It is probable that the common term "tone-color" is not a mere figure of speech based upon analogy.'

In order to summarize the results more concisely, I converted the data into scores on each of three bipolar dimensions: yellow–blue, red–

green, and white–black. These three dimensions are the usual ones for opponent-process theory of color vision (e.g. Hering 1878; Hurvich and Jameson 1957), and they may also be used conveniently to describe the coordinates of three-dimensional color space. Not only does the reduction to three dimensions help compress the color data, but it also puts the data into a form that is psychologically meaningful.

The calculations themselves were made simply by subtracting the number of blue responses from the number of yellow responses (or vice versa), of red from green (or green from red), and of white from black (or black from white). Thus, the score on each vowel–color dimension represents a difference between response frequencies.

Somewhat arbitrary decisions had to be made about how to analyze reports of violet and brown. I decided to divide each violet response into .5 blue and .5 red, even though violet light (wavelengths of 400–440 nm) is usually reported to appear more blue than red (e.g. Boynton and Gordon 1965). And it turns out that the breakdown into equally weighted blue and red components was a valid decision because this choice tended to diminish the magnitudes of the differences that were finally calculated. Responses of brown were divided into .5 black, .25 red, .25 yellow; that is, brown was treated as dark orange.

Table 4.2 gives the final results of the tridimensional analysis. Needless to say, several objections may be raised to the procedure used and, to a certain extent, the objections may be justified. Nevertheless, the procedure has the great value of reducing the data to a readily manageable quantity and of revealing something about the probabilities of associations between vowels and colors when the colors are organized into a scheme of bipolar dimensions.

Table 4.2 Synesthetic colors induced by vowel sounds, presented as scores on three opponent-color dimensions

Vowel	*Blue–yellow*	*Red–green*	*White–black*	N
a	39.62 blue	111.88 red	34.75 black	419
e	54.5 yellow	11.5 green	49.5 white	400
i	47.75 yellow	44.75 red	67.5 white	400
o	44.5 yellow	93.25 red	54.5 black	372
u	36.75 blue	8.0 green	84.0 black	362
$u_{(French)}$	18.75 blue	31.0 green	23.5 black	195
$u_{(German)}$	14.25 blue	20.25 red	44.25 black	146
ou	0.37 yellow	21.88 red	35.75 black	157

Data derived from Fechner (1876), Bleuler and Lehmann (1881), Flournoy (1892, 1893), and of 35 small-scale studies enumerated in text.

The most notable feature of the colors of vowels is the way their brightness varies: *i* and *e* are brightest, *o* and *u* are darkest. Flournoy (1893) noted that this relation was generally true, for he too had analyzed data reported by Fechner (1876) and by Bleuler and Lehmann (1881), as well as his own data. Flournoy proposed as a general principle a *'loi de charté'*, and Bleuler and Lehmann proposed a *'Helligkeitsgesetz'*. These translate into *law of brightness* and it says that bright-sounding vowels induce bright auxiliary visual sensations. We noted previously the general finding that photisms vary in their brightness as the sounds that produce them vary in their frequency (subjectively, in pitch or brightness). These results for synesthesia produced by vowels (as exemplified by the law of brightness) manifest the generality of the correlation between auditory pitch and visual brightness.

Vowel spectra and vowel colors The obvious question to ask at this point is, What is the relation between the sound structure of vowels and the secondary visual sensations? Henning (1923) suggested that the differences among colors aroused synesthetically by various speech sounds might be due to phonetic differences among the sounds. Wehofer (1913), and later Masson (1952), pointed to the formant structures of vowels as possible bases for synesthetic vowel colors.

The obvious place to begin a systematic inquiry into the structural basis of the colors of vowels is with the fact that the brightness or pitch of vowels appears to correlate with the brightness of the associated photisms. The vowels *o*, *ou*, and *u* (phonetically, for example, /o/ as in b*oa*t, /u/ as in b*oo*t, /U/ as in b*oo*k) sound relatively low in pitch, as compared to *e* and *i* (e.g. /ɛ/ as in b*e*t or /e/ as in b*ai*t, /I/ as in b*i*t or /i/ as in b*ee*t), which sound relatively high.

Studies of the pitch of vowels trace back at least to the early nineteenth century, when Willis (1830) attempted to produce synthetic vowel sounds. Donders (1857), Helmholtz (1863), and Koenig (1870) tried to determine what the resonance frequencies of the oral cavity are during the production of vowels. Those studies all agreed in demonstrating *u* and *o* to be lowest in frequency, *e* and *i* to be highest. Köhler (1910) was apparently the first to try to match pure tones to vowels. He obtained the following order of increasing frequencies (pitches): *u*, *o*, *a*, *e*, *i*. Köhler's results were later confirmed by Modell and Rich (1915). Vowels are not pure tones, of course, but vowel quality can be mimicked satisfactorily by sounds with spectra that contain two formants. In the case of artificial two-formant vowels, it is the frequency of the second formant (F_2) that is most closely related to a vowel's pitch (cf. Delattre et al. 1952).

At this point, it becomes useful to derive, for every vowel, a scale value on each of the three bipolar color dimensions. Because the total number of observations (*N*) differs from one vowel to another, it is necessary to calculate proportions, that is, to take the ratio of each color score to *N*. When that is done, values on the white–black dimension come out: *a* = .084 black; *e* = .124 white; *i* = .169 white; *o* = .147 black; *u* = .232 black; *ou* = .228 black. The order of increasing vowel-induced brightness is *u* – *ou*, *o*, *a*, *e*, *i*, the same order that defines increasing vowel pitch. Figure 4.1 shows how the scale values of vowel-induced brightness plot against the corresponding log sound frequencies obtained by Köhler, Modell and Rich, and Delattre et al. That the relation is almost linear may be fortuitous; nevertheless, the strength of the correlation is impressive and serves to emphasize the close connection between synesthetic color brightness and vowel pitch.

Perhaps the greatest complication to the present analysis is the difficulty involved in deciding on the sound structure of some of the vowels, at least as far as most of the studies on synesthesia are concerned. With regard to the experiments on vowel pitch by Köhler (1910) and Modell and Rich (1915), even though the phonetic forms of

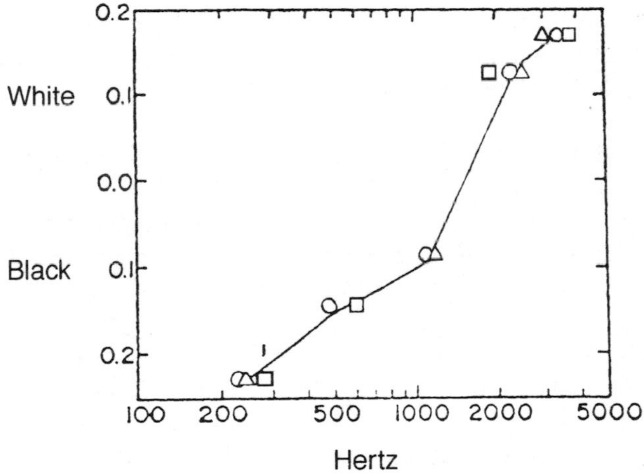

Figure 4.1 Relation of brightness to pitch in visual–auditory synesthesia

Note: The ordinate shows scores on a dimension of visual brightness, derived from probabilities of synesthetic responses to vowel sounds. The abscissa gives the sound frequencies of the pitch of the vowels as determined by Köhler (1910): circles; Modell and Rich (1915): squares; and Delattre et al. (1952): triangles. The vowels are, in terms of increasing sound frequency, /u/, /o/, /a/, /e/, /i/.

the cardinal vowels *a, e, i, o,* and *u* are known (they were the same /a/, /e/, /i/, /o/, and /u/ that were employed in the experiment of Delattre et al., 1952), we cannot always be certain these are the same phonetic forms that apply to vowels described in studies on synesthesia; it is a good guess that they do, but we cannot be absolutely sure.

However, the situation is not desperate. Two of the vowels, *a* and *o*, pose no problem since they are given constant and identical pronunciation, as /a/ and /o/, in French and German, which are the languages that comprise by far the majority of the examples of colored vowels. The other vowels can differ, though, both within and between languages: *u* can be either /y/ or /u/ in French, /u/ or /U/ in German; the vowel *e* can be /e/ or /ɛ/; and *i* can be /i/ or /I/ in both languages. Fortunately, some of the studies on synesthesia do indicate phonetic forms. Reichard, Jakobson and Werth (1949) and Masson (1952) stated their vowels in IPA (International Phonetic Alphabet) notation. More significantly, several other studies compared colors induced by alternate pronunciations of the same vowel *e*. Lauret (reported by Suarez de Mendoza 1890), Suarez de Mendoza (1890), Philippe (1893b), Laignel-Lavastine (1901), Ulrich (1903), Coriat (1913b), and Collins (1929) all described the colors induced by the French vowels è and é (/ɛ/ and /e/). In every case, both sounds yielded the same colors. Only two studies did not give this result: Baratoux (1887) and Binet and Philippe (1892) each described the colored vowels of a single synesthete. As it turned out, these two reports exactly cancel each other out, for Baratoux's subject said é aroused yellow and è white, Whereas Binet and Philippe's subject said é aroused white and è yellow!

Some of the other ambiguities with respect to phonetic form make little or no difference to our interpretations of colored vowels. For instance, the second formants of both /i/ and /I/ are higher in frequency than those of /a/, /ɛ/, /e/, /o/, /u/, /y/, and /U/. Thus, the overall relation between color brightness and vowel pitch remains basically the same in spite of changes in choice of phonetic forms of vowels. Regardless of the particular phonetic representations of vowels, it is clear that vowel pitch predicts the whiteness or blackness of associated photisms.

With the white–black dimension taken care of, it is now possible to examine whether the two chromatic dimensions of colored vowels are also accountable in terms of their sound spectra. Since the first two formants of vowels appear most crucial to the determination of vowel quality, it is likely that one or both chromatic dimensions of vowel-induced colors depend on the frequencies of F_1 and F_2. Figure 4.2 plots scale values on the red–green dimension as a function of the ratio of

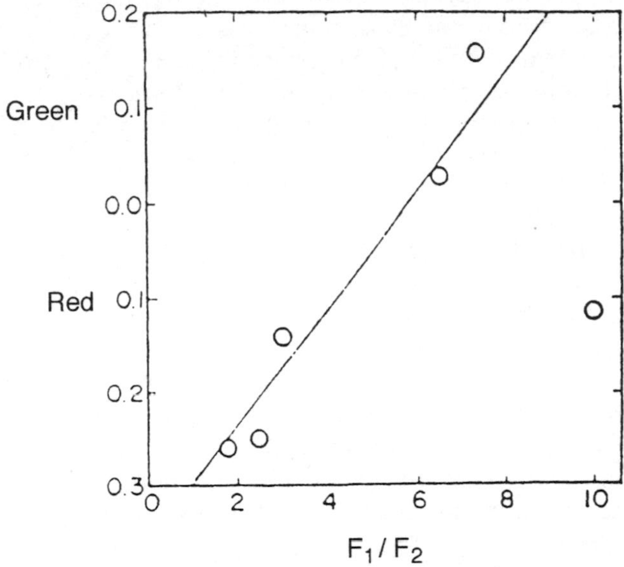

Figure 4.2 Relation of hue to sound structure in visual–auditory synesthesia

Note: The ordinate shows scores on a dimension of greenness–redness, derived from probabilities of synesthetic responses to vowel sounds. The abscissa gives the ratio of the sound frequencies of the second and first formants of the vowels. The vowels are, in terms of increasing ratio F_2/F_1, /a/, /o/, /u/, /e/, /y/ and /i/.

the frequencies of F_1 and F_2. The various vowels have been assigned to the following phonetic categories: /a/, /e/, /i/, and /o/ to *a*, *e*, *i*, and *o* in all languages; /u/ to the French *ou* and to the German *u*; and /y/ to the French *u*. Except for /i/, there is a direct increasing relation between greenness–redness and the ratio F_2/F_1: As the ratio increases, greenness increases and redness decreases.

In this manner we are able to account for a second of the three dimensions of colors as they are linked synesthetically to vowel sounds. The third dimension, yellow–blue, is more difficult to interpret. Simpson, Quinn and Ausubel (1956) played pure tones to children and asked them to name the hues that the tones conjured up. Yellowness was most often associated with tones of high frequency, blueness with tones of low frequency. Extrapolation of this outcome to the synesthetic colors of vowels would suggest that sound frequency, probably frequency of the second formant, should predict yellowness. Yet we have already seen that sound frequency correlates with whiteness, and in fact, F_2 fails to predict perfectly yellowness of colored vowels, at least when the latter are analyzed in the present way. The failure may be due in some measure to the nature of colored vowels and/or to the present method of analysis.

It is important to bear in mind that the scale values presented here are based only on frequencies of association, not necessarily on strength of association. It is not as though every synesthetic person reported how every vowel varied along each of the three bipolar dimensions. All that the data show is an overall tendency *across subjects* for correlations to exist between whiteness–blackness and pitch (frequency, presumably of F_2) and between greenness–redness and the ratio F_2/F_1. Note, too, that it was not necessarily the case for any particular synesthete that all the colors of vowels were determined by just one of the dimensional associations. Some vowels might yield colors that express whiteness–blackness; others, colors that express yellowness–blueness; others, colors that express greenness–redness. For example, the vowel *a* might be called red because the dimension of redness–greenness dominated, whereas *i* might be called white because the dimension of whiteness–blackness dominated. If there exists competition between dimensions – for example, if yellowness–blueness and whiteness–blackness both vie for association with pitch (frequency of F_2) – then to the extent that one of the associations is stronger, the other could fail to manifest itself. What this boils down to is the possibility that a strong connection between pitch and brightness might overwhelm a weaker connection between pitch and yellowness. Even so, there was some overall positive correlation between the yellow–blue dimension and F_2: The value of the Spearman rank-order coefficient of correlation between yellow–blue and F_2 was .43. Of course, there always exists the possibility that yellowness–blueness correlates with some paramether whose nature has eluded the present author. The appeal of this possibility is that it implies that there are three crucial dimensions of sound structure, one applicable to each of the three bipolar dimensions of color. In any case, at least two visual dimensions show empirical correlation with sound (formant) frequency of vowels.

Vowel colors and distinctive features The reader familiar with speech perception may have already noted that the acoustical properties of vowels that are responsible for synesthetically induced colors are also the properties theorized to be responsible for the auditory identification of vowels themselves. The frequency of the second formant and the ratio of the second to first formant are acoustical descriptions of two of the so-called *distinctive features* (Jakobson, Fant and Halle 1963).

The distinctive features of speech consist of a set of bipolar dimensions that are presumed to be critical for phonetic identification. One of these features is termed *gravity*: Its two values differentiate high-pitched (acute) from low-pitched (grave) vowels (e.g. /i/ and /e/ versus /o/ and /u/). We might say that gravity as a distinctive feature of vowels correlates with darkness of synesthetically perceived colors.

A second important distinctive feature is termed *diffuseness*: Its two values differentiate compact from diffuse vowels (e.g. /a/ versus /i/). Compact vowels concentrate most of their energy in a small region of the spectrum, whereas diffuse vowels spread energy over larger spectral regions. Hence, given a sound structure containing two formants, a large ratio of F_2 to F_1 implies diffuseness, a small ratio implies compactness. Diffuseness as a distinctive feature of vowels correlates with greenness of synesthetically perceived colors.

Not only do distinctive features provide a logically satisfactory basis for phonetic discrimination, but they appear to have psychological relevance as well. If there do exist a small number of dimensions by means of which all speech sounds are classified, it is small wonder that the same features are responsible for other speech-related phenomena – in the present matter of concern, the synesthetically perceived colors of vowels.

Summary Analysis of reports on vowel–color synesthesia yield several general principles:

1 Most vowel–color synesthesiae reflect regular correlations between dimensions of visual and auditory experience.
2 The brightness of the induced visual 'sensation' is a direct function of the pitch of the vowel (frequency of its second formant). Vowel brightness correlates with the distinctive feature *acuteness*. Acute (high-pitched) vowels yield bright colors; grave (low-pitched) vowels yield dark colors.
3 The greenness and redness of induced colors depend systematically on the ratio of the frequencies of the second to first formants and, thus, on the distinctive feature *compactness*. Compact vowels yield red colors; diffuse vowels yield green colors.

Sound quality and perceived size of photism

Although the major interest here, and the preponderance of data, concerns the relation between color and sound quality, a significant number of reports on synesthesia also note that the sizes of photisms vary from one sound to another (Anschütz 1925; Bleuler and Lehmann 1881; Dudycha and Dudycha 1935; Karwoski and Odbert 1938; Riggs and Karwoski 1934; Vernon 1930; Voss 1929; Zigler 1930). Universally present in those reports was the observation that visual size increased as auditory pitch decreased. High-pitched sounds produce synesthetic visual sensations that are small in size; low-pitched sounds produce synesthetic sensations that are large in size.

Taken at face value, these results imply a second (or perhaps a third) visual correlate to auditory pitch. In addition to visual brightness (whiteness–blackness) and possibly visual yellowness, we also have visual size varying with auditory pitch. There are some additional facts, however, to bear in mind. Just as several studies found that visual brightness depends on loudness as well as increasing pitch – the louder the sound, the brighter the photism (e.g. Pedrono 1882; Wheeler 1920; to some extent, Ortmann 1933) – so too does visual size depend on loudness – the louder the sound, the larger the photism (e.g. Bleuler and Lehmann 1881; Voss 1929). The importance of these additional functional relations is made apparent shortly. Meanwhile, let it suffice that induced size is not related solely to pitch, so it may not be pitch per se that is the relevant auditory variable.

Colored music

Given the penchant these days for multimedia exhibitions – in the arts, in educational technology, to name but two manifestations – one might gain the impression that the association of sound and color in music is a conception of only recent development. In fact, presentation of mixed-mode concerts (patterns of light together with musical sounds) was not uncommon in late nineteenth-century Paris. (Sometimes odors too were included!) The composer Alexander Scriabin, for one, was synesthetic, and some of his compositions were written for and performed in both light and music; by means of polysensory works he hoped to give expression to his mystic world view. An example is Scriabin's (1911) composition *Prometheus*, which was written for orchestra, piano, organ, chorus, and color keyboard; it was performed in New York on March 20, 1915. In order to produce it, Carnegie Hall was specially equipped with a color organ; colors were played on a keyboard and projected onto a screen behind the orchestra. The correlation between tone and color was systematic in that C was accompanied by red, D by yellow, E and F-sharp by blues, A by green, and B-flat by gray. For a description of the concert, see Plummer (1915).

Actually, the current vogue for color organs traces back in history at least to the eighteenth century. At that time, a Jesuit named L.-B. Castel proposed (1725) and later built (1735), a color organ on which one could play music that simultaneously expressed itself in color: 'For we are born in music, & we have only to open our ears in order to taste it . . . and . . . one has only to open one's eyes in order to taste a Music of colors & to judge it' (Castel 1735: 1621). Castel's color organ was exhibited in 1735. As in Scriabin's compositions, to each note of the scale there corresponded a particular color; furthermore, the associations were, according to the creator Castel, real, not arbitrary: blue was assigned to do, green to re, yellow to mi, and red to sol not by whim but because of some presumably intrinsic appropriateness. The association between blue and do was thought special, for Castel believed blue to be the tonic and fundamental color both of nature and of art. He also believed that the colors formed a harmonic series like that of the notes, a scale of colors, an idea that he may have derived directly or indirectly from Newton (1704; Castel 1735, 1740). It is certain that his theory derived from Athanasius Kircher's *Musurgia Universalis* of 1650 (Castel 1725, 1735). Kircher had written of sound as 'mimic of light'. It is also possible that Castel was influenced by the work of the painter Arcimboldo, who in the sixteenth century conceived a color music (Eastlake 1840).

A luminous music, played with colored lights that are synchronized to a harpsichord, was proposed again a half-century later by Clarles Darwin's grandfather Erasmus Darwin (1790). Like Castel, Darwin suggested that there exist certain natural relations between colors and sounds. By the late nineteenth century and early twentieth century, interest in color organs had blossomed into what might almost be called an epidemic (e.g. Sullivan 1914).

When it comes to reports on musical synesthesia, we find that the important principles of visual–auditory association that manifest themselves in colored music are basically the same principles that manifest themselves in colored vowels – that is, the relations of visual brightness and size to auditory pitch and loudness. As we shall see, other sorts of associations between light and sound in music tend to be more idiosyncratic. For that reason, consideration of colored music is only cursory.

Colors of musical instruments First, we may note the associations of colors with the sounds of particular musical instruments (as in Locke's 1690, and Leibniz's 1704, references to a blind man understanding what scarlet is by the sound of a trumpet). Reports of colors associated with musical instruments were made by L. Hoffmann, Raff and Lauret (as cited by Krohn 1892) and by Bleuler and Lehmann (1881), de Rochas (1885), Lomer (1905), Mudge (1920), Anschütz (1926), and Ortmann (1933). Interestingly, the composer Raff perceived the color of the trumpet's sound as scarlet, and Hoffmann's and Ortmann's subjects reported it as bright red (de Rochas's subject called it yellow, Lomer's subject called it yellow red and Anschütz's two subjects called it blue green and yellow). The painter Kandinsky (1912) described colors of musical instruments, and although the trumpet's color was not included on his list, the tuba was said to arouse red.

It is both easy and difficult to dismiss correspondences between instrument sounds and colors. It is easy to the extent that the correspondences are idiosyncratic, as they often are; and it is difficult to the extent that they are universal, as perhaps some are. Kandinsky (1912) wrote that, musically, the flute resembles bright blueness, *'helles Blau'*. Was he, then, drawing the same analogy as that of the German poet Tieck (1828: 291), who said of the flute *'Unser Geist ist himmelblau / Führt dich in die blaue Ferne'*?

Mudge's (1920) study is of some importance because it recounts visual responses to music obtained from 42 subjects. Of that number, 34 said that low tones yield dark colors, 26 said medium tones yield medium bright colors, and 36 said high tones yield bright colors. Among the musical instruments, the violin's sound was typically reported to be blue or violet; the trombone's to be dark, usually brown; and the clarinet's and flute's to be bright.

Colors of musical notes Musical key, musical notes in particular, can also determine the specific colors aroused by music. One can see as well as hear the 'Music' of Conrad Aiken (1942):

> The calyx of the oboe breaks,
> silver and soft the flower it makes.
> And next, beyond, the flute-notes seen
> now are white and now are green.

The assignment of specific colors to specific musical notes is quite common, though nowhere near universal, among musical synesthetes. Recall the supposed intrinsic relations described and used by Castel. One of the associations he conjectured to be 'natural' was between sol and red. A fascinating, though not quite believable, report by Albertoni (1889) claimed not only that sol is in fact usually called red but, furthermore, that a red-blind subject (what we would now call a protanope) failed also to name correctly the note G (sol). Albertoni named this condition of auditory color blindness *auditory daltonism*. One almost hesitates to bring facts to bear on such a claim, but there are some important points to make. First, the tacit assumption that protanopia consists of a loss of 'red sensation' oversimplifies the nature of color blindness. And second, sol (the note G) has been seen (or I should properly say heard) to arouse not just red but also blue (Langfeld 1914; Ortmann 1933), yellow (Scriabin, as reported by Vernon 1930), and white (Starr 1893). A survey by Gruber (reported by Marinesco 1912) found ten respondents who reported coloring musical notes; to sol two of them assigned green, three assigned blue, one red, and one yellow.

An interesting fact is that, as the reports by Langfeld (1914), Ginsberg (1923), Vernon (1930), Dudycha and Dudycha (1935), and Karwoski and Odbert (1938) make clear, the colors associated with music, like the colors associated with vowels, vary along a bright–dark dimension, a psychological dimension that itself correlates with a high–low dimension of sound frequency. Perhaps we should not be too surprised that music and speech sounds are similar in this respect. Slawson (1968) showed that artificial, two-formant sounds are readily interpretable both as vowels and as musical notes and that vowel quality and musical timbre depend in similar ways on the structure of the sound (formant frequencies and spectrum envelope). However, just as there is more to music than the frequency structure of the component sounds, so too is it that sometimes only the more complex features of music suffice to arouse secondary visual sensations.

Colors of musical keys Vernon (1930) categorized two major types of musical synesthesia besides the three that are already familar to us – the three being (a) brightness and (b) size of photism as functions of sound structure, especially fundamental frequency, and (c) colors proper to musical instruments. Another is the relation between colors and tonalities. Musical composers in particular display such synesthesiae with relatively high occurrence. For instance, Beethoven called the key of B-minor black. The composers Scriabin and Rimsky-Korsakov were both synesthetic, and it has been reported that they agreed on the colors of some musical keys (e.g. that D-major is yellow). I am reminded, in this regard, of E.T.A. Hoffmann's ([1810] 1899: 61):

> auch hatte ich gerade ein Kleid an, das ich ernst im höchsten Unmut über ein misslungenes Trio gekauft, und dessen Farbe in Cis-Moll geht, weshalb ich zu einiger Beruhigung der Beschauer einen Kragen aus E-dur-Farbe daraufsetzen lassen.

Colors of musical patterns Interestingly, music may be reported as colored according to the individual composer. Raines (1909) described the several synesthesiae of a young woman. Included was the observation that she found works of Chopin to be purple, of Mozart to be green, and of Wagner to be red. Colors specific to composers were also described by Anschütz (1926) for one of his three synesthetic subjects.

Vernon (1930) and Anschütz (1926) pointed out that synesthesiae can be based on other musical patterns, particularly on complex temporal patterns such as progressions, styles, and so forth. It is not surprising then that individual compositions may evoke specific synesthetic reactions. Schumann (in Erler 1887) was reported to have assigned special colors to specific musical works. A similar conclusion was reached by Karwoski and Odbert (1938). They found that synesthetic responses often depended on musical patterns, at least in the relatively simple musical materials (e.g. 'Jingle Bells') that were studied.

Just as the important dimensions of the auditory stimulus that are responsible for musical synesthesiae can be quite complex, so too can be the synesthetic responses themselves (Karwoski and Odbert 1938). Visual sensations aroused by music need not be limited or confined to simple spots of color. Often the entire visual field fills with colors that change over time with the music; some subjects report several colors simultaneously, each color reflecting a particular aspect of the music. The shapes of the photisms also vary, particularly with musical tempo; the faster the music, the sharper and more angular the photism.

An important study was conducted by Karwoski, Odbert and Osgood (1942), who applied verbal tests of bipolar opposites (like the semantic differential that Osgood, Suci and Tannenbaum 1957 developed later) to non-synesthetic subjects. Verbal reports concerning relations of color and form to music were similar to responses to music that are obtained from synesthetic subjects.

Can sounds produce visual sensations?

Several of the small-scale reports that yielded part of the data in Table 4.2 appear to provide examples of what we may call strong synesthesia. Typically, the subjects of those studies claimed that sounds produced visual sensations. The same appears to be true of the many cases described by Bleuler and Lehmann (1881). On the other hand, the report of Flournoy (1892, 1893) was based on responses to a questionnaire. Without careful examination of subjects, it is difficult to know whether many or even most of the examples might have consisted of relatively weak associations between color and sound.

In any event, it is probably difficult to prove in any given circumstance that strong rather than weak synesthesia is evident. For it is not clear just how one would go about discovering whether a stimulus appropriate to one modality (say a sound) actually produces a sensation appropriate to another (such as a color), though classical conditioning of sensations does appear to be possible (Leuba 1940). Sometimes synesthetic subjects report the associated visual sensation to appear not in visual space but rather in the sound itself. A relevant datum is the observation by Ortmann (1933), on a synesthetic young woman, that there was no interaction between synesthetically induced color and color produced simultaneously by a visual stimulus except when the colors were the same. Under that condition, synesthetic color and real color fused!

Perhaps it is more appropriate to speak of synesthetically induced 'images' than of synesthetically induced sensations. Colors induced by sounds are usually quite distinguishable from colors induced by light. Synesthetic images are secondary and contingent; often they appear with some delay after the onset of primary sensations. This is not to say that synesthetic images do not have many of the properties of sensations nor that they are never as strong or vivid. Imagery can strongly resemble perception, as several experiments have demonstrated. In Perky's (1910) well-known study, very weak visual percepts of objects such as a tomato and a banana were often interpreted as visual images, from which result Perky deduced that 'the materials of imagination are closely akin to those of perception' (p. 451). Perky's result was later confirmed by Segal and Nathan (1964). In a study that employed analytical tools of the theory of signal detectability, Segal and Fusella (1970) found that imagery interferes with sensory detection, particularly when the test stimuli were presented in the same modality as the images.

To some extent then, dimensions or attributes of images overlap dimensions or attributes of sensations. As Paivio (1971) concluded, 'imagery and perception are continuous modes of experience' (p. 144). It might be convenient to think of the conjunction of imagery and sensation in terms of some common portion of the neural system that both actuate. Ortmann (1933) argued that the colored hearing of his subject was not imagery but rather sensation. If imagery and sensation lie on a continuum, it may be unnecessary to make Ortmann's distinction.

Status of visual–auditory synesthesia

An important issue to consider now is the status of the synesthetic correspondences between auditory and visual sensations. One approach is to treat synesthesia as a special phenomenon distinctive in its own right. This approach is based on the supposition that in synesthesia, sounds truly arouse sensations of color and that such a condition is not normal.

Of course, it may not be possible to decide whether sounds can actually yield visual sensations. But even if they do, there exists an alternative approach whereby synesthesia is regarded not so much as a distinct, non-normal entity but as the end point of a continuum on which sensory correspondences vary in strength. Much of the evidence on colored hearing tends to support the latter approach in that synesthetic relations appear to express correspondences between dimensions of sensory experience that are fundamental to sensation in general. Given the marked similarity among results obtained in the studies just reviewed, the generality of at least some of the visual–auditory correlations can hardly be denied. The correlations between vowel quality and color are similar with native speakers of French and German, and Reichard et al. (1949) argued that they are similar in German, Czech, Serbian, and Russian.

The second half of the argument is that correspondences between light and sound that are general to synesthetes are also general to nonsynesthetes. Results reported by Karwoski et al. (1942) imply equivalent responses to music by both synesthetic and non-synesthetic subjects. Wicker (1968) obtained similarity judgments and semantic judgments of colors and tones from non-synesthetic subjects; his results indicated a correlation between visual brightness and auditory pitch. Recently, I (Marks 1974) asked non-synesthetic subjects to search for tones that matched gray surfaces. The results showed general agreement that increasing auditory pitch goes with increasing surface brightness, as can be seen in the averaged data plotted in Figure 4.3. Most subjects also aligned increasing loudness with increasing brightness, but others did the reverse, aligning loudness with dardness.

There are two additional lines of evidence to support the contention that synesthetes translate sensations from one modality to another in basically the same way that non-synesthetes do and that these translations reflect fundamental properties of sensation and cognition. These lines of evidence comprise synesthesia under drugs and phonetic symbolism.

Synesthesia under drugs Mescaline and hashish often produce strong synesthetic experiences in normal (non-synesthetic) subjects, as has been noted time and again over the past century. The French poet Théophile Gautier (1843) described how he would hear colors when he was under the influence of hashish:

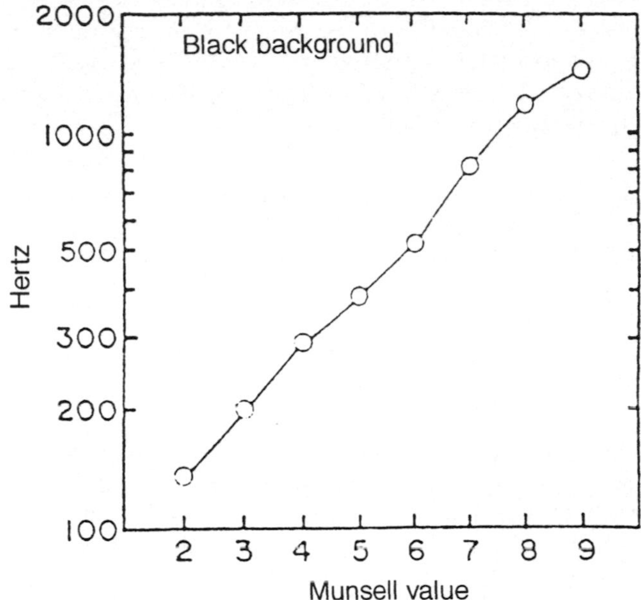

Figure 4.3 Matching of auditory pitch and visual brightness by non-synesthetic subjects

Note: Average settings of sound frequency (loudnes held constant) to gray surfaces that varied in luminous reflectance from 3 per cent to 80 per cent.
Source: Marks (1974).

> mon ouïe s'était prodigieusement développée; j'entendais le bruit des couleurs. Des sons verts, rouges, bleus, jaunes, m'arrivaient par ondes parfaitement distinctes. Un verre renversé, un craquement de fauteuil, un mot prononcé tout bas, vibraient et retentissaient en moi comme des roulements de tonnerre. Chaque objet effleuré rendait une note d'harmonica ou de harpe éolienne. (1846: 530)

And he described his response to piano music, '*Les sons en jaillissaient bleus et rouges.*'

Charles Baudelaire ([1860] 1923), no slacker in the hashish department, wrote similarly of its effect on sensation, namely, how '*L'odorat, la vue, l'ouïe, le toucher participent également*', and '*Les sons se revêtent de couleurs, et les couleurs contiennent une musique.*' Interestingly and importantly, Baudelaire followed these statements with a dialogue between author and reader, in which the reader commented that the synesthetic correspondences are not unique to hashish but appear also in the non-drugged state (i.e. to the poet); to this comment the author, Baudelaire, responded in turn that hashish has, of course, no supernatural effect. What it does is to make more vivid those correspondences that exist in the normal state:

> Les sons se revêtent de couleurs, et les couleurs contiennent une musique. Cela, dira-t-on, n'a rien que de fort naturel, et tout cerveau poétique, dans son état sain et normal, conçoit facilement ces analogies. (p. 218)

The vividness of synesthesia provoked by hashish is also apparent in Ludlow's (1857: 149–50) account:

> Thus the hasheesh-eater knows what it is to be burned by *salt* fire, to *smell* colors, to *see* sounds, and, much more frequently, to *see* feelings. How often do I remember vibrating in the air over a floor bristling with red-hot needles, and, although I never supposed I came in contact with them, *feeling* the sensation of their frightful pungency through *sight* as distinctly as if they were entering my heart.

Both Gautier and Baudelaire emphasized the correspondences between sounds and colors that manifested themselves under hashish intoxication. Cairns (1929) described the visual images that music aroused in him after he was injected with peyote extract (mescaline). Delay, Gérard and Racamier (1951) noted that auditory–visual synesthesia is found under mescaline intoxication, and Beringer (reported by Werner 1940) found that mescaline produces experiences of colored hearing in which visual brightness correlated with auditory pitch. It would appear then that there is an especially intimate connection between vision and hearing, at least to the extent that the auditory–visual forms dominate both normal and drugged synesthesiae and, furthermore, that synesthesiae induced by drugs consist predominantly, if not exclusively, of enhancements of normal crossmodal interrelations.

Synesthesia and phonetic symbolism Some of the strongest evidence to support the view that visual–auditory correspondences found in synesthetes are similar or identical in nature to correspondences found in normal persons (non-synesthetes) adduces from studies of sound symbolism in speech – what is often termed *phonetic symbolism*. The notion that the sounds of words convey meaning has a history that goes back at least to Plato (*Cratylus*) and was echoed, in one form or another, by

Rousseau ([1753] 1839) and later by Balzac ([1832]1961) who asked, rhetorically, 'Are not most words colored with the idea that they represent externally?' (p. 507). Werner (1940) called the intrinsic meaning of sounds an example of the *physiognomic* aspect of language – language is not just an abstract, formal system of symbols. To some extent, words 'belong to' objects.

Sapir (1929) was among the first to verify experimentally that vowel sounds differ with respect to the sizes of the objects they suggest. For instance, objects named with nonsense syllables containing the sound /a/ appear larger than objects named with syllables containing /i/; this is true of children as well as of adults and of native speakers of Chinese as well as of native speakers of English. Since Sapir's report, many studies have been carried out with the aim of discovering whether different speech sounds bear some intrinsic, connotative relation to the objects their words represent.

Newman (1933) constructed pairs of nonsense syllables that contained different vowel sounds and asked subjects both which syllable of each pair seemed larger and also which syllable seemed brighter. From large to small the order of the vowels was /o/, /a/, /æ/, /ε/, /e/, and /i/; from dark to bright the order was /u/, /a/, /æ/, /e/, /ai/, /I/, and /i/. First of all, we note that the two orders correlate highly with one another. Second, we note that both orders also correlate strongly with pitch of the vowel (i.e. with frequency of the second formant). The relations between vowel sound and the dimensions of size and brightness obtained in Newman's experiment on phonetic symbolism are the same as the relations manifested in colored hearing. In the African language Ewe, high-pitched words describe small objects, low-pitched words describe large objects (Kainz 1943). Studies on phonetic symbolism by Czurda (1953) and on onomatopoeia by Wissemann (1954) support Sapir's and Newman's results. Czurda found /a/, /o/, and /u/ to be large vowels and /ε/ and /I/ to be small vowels; Wissemann found /u/ and /o/ to be dark and /i/ to be bright. Of theoretical importance is the finding that phonetic symbolism is absent in deaf people who have learned to talk (Johnson, Suzuki and Olds 1964). Thus, the cues to phonetic symbolism appear to be in sounds, not in kinesthesis of speech production. This interpretation is supported by the study of Bentley and Varon (1933), who verified Sapir's and Newman's findings and then went on to make an important additional observation, namely, that the sounds *themselves* vary in size and brightness. Not only do sounds *imply* differences in brightness and size, but they *can be* more or less large, more or less bright.

These experiments on phonetic symbolism were conducted, presumably, with non-synesthetic subjects. The simplest hypothesis, then, is that sounds, such as vowels, differ among themselves with regard to the dimensions of brightness and size and that in synesthesia, the visual images (photisms) that are aroused by the sounds correspond in their brightness and size to the brightness and size of the (vowel) sounds.

It is worthwhile, in this regard, to note and modify Brown's (1958) caution against equating phonetic symbolism with synesthesia. His reason was that the results of experiments on phonetic symbolism tend to produce a body of results that is stable and consistent from person to person, whereas results on synesthesia show large individual differences. Although it is true that individual differences in synesthesia are sizable, there exist several common, underlying currents that are consistent from synesthete to synesthete; furthermore, at least some of the common principles governing synesthesia are similar to those governing phonetic symbolism.

What dimensions correspond in visual–auditory synesthesia?

After cutting through the idiosyncratic differences among synesthetes, we find several general principles underlying auditory–visual correspondences in synesthesia. First, low-pitched sounds arouse dark photisms, high-pitched sounds arouse bright ones. Second, low-pitched sounds arouse spatially large photisms, high-pitched sounds arouse smaller ones. At first glance, it would appear that we have a single auditory dimension, namely pitch, which maps itself onto two visual dimensions, namely brightness and size. This interpretation is in line with a conclusion of Karwoski et al. (1942). They proposed as the fifth of a set of general principles of colored music, the 'principle of alternate visual polarities and gradients', which states that more than one visual dimension may parallel a single auditory dimension.

There are some additional facts, which were mentioned earlier, that bear on this interpretation. First, louder sounds arouse brighter photisms than do softer sounds; and second, louder sounds arouse larger photisms than do softer sounds. If we were to extrapolate the logic just employed, we would have to conclude also that a second auditory dimension, namely loudness, maps onto the same two visual dimensions of brightness and size.

There exists an alternative interpretation. Note that psychophysical studies of hearing show that even simple sounds vary along at least four different psychological dimensions. Besides pitch and loudness, sounds are often described as more or less *voluminous* and more or less *dense*. Low-pitched loud sounds are large; high-pitched loud sounds are dense. Thus, pitch, loudness, volume, and density all depend in different ways on sound frequency and intensity.

Early in the twentieth century several references were published to yet another dimension of auditory experience, brightness. Hartshorne (1934), Hornbostel (1931), Rich (1919), and others identified brightness with pitch; and Hartshorne and Hornbostel argued for the analogy (if not the identity) of auditory and visual brightness. However, other evidence was brought to bear that suggested brightness is not merely pitch; for one, brightness also depends on sound complexity (Abraham 1920). Troland (1930) argued that brightness increases not only with increasing pitch, but also with increasing loudness; and most importantly, Boring and Stevens (1936) found brightness to be the same as density.

Recent work involving the scaling of auditory density by magnitude estimation (Guirao and Stevens, 1964; Stevens, Guirao and Slawson 1965) demonstrates the way that auditory density increases both with sound frequency and sound intensity. If brightness and density are one and the same attribute of sounds, but different from pitch, then Hartshorne and Hornbostel are partially correct. Auditory brightness does correspond to visual brightness, at least in colored-hearing synesthesia. (Recall, as was described earlier, the 'law of brightness' proposed by Bleuler and Lehmann 1881 and by Flournoy 1893). However, brightness is not the same as pitch. Brightness increases markedly with increases in sound frequency, and at a given constant level of loudness, brightness correlates closely with pitch. But brightness increases also with loudness; pitch may do so too at times, but not always and not in the same way. If sound frequency is held constant and low, pitch increases as intensity increases; but if sound frequency is held constant and high, pitch decreases as intensity increases (Stevens 1935). Increasing the complexity of sound decreases auditory brightness (Abraham 1920), and increasing sound complexity also decreases synesthetically induced visual brightness (Riggs and Karwoski 1934).

A similar argument can be made with respect to auditory volume and visual size. Auditory volume increases as frequency decreases (and, concomitantly, as pitch decreases), but it increases as intensity increases (and, therefore, as loudness increases) (Terrace and Stevens 1962). Synesthetically induced visual size follows the same pattern. Thus, it appears that the size of photisms in auditory–visual synesthesia corresponds to, or at least correlates with, the size (volume) of the sound. Like brightness, volume does bear a relation to pitch, but it is not auditory pitch proper that determines visual size, just as it is not pitch proper that determines visual brightness.

These interrelations are depicted in Figure 4.4, which is a schematic representation of two-dimensional auditory space. Pitch and loudness are given as orthogonal dimensions; brightness and volume are also orthogonal but are displaced approximately 45 degrees from pitch and

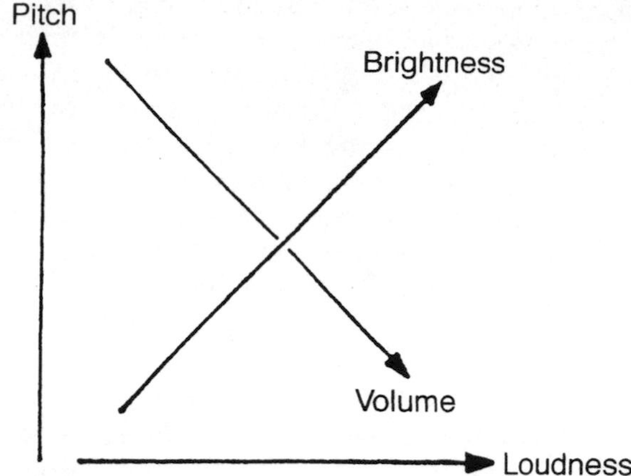

Figure 4.4 Schematic representation of the psychological space for simple sounds

loudness. To the extent that this space can also represent synesthetic visual dimensions, it follows that visual brightness and size fall along the corresponding auditory dimensions of brightness and volume.

The present interpretation is diametrically opposed to the initial one. Instead of visual brightness and size both corresponding to auditory pitch, neither corresponds to pitch Brightness parallels brightness and size parallels size. It seems fair to venture that the same basic correlations arise both in synesthetes and in nonsynesthetes and that these two correlations are therefore fundamental to the normal sensory and conceptual systems of humans.

Summary

It does no matter whether one considers perception by synesthetes or by non-synesthetes; in both cases the correlations between dimensions of visual and auditory experience are nearly identical. These dimensional, cross-modal correlations express themselves most vividly in people not normally synesthetic by means of hashish and mescaline intoxication. The same correlations express themselves in the non-drugged states, less vividly to be sure, in the way that sounds of speech as such can convey particular meanings (phonetic symbolism). Interpreting the correlations of visual and auditory experience in terms of known dimensions of sensory experience, it seems that there exist two outstanding, universal, cross-modal relations: one between auditory brightness or density and visual brightness, the other between auditory volume and visual size.

What is Synesthesia All About?

There has perhaps been as much written about *why* synesthesia is as about *what* it is. In their impact and significance, theories of synesthesia vary from predictable to unpredictable, from cogent to absurd. Mahling (1926) and Ortmann (1933) reviewed at length many of the early theories, and the interested reader may wish to consult those works. The present exposition deals only with some of the more interesting and important hypotheses.

All theories of synesthesia are theories of mediation. Sensations or sensory dimensions linked to one another must be linked by something. We may call that link a learned association – a psychological entity, perhaps with overtones of neural basis. We may call the link a physiological response – a neural, muscular, or other physiological entity of actual or mythological status. Or by response we may mean some tidbit of behavior, again either actual and measurable or covert and mythical. Finally, we may call the link cognitive, by which we mean none of the above or perhaps all of them. To say the link is cognitive, empty though that statement may seem, is foremost to propose that the plane of explanation should be psychological. Moreover, to say that the link is cognitive implies that synesthesia is involved in thought, in knowledge, in the way that the world is *represented* in consciousness.

Synesthesia as learned associations

As might be expected, several investigators (Calkins 1893; Claparède 1903; Dresslar 1903; Harris 1908; Laignel-Lavastine 1901; Langenbeck 1913) postulated that synesthesia is the outcome of experienced conjunctions between stimuli encountered early in life. Harris qualified his opinion by theorizing that the tendency to be synesthetic is strongly determined by genetic factors, but he believed that the actual associations are themselves totally the result of chance contiguities. In a few instances no doubt this view is correct, as, for example, in the synesthesia described by English (1923). He reported the colored music of a 3-year-and-11-month-old boy: Soft music was yellow, loud music was black. The basis for the correspondences was, according to the child, that yellow crayon cannot readily be seen on a wall, whereas black can, just as soft music may not easily be heard, but loud music can. Whether associations like these can explain any sizable proportion of synesthesiae, if in fact they even *explain* this one, is a question that may be impossible to answer. Nevertheless, the existence of even a single case of synesthesia based on experienced conjunctions would serve to make associative learning a factor to consider.

Certainly to the extent that experienced conjunctions are assumed to be *fortuitous*, it is difficult to see how they can lead to the regularities that are observed in synesthesia, particularly those in colored hearing. The visual brightnesses and hues associated with vowel sounds cannot easily be explained in such a manner. It is curious that Colman (1894) gave such an interpretation to the data on auditory–visual synesthesia he compiled, particularly since he noted that the colors produced by vowel sounds showed less variation from subject to subject than did the colors produced by written letters of the alphabet.

Of course, one might attempt to adhere to the associative theory but endeavor to account for the observed regularities by hypothesizing some universal experience as the basis for the associations. That is, as most youngsters grow up they may encounter the same conjunctions of visual and auditory stimuli and sensations in their environments. This appears to be the view that Binet (1892, 1893) hinted at. Although Binet argued for an associative basis to synesthesia, he was aware of the regularities that govern connections between color and sound.

If the associative hypothesis is to be taken seriously, then some attempt should be made to find the source of the common conjunctions between dimensions of different modalities. With respect to colored vowels, one possible explanation that comes to mind is that children's books often present letters and words in colors. Thus, by the association of sound with the printed letter, printed letter with its color, children may tend to associate sounds with colors. This very explanation was actually propounded to account for the vowel colors that Rimbaud expressed in his 'Le Sonnet des Voyelles' (see Starkie 1961).

But regardless of the correctness of its application to Rimbaud's invention, it would seem difficult to maintain this explanation for colored vowels in general. First of all, if the sequence of events given above were correct, we would expect the association between color and written letter to be much stronger than the association between color and sound, since the former association would be more direct. Yet the reverse is actually true. It is vowel sounds that are potent as synesthetic stimuli. Second, in order to explain the great (i.e. cross-linguistic) generality of vowel brightness and darkness, we would have to postulate that the same vowels are connected with bright and dark colors in children's books printed in English, German, French, and perhaps several other languages as well. The only way to account for such a remarkable cross-linguistic occurrence would be in terms of some other, more general, basis to the linking of sound and color, in which case the explanation in terms of colors in alphabet books itself becomes secondary if not superfluous.

If there is any truth to the theory just described, there may now be ample opportunity for experimental verification, for one of the recently developed means to teach reading to children is called 'Words in Color' (Gattegno 1962). Every letter of the alphabet (actually every sound) is represented by a different color, 39 in all. Thus, there now exists a sizable number of primary grade students who are exposed on a regular basis to similar correlations of sound and color.

Before taking leave of the hypothesis that synesthesia is learned, we may ask a closely related question, namely, Can synesthesia be learned? Binet (1893) artificially paired colors and sounds, which he proceeded to teach to himself. His proficiency at naming the colors in response to the sound stimuli became great – equal to that of a synesthete. Binet took this result as some evidence in favor of his suspicion that synesthesia is learned, based on contiguities encountered in childhood.

Subsequent experimentation has failed to shed much more light on the role of learning in the development of synesthesia. Several experiments investigated the capacities of adults to associate colors with sounds. In the first (Kelly 1934), 18 subjects were given eight pairs of colors and sounds (notes from the tonic C scale played on an accordian). With repeated presentations some learning occurred, but there was no tendency for the subjects actually to 'see' the colors when the notes were played.

In a second experiment (Howells 1944), eight subjects heard an organ note, which was followed by a color (red or its blue-green complement). During training the colors were presented at maximal saturation, but during subsequent testing the saturations were reduced. Furthermore, on some trials during the test period the complementary color was presented instead of the primary one that had been used throughout training. That is, note C might be paired with red during training and, usually, also in testing; but occasional test trials would consist of C followed by blue green. The experimental question was, Will the prior pairing of C and red lead the subject to see red instead of blue green on those trials? Howells did find a positive effect. However, whether the organ notes actually influenced the color perception is moot. The training period might have led only to the development of particular verbal response tendencies, either direct or mediated.

A study reported by Ellson (1941b) suggests that the conditioning of sensation is possible. Ellson repeatedly paired a 1000-Hz tone with a white light, and he found that 'auditory hallucinations' developed. Sometimes, these light-invoked sensations of sound could not be distinguished from sensations produced by auditory stimuli. Furthermore, conditioned auditory sensations appeared quite resistant to extinction (Ellson 1941a). Similar results were obtained by Leuba (1940) and by Leuba and Dunlap (1951). In these experiments, the conditioning sessions were conducted while the subjects were under hypnosis. Test sessions were conducted after hypnosis, but the conditioning sessions were not remembered. (The subjects were told, under hypnosis, not to recall the conditioning.) Sensations of touch and smell, conditioned to sound, came on automatically and involuntarily, and again on several occasions the conditioned sensations could be mistaken for primary sensations.

Despite the positive results, one might reasonably argue that none of the attempts to induce experimental synesthesia has any relevance to the question of the ontogeny of synesthesia as it actually or normally takes place. For one thing, synesthesia usually begins in childhood. Thus, even if regularly experienced conjunctions of particular lights and sounds are important to the development of auditory–visual synesthesia, there is always a possibility that the formation of associations will proceed differently in children than in adults. For another thing, the consistent relations that are observed in synesthesia require either that the same types of visual and auditory stimuli actually appear with greater-than-chance regularity in different parts of the world or, alternately, that people are somehow intrinsically turned or programmed to develop certain associations more readily than to develop others. Under this last interpretation, one could hardly expect stimuli that were paired artificially to yield the same sort of affiliation as that which would derive from stimuli that were 'properly' paired.

There is a final point concerning the role of experienced contiguity. We may take a moment to consider the relation between sound sensation and induced visual size. As has been mentioned several times, sounds vary along the attribute of volume: High-intensity, low-frequency sounds appear to be large; low-intensity, high-frequency sounds appear to be small. Similarly, size of visual photism in synesthesia follows auditory volume. Now, it might be that the perceived sizes or volumes of sounds are themselves learned characteristics, in which case the synesthetic relations, to the extent they follow directly, would also have an experiential basis. The rationale behind attributing the auditory dimension of volume to learning is that, as the laws of physics tell us, large objects tend to produce lower sound frequencies (when set into resonant motion, for instance) than do smaller objects. The frequency range of a piccolo is displaced well above that of a bassoon. Large objects thud when they fall or are stricken, small objects ping and tinkle.[3] Such an argument was used by Osgood et al. (1957) to explain synesthesia and metaphor, and a similar explanation was presented by Brown (1958) to explain phonetic symbolism.

There is one item of evidence to suggest that experienced conjunctions of visual and auditory stimulation are not necessary to the perception of correspondence between visual size and auditory volume. Stevens (1934) found that a congenitally blind woman responded essentially the way sighted subjects do with respect to auditory volume, once the existence of this attribute was pointed out to her. If this is correct, then it would suggest that experience of simultaneous visual and auditory stimulation is not necessary for the appreciation of volumic differences among sounds. Of course, physical differences in size among objects can be comprehended by other means (e.g. touch and verbal description) and thereby perhaps provide a basis for associative learning.

Of some relevance in this context is an observation made by von Békésy (1959) to the effect that the sensation produced by a vibrator resting on the skin feels smaller the higher the vibratory pitch (the higher the stimulus frequency). Thus, psychophysical responses of the vibration sense of the skin parallel psychophysical responses of the vibration sense of the ear. It is difficult to see how an association theory could account for the dependence of perceived vibratory size on vibration frequency.[4]

Synesthesia as neural short circuit

A theory described by Clavière (1898) states that synesthesia is pathological. Perhaps. And perhaps we all are crazy. One version of this theory attempts to account for synesthesia in terms of the cross-excitation of sensory centers in the brain. Pedrono (1882) and de Rochas (1885) proposed such a physiological theory. In essence, it implies either some sort of neural short circuit or else an anastomosing of neurons from two or more senses. A first cousin to this theory is Coriat's (1913a) hypothesis of incomplete physiological differentiation. Basically, all of these theories postulate some abnormal condition; thus, this type of theory is really a variant of the view that synesthesia is pathological. But the generality of so very many synesthetic correspondences tends to diminish the value of the theory, since apparently it would have to apply as well to nonsynesthetes. (Unless we wish to adhere to the aforestated view that insanity prevails.) Of course, to the extent that one believes that all psychological phenomena have direct physiological correlates, some type of physiological theory must be correct. But there is no guarantee that a physiological theory will be useful in elucidating psychological mechanisms.

The mediation of synesthetic correspondences

The theory described by Clavière that is of greatest potential is the theory of equivalent excitation. It was propounded by Féré (1892), Bleuler and Lehmann (1881), and Flournoy (1893). In essence, the theory proposes that synesthetic correspondences derive ultimately from the existence of common properties of responses to sensory stimulation. Fété's view was that stimuli that impinge on all of the senses produce general physiological reactions, such as changes in muscular tonicity, and that these physiological responses act as mediators in the development of synesthesia. When two stimuli excite different senses, but produce physiological responses that have some common properties, those stimuli will tend to be associated; the greater the degree of commonality in response, the more closely associated in synesthesia the stimuli will be.

The views of Bleuler and Lehmann and of Flournoy were that the common responses are emotional (i.e. that the linkage between sensations in synesthesia derives from commonality of affect). Frequently, sensations linked synesthetically do appear to show an affective basis, as Calkins (1895), Whipple (1900), Riggs and Karwoski (1934), and Odbert, Karwoski and Eckerson (1942) noted. As early as the eighteenth century, Herder (1772) wrote of an affective synesthetic bond among various senses. In *Abhandlung über den Ursprung der Sprache*, in which he proposed an onomatopoetic theory of the origin of language, Herder argued that sound and color interrelate via feeling.

A more recent version of Féré's theory is that of Börnstein (1936, 1970), who also argued that sensory stimulation has a general effect on muscular tonicity. Börnstein claimed that this generalized tonic response serves to unite the senses. The most important manifestation of the unity of the senses is, according to Börnstein, the general sensory attribute of brightness, which he stated is correlated with heightening of muscular tone, regardless of the particular sense modality that is aroused. In a similar vein are Vernon's (1930) hypothesis that musical synesthesia relates to a primitive autonomic response and, even more closely, Werner and Wapner's (1949) sensori-tonic field theory, which is based on empirical evidence that muscular tone and perceived body orientation can be influenced by stimulation of several modalities.

Be these as they may, the wide variety of sensory correspondences that appear in synesthesia (the number of different corresponding pairs of dimensions found in various synesthetes) would hardly seem accountable solely in terms of anything as universal and general as body tonus. A similar conclusion may be reached about emotion or affect. Downey (1911), for example, rejected affect as a general basis for the visual–gustatory synesthesiae that she described. Affect (emotion), like tonus, appears to be too narrow a basis to account by itself for all of synesthesia.

A theory of synesthesia

But even though the simple hypotheses just described are deemed insufficient to account adequately for synesthesia in all of its sundry forms, the general approach seems correct; and, furthermore, the specific proposals just examined (that synesthesia emerges from certain common tonic and affective responses to stimulation) may turn out to provide at least part of an adequate theory. To repeat the general hypothesis, synesthesia derives from responses common to stimulation of all sense modalities. A little thought on the matter leads us to consider the possibility that the two common responses already considered (tonus and affect) are manifestations of the general factors of connotative meaning that Osgood et al. (1957) derived by means of semantic differentiation. Osgood et al. discovered that three factors are of wide applicability to the meanings of concepts; they even noted that the use of bipolar dimensions for semantic evaluation itself derived from the bipolarity of dimensions obtained in the study of synesthesia. Thus, it is not at all surprising that we come full circle and invoke those same factors of connotative meaning in a theory of synesthesia. (I shall continue to employ the term *connotative meaning* even though Osgood later (e.g. 1969, 1971) used the term *affective meaning*. In the present usage, *affect* has a more restricted meaning, closer to the single dimension of pleasantness–unpleasantness.)

The three bipolar factors derived from semantic differentiation of concepts are called *evaluation*, *potency*, and *activity*. The dimension of evaluation includes an affective component, so to the extent that affect provides a cross-modal link in synesthesia, it may be subsumed under this first factor. Unfortunately, no other one-to-one correlation reveals itself. Tonus, for instance, cannot very easily be ascribed either to the factor of activity or that of potency, though it contains characteristics of both. More to the point, it does not appear that we can apply to synesthesia in any simple, one-to-one manner the three factors obtained from semantic differentiation – no more than we were able to apply affect and tonus in that way, two possible dimensions of equivalent excitation. We cannot say, for example, that visual brightness correlates with auditory pitch because both reflect a single, underlying cognitive dimension like evaluation. They may also reflect activity. Every pair of synesthetically correlated sensory dimensions probably partakes to various extents of several underlying cognitive dimensions of factors.

Perhaps the solution to the problem lies merely in how the pie gets divided. It might be that some different set of factors besides evaluation, potency, and activity could provide a more direct, one-to-one correspondence with underlying synesthetic dimensions. But just as likely, or even more likely, the synesthetic dimensions are actually complexes that themselves vary along several component dimensions, just as sensations of sound and light vary with respect to several psychological attributes or dimensions.

It is useful in this context to look at the way Osgood (1971) interpreted the three factors of connotative meaning. According to his theory, meaning consists of a process of mediation, whose connotative components correspond to the dimensions that obtain via semantic differentiation. The mediation processes themselves are treated as learned representations of responses that become attached to their signs through learning (i.e. via differential reinforcement). More importantly to our present concern, the representational components are not simple responses but complexes derived from several reaction systems. For our purposes, we might interpret these systems to include affect (as that term is used in the present article), muscular tonic reactions, and so forth. Viewed in this manner, the present theory agrees in several fundamental respects with Osgood's, particularly as to the multidimensional mediation of synesthesia. A major difference, however, is that the present theory suggests that several of the dimensions of intersensory correspondence derive not from learning based on common and regular features of the environment but from the basic structure of people's sensory and nervous systems.

We may attribute synesthesia to some sort of fundamental processes or functions, perhaps those with their own special neural loci, at which stimulation of different sense organs produces common effects. This is in some manner equivalent to saying that synesthesia derives from what Aristotle called the *common sense* (e.g. *De anima,* 442b). Much the same point was made by Werner (1934), who argued that sensory stimulation first arouses a common, synesthetic sense before differentiating into specific, modal perception. The response at the first level is presumably more diffuse and malleable.

An interesting and important study was conducted by Osgood (1960) on the cross-cultural generality of synesthetic thought. Verbal concepts such as good, bad, white, and black were evaluated on visual scales such as light–dark, large–small, and up–down by Anglo-Americans, Navajos, Mexican-Spanish, and Japanese. Not only were the verbal–visual synesthetic tendencies much the same for members of each cultural and linguistic group, but there were good correlations between groups as well. For instance, Anglos, Navajos, and Japanese all agreed that *white* is *thin* and *calm*; that *fast* is *thin, bright,* and *diffuse*; that *heavy* is *down, thick, dark,* and *near*. Because of their cross-linguistic generality, Osgood interpreted his results as casting doubt on the importance of Whorf's (1956) hypothesis that cognition (meaning) is tied to and dependent on linguistic structure. Instead, the generality must mean that universal experiences are more important and/or that innate determinants are more important. Osgood also reported results of semantic differentiation of actual color samples on the part of Navajo and Anglo subjects. There was general cross-cultural agreement as to the connotative meanings of colors. Interestingly, Osgood noted that the agreement seemed somewhat better with respect to the meanings of the actual color samples than it did with the color names used in the prior study. Such an outcome is not surprising, and it serves as a caution against too readily equating verbal and sensory synesthesia.

Two conclusions from Osgood's study are of theoretical import. The first is that synesthetic tendencies (at least those on the verbal–visual level) show generality across members of different linguistic and cultural groups. The generalization in itself may seem merely to affirm the conclusion that was arrived at earlier with respect to pure sensory synesthesia (colored hearing). But the implication of Osgood's results leads further, for a second conclusion we may derive from his findings is that synesthesia is primarily a cognitive phenomenon; synesthesia is related to connotative meaning in general. Similar conclusions were reached earlier by Wheeler and Cutsforth (1922), Vernon (1930), Riggs and Karwoski (1934), and Karwoski and Odbert (1938). This same conclusion is implicit, if not explicit, in the view expressed by Bleuler (1913), who pointed out that certain synesthetic relations (like pitch–brightness) are universal and that colors act as symbols. The dimensions that underlie synesthesia are the same as those that appear to underlie connotative meaning in general.

What synesthesia provides to cognition is, in essence, a shorthand. Synesthesia is not just something that is tacked onto ordinary sense perception and cognition. Rather, it is an integral part of perception and cognition. One of its special roles is to summarize important cognitive distinctions in a convenient and economical way. To use an example of Boring, Langfeld and Weld (1935), we are capable of *perceiving* ice as cold and heavy or an object as light or heavy by the sound of its fall, and so on. Those are economical modes of perceiving. So too is it often with synesthesia. The cross-modal correspondences between and among the senses serve to highlight, in a convenient manner, important dimensions held in common (brightness, size, affect, etc.). Even when synesthetic responses extend the domain of reference (i.e. when the induced sensations add new qualities, new dimensions) synesthesia is not uneconomical. Rather, it is both enriching (as in the synesthetic responses to music) in its content and economical in its mode – economical, that is, as compared to alternative means of cognitive enrichment, such as linguistic elaboration. In this sense, it may be of some use to treat synesthetic cognition as an *adjunct* (*alternative* being too strong a contrast) to verbal cognition. Synesthetic, cross-modal, sensory cognition is both less abstract and more dense in informational content.

The present interpretation may help to shed some light on one unresolved problem, namely, why synesthesia often seems to disappear as a person grows and matures from childhood to adulthood. Synesthesia has been claimed to be a significant mode of thought in children (Werner 1940). That synesthesia typically arises in childhood has been noted in nearly every study, although there are occasional exceptions (e.g. Vernon 1930 reported that his own musical synesthesiae began only around age 14–15). The origin of synesthesia in childhood is in part the reason for the many reports of children's synesthesia (e.g. English 1923; Lenzberg 1923; Riggs and Karwoski 1934; Werner 1940).

Synesthesia is also more common in children than in adults. G. Stanley Hall (1883) found that 21 children of 53 (39.6 per cent) described the sounds of musical instruments as colored. Révész (1923) estimated that 50 per cent of children are synesthetic. Estimates vary as to the frequency of occurrence in adults. Bleuler and Lehmann (1881) reported that 76 of 596 adults (12.7 per cent) had colored hearing; Calkins (1895) gave a similar value, 15.7 per cent; and Rose (1909), a somewhat lower value, 9.1 per cent. On the other hand, Philippe (1893a) reported that 30 of 150 blind subjects (20 per cent) had colored hearing; many claimed their synesthesiae developed after the loss of vision. In sum, the frequency of synesthesia in children appears to be two to three times that in adults. Because most synesthetes report remembering their synesthesia as far back as childhood, it would seem a reasonable conclusion that whereas synesthesia originates in childhood, some or many child synesthetes lose their synesthesia when they grow up.

Why does synesthesia tend to be lost with age? Probably because it is replaced by another, more flexible mode of cognition (i.e. abstract language). Although synesthesia is a direct and economical mode of cognitive organization, it is not only an overly general and imprecise mode but also an inflexible one. The connotative meanings borne by synesthetic relationships are compact and salient but tend to be relatively fixed. As a child matures and cognitive development ensues, it becomes valuable, indeed necessary, for the child to transfer the meanings from the perceptual-synesthetic to the verbal realm, in which they may be used within a much less restrictive and more tractable framework. This is what Bruner (1964) called the transition from iconic to symbolic modes of representation. Considered in this manner, to the extent that synesthesia transcends childhood and lasts into adulthood, we may view it as somewhat vestigial.

Earlier in this article it was pointed out that synesthesia in its sensory form may conveniently be classified under the general rubric of *imagery*. Given the significant role that imagery plays in cognitive development (e.g. Bruner 1964), it is not surprising that Werner (1940) called attention to the importance of synesthesia in childhood. Synesthetic perception is a mode of iconic representation. Its importance, indeed the importance of imagery in gerneral, diminishes with the augmented importance of language, that is, of symbolic representation. The present interpretation of synesthesia as imagery is consistent with Paivio's (1971) model, in which imagery precedes language but both develop concurrently as the means to process information. Paivio gave an excellent account of the extent to which imagery in general continues to be an important system in cognition.

Implicit in this discussion is the view that synesthesia is not an isolated phenomenon, separated from nonsynesthetic perception and thought. Rather, synesthesia is a cross-modal manifestation of meaning in its purely sensory, and in one sense its strongest, form. But in its essence synesthesia is not really different from nonsynesthetic, cross-modal meaning nor, in much of its content, from abstract verbal meaning. A corollary is that synesthesia is probably not really lost in the cognitive transition from childhood to adulthood but is merely diminished in its magnitude, importance, and/or salience. The cross-modal matches shift from a purely sensory to a sensory–verbal or even purely verbal realm.

Though verbal synesthesia proper falls beyond the scope of the present article, a few words are in order. There are two forms of metaphoric or poetic expression of cross-sensory relation. One form simply symbolizes sensory synesthesia (i.e. expresses some intrinsic cross-modal relationship). In 'Al Aaraaf', Poe asked us to 'Witness the murmur of the grey twilight' The other, probably more typical, form creates or points to new or original sensory correspondence (i.e. expresses some extrinsic cross-modal relationship that is imposed). In 'The Anunciation', W.S.

> Merwin asked us to witness 'the blackness / of their shadow growing as it came down / Whirring and beating, cold and like thunder.'

Now we are led to consider a significant difference between synesthetic and non-synesthetic sensory correspondences. For, whereas synesthetic correspondences tend to be fixed and inflexible, non-synesthetic correspondences can be quite flexible. Some non-synesthetic subjects may correlate auditory loudness with visual brightness, others may correlate loudness with darkness, and still others may correlate loudness with brightness on some occasions but may correlate loudness with darkness on other occasions (Marks 1974). Most likely, such reversals in the way that dimensions align are themselves mediated by language. Synesthetic correspondences may provide a primitive origin containing fixed relationships upon which abstract language can build and provide flexibility.

Verbal synesthesiae (representations of cross-sensory equivalence in language) need not rely on fixed responses to mediate between dimensions on different modalities; indeed, verbal synesthesiae cannot rely on such. In order for verbal manipulations to permit reversals of dimensional alignment, they must rely on a mechanism more complex than mediating responses. Just how that verbal mechanism operates remains a question, but whatever it is, a price is paid for the flexibility it provides: The symbolic manipulations arise at least one step, probably several steps, removed from the sense perceptions described, and thereby we lose the immediacy, the richness, and the vivacity of sensory synesthesia. Sometimes the purely sensory correspondences can be reached or regained, for instance, under the influence of drugs. Thus, Baudelaire (1860) the hashish smoker could perceive, as Baudelaire (1857) the poet cognized, how *'Les parfums, les couleurs et les sons se répondent'*.

Notes

1 Each author made good use of previous bibliographies, and some (e.g. Mahling 1926) unabashedly listed works not verified. Although Mahling's

list of references is most extensive, the reader is warned that it contains numerous errors.

2 There is no systematic relation between colors of vowels and the vowels in color names. If there were, we would expect the French *ou* to be red (rouge), *e* to be green (vert), *a* to be white (blanc) or perhaps yellow (jaune), and possibly both *o* and *i* to be black (noir).

3 I assume the sound symbolism in the last sentence was not lost to the reader.

4 One explanation might be that low-frequency vibrations actually spread out over larger areas of skin. Though this is possible, note that measurements of lateral spread (Sherrick 1953) show a non-monotonic effect of increasing vibratory frequency.

References

Abraham, O. 1920: Zur psychologischen Akustik von Wellenlänge und Schwingungszahl. *Zeitschrift für Sinnesphysiologie*, 51, 121–52.

Aiken, C. 1942: Music. In C. Aiken, *Brownstone Eclogues and Other Poems*, New York: Duell, Sloan & Pearce.

Albertoni, P. 1889: Ueber Beziehungen zwischen Farben und Tonen. *Centralblatt für Physiologie*, 3, 345–7.

Anschütz, G. 1925: Untersuchungen zur Analyse musikalischer Photismen. *Archiv für die Gesamte Psychologie*, 51, 155–218.

Anschütz, G. 1926: Untersuchungen über komplexe musikalische Synopsie. *Archiv für die Gesamte Psychologie*, 54, 129–273.

Argelander, A. 1927: *Das Farbenhören und der synästhetische Faktor der Wahrnehmung*. Jena: Fischer.

Aristotle [C4BC] 1931: *De anima*. In *The Works of Aristotle*, ed. W.D. Ross, Oxford: Clarendon Press.

Balzac, H. de. Louis Lambert [1832] 1961: In G. Le Prat (ed.), *Oeuvres complètes*, vol. 20, Paris: Le Prat.

Baratoux, J. 1887: De l'audition colorée. *Le Progrès Médical*, 6, 495–6; 515–17; 538–9.

Baudelaire, C. 1887: Les Correspondances. In *Les Fleurs du mal*, Paris: Calmann-Lévy.

Baudelaire, C. [1860] 1923: Les Paradis artificiels. In Y.G. Le Dantée (ed.), *Oeuvres complétes de Charles Baudelaire*, vol. 3, Paris: Gallimard.

Beaunis, H. and Binet, A. 1892: Sur deux cas d'audition *colorée. Revue Philosophique*, 33, 448–60.

Békésy, G. von. 1959: Similarities between hearing and skin senses. *Psychological Review*, 66, 1–22.

Bentley, M. and Varon, E.J. 1933: An accessory study of 'phonetic symbolism'. *American Journal of Psychology*, 45, 76–86.

Binet, A. 1892: Le problème de l'audition colorée. *Revue des deux-mondes*, 113, 586–614.

Binet, A. 1893: L'application de la psychométrie à l'étude de l'audition colorée. *Revue philosophique*, 36, 334–6.

Binet, A. and Philippe, J. 1892: Étude sur un nouveau cas d'audition colorée. *Revue philosophique*, 33, 461–4.

Bleuler, E. 1913: Zur Theorie der Sekundärempfindungen. *Zeitschrift für Psychologie*, 65, 1–39.

Bleuler, E. and Lehmann, K. 1881: *Zwangsmässige Lichtempfindungen durch Schall und verwandte Erscheinungen*. Leipzig: Fues' Verlag.

Boring, E.G., Langfeld, H.S. and Weld, H.P. 1935: *Psychology*. New York: Wiley.

Boring, E.G. and Stevens, S.S. 1936: The nature of tonal brightness. *Proceedings of the National Academy of Sciences*, 22, 514–21.

Börnstein, W. 1936: On the functional relations of the sense organs to one another and to the organism as a whole. *Journal of General Psychology*, 15, 117–31.

Börnstein, W.S. 1970: Perceiving and thinking: their interrelationship and organismic organization. *Annals of the New York Academy of Sciences*, 169, 673–82.

Boynton, R.M. and Gordon, J. 1965: Bezold-Brücke hue shift measured by color-naming technique. *Journal of the Optical Society of America*, 55, 78–86.

Brown R. 1958: *Words and things*. New York: Free Press.

Bruner, J.S. 1964: The course of cognitive growth. *American Psychologist*, 19, 1–15.

Cairns, H. 1929: A divine intoxicant. *Atlantic Monthly*, November 638–45.

Calkins, M.W. 1893: A statistical study of pseudo-chromesthesia and of mental-forms. *American Journal of Psychology*, 5, 439–64.

Calkins, M.W. 1895: Synaesthesia. *American Journal of Psychology*, 7, 90–107.

Castel, L.-B. 1725: Clavecin par les yeux, avec l'art de peindre les sons, & toutes sortes de pieces de musique. *Mercure de France*, 2552–77.

Castel, L.-B. 1735: Nouvelles experiences d'optique & d'acoustique. *Mémoires pour l'histoire des sciences et des beaux arts*, 1444–82; 1619–66; 1807–39; 2018–53; 2335–72; 2642–768.

Castel, L.-B. 1740: *L'Optique des couleurs, fondée sur les simples observations, & tournée sur-tout à la pratique de la peinture, de la teinture & des autres arts coloristes*. Paris: Briasson.

Claparède, E. 1903: Persistance de l'audition colorée. *Comptes Rendus de la Société de Biologie*, 55, 1257–9.

Clavière, J. 1898: L'audition colorée. *L'Année Psychologique*, 5, 161–78.

Collins, M. 1929: A case of synaesthesia. *Journal of General Psychology*, 2, 12–27.

Colman, W.S. 1894: On so-called 'colour hearing'. *Lancet*, 795–6; 849–51.

Coriat, I.H. 1913a: A case of synesthesia. *Journal of Abnormal Psychology*, 8, 38–43.

Coriat, I.H. 1913b: An unusual case of synesthesia. *Journal of Abnormal Psychology*, 8, 109–12.

Czurda, M. 1953: Beziehungen zwischen Lautcharakter und Sinneseindrücken. *Wiener Archiv für Psychologie, Psychiatrie, und Neurologie*, 3, 73–84.

Darwin, E. 1790: *The Botanic Garden*, vol. 2: *The Lives of the Pants*. Dublin: J. Moore.

Delattre, P., Liberman, A.M., Cooper, F.S. and Gerstman, L.J. 1952: An experimental study of the acoustic determinants of vowel color; observations on one- and two-formant vowels synthesized from spectrographic patterns. *Word*, 8, 195–210.

Delay, J., Gérard, H.-P. and Racamier, P.-C. 1951: Les synesthésies dans l'intoxication mescalinique. *L'Encéphale*, 40, 1–10.

de Rochas, A. 1885: L'audition colorée. *La Nature*, Pt 1, 306–7, 406–8; Pt 2, 274–5.

Donders, F.C. 1857: Über die Natur der Vokale. *Archiv für die Holländischen Beiträge zur Natur und Heilkunde*, 1, 157–62.

Downey, J.E. 1911: A case of colored gustation. *American Journal of Psychology*, 22, 528–39.

Dresslar, F.B. 1903: Are chromaesthesias variable? *American Journal of Psychology*, 14, 368–82.

Dudycha, G.J. and Dudycha, M.M. 1935: A case of synesthesia: visual–pain and visual–audition. *Journal of Abnormal and Social Psychology*, 30, 57–69.

Eastlake, C.L. 1840: Notes to *Theory of colours* by J.H. von Goethe. *London: Murray*.

Ellson, D.G. 1941a: Experimental extinction of an hallucination produced by sensory conditioning. *Journal of Experimental Psychology*, 28, 350–61.

Ellson, D.G. 1941b: Hallucinations produced by sensory conditioning. *Journal of Experimental Psychology*, 28, 1–20.

English, H.B. 1923: Colored hearing. *Science*, 57, 444.

Erler, H. 1887: *Robert Schumanns Leben aus seinen Briefen geschaldert*, vol. 2. Berlin: Ries und Erler.

Fechner, G.T. 1876: *Vorschule der Aesthetik*. Leipzig: Breitkopf & Härtel.

Féré, C. 1892: *La Pathologie des emotions*. Paris: Alcan.

Flournoy, T. 1892: L'audition colorée. *Archives des Sciences Physiques et Naturelles*, 28, 505–8.

Flournoy, T. 1893: *Des phénomènes de synopsie*. paris: Alcan.

Galton, F. 1883: *Inquiries into Human Faculty and its Development*. London: Macmillan.

Gattegno, C. 1962: *Words in Color*. Chicago: Learning Materials.

Gautier, Th. 1843: Le club des hachichins. *La Presse* (Paris), 10 July.

Gautier, Th. 1846: Le club des hachichins. *Revue des deuxmondes*, 13, 520–35.

Ghil, R. [1887] 1938: Traité du verbe. In A. Messein (ed.), *Oeuvres complètes*, vol. 3, Paris: Messein.

Ginsberg, L. 1923: A case of synaesthesia. *American Journal of Psychology*, 34, 582–9.

Giradeau, C. 1885: De l'audition colorée. *L'Encéphale*, 5, 589–97.

Grafé, A. 1897: Note sur un nouveau cas d'audition colorée. *Revue de mèdecine*, 17, 192–5.

Grafé, A. 1898: Sur un cas à rattacher à ceux d'audition colorée. *Revue de médecine*, 18, 225–8.

Gruber, E. 1893: Questionnaire psychologique sur l'audition colorée, figurée et illuminée. *Revue philosophique*, 35, 499–502.

Guirao, M. and Stevens, S.S. 1964: Measurement of auditory density. *Journal of the Acoustical Society of America*, 36, 1176–82.

Hall, G.S. 1883: The contents of children's minds. *Princeton Review*, 249–72.

Harris, D.F. 1908: Colored thinking. *Journal of Abnormal Psychology*, 3, 97–113.

Hartshorne, C. 1934: *The Philosophy and Psychology of Sensation*. Chicago: University of Chicago Press.

Helmhotz, H. von 1863: *Die Lehre von den Tonempfindungen*. Braunschweig: Viewig und Sohn.

Henning, H. 1923: Eine neuartige Komplexsynästhesie und Komplexzuordnung. *Zeitschrift für Psychologie*, 92, 149–60.

Herder, J.G. van. 1772: *Abhandlung über den Ursprung der Sprache*. Berlin: Voss.

Hering, E. 1878: *Zur Lehre vom Lichtsinne*. Vienna: C. Gerold's Sohn.

Hilbert, R. 1895: Zur Kenntnis der sogenannten Doppelempfindungen. *Archiv für Augenheikunde*, 31, 44–8.

Hoffmann, E.T.A. 1899: *Kreisleriana. II* (originally published, *c.*1810). In *Musikalische Schriften*. Köln and Leipzig: Leuckert.

Hornbostel, E.M. von. 1925: Die Einheit der Sinne. *Melos, Zeitschrift für Musik*, 4, 290–7 (translated as: The unity of the senses. *Psyche*, 1927, 7, 83–9).

Hornbostel, E.M. von. 1931: Über Geruchshelligkeit. *Pflügers Archiv für die Gesamte Physiologie*, 227, 517–38.

Howells, T.H. 1944: The experimental development of color–tone synesthesia. *Journal of Experimental Psychology*, 34, 87–103.

Hurvich, L.M. and Jameson, D. 1957: An opponent-process theory of color vision. *Psychological Review*, 64, 384–404.

Hug-Hellmuth, H. von 1912: Über Farbenhören. *Imago*, 1, 228–64.

Jakobson, R., Fant, C.G.M. and Halle, M. 1963: *Preliminaries to Speech Analysis*. Cambridge, Mass.: MIT Press.

Johnson, R.C., Suzuki, N.S. and Olds, W.K. 1964: Phonetic symbolism in an artificial language. *Journal of Abnormal and Social Psychology*, 69, 233–6.

Kainz, F. 1943: *Psychologie der Sprache*. Stuttgart: Enke.

Kandinsky, W. 1912: *Über das Geistige in der Kunst, inbesondere in der Malerei*. Munich: Piper.

Karwoski, T.F. and Odbert, H.S. 1938: Color-music. *Psychological Monographs*, 50 (2, whole no. 222).

Karwoski, T.F., Odbert, H.S. and Osgood, C.E. 1942: Studies in synesthetic thinking. II. The role of form in visual responses to music. *Journal of General Psychology* 26, 199–222.

Kelly, E.K. 1934: An experimental attempt to produce artificial chromaesthesia by the technique of conditioned response. *Journal of Experimental Psychology*, 17, 315–41.

Kircher, A. 1650: *Musurgia universalis, sive Ars magna consoni et dissoni in X. libros digesta*. Rome: Carbelletti.

Klinckowström, A. 1890: Trois cas d'audition colorée dans la même famille. *Biologiska Föreningens i Stockholm Förhandlingar*, 3, 117–18.

Köhler, W. 1910: Akustische Untersuchungen, II. *Zeitschrift für Psychologic*, 58, 59–140.

Koenig. R. 1870: Sur les notes fixes charactéristiques des diverses voyelles. *Comptes Rendus de l'Académie des Sciences*, 70, 931–3.

Krohn, W.D. 1892: Pseudo-chromesthesia, or the association of colors with words, letters, and sounds. *American Journal of Psychology*, 5, 20–41.

Laignel-Lavastine (sic). 1901: Audition colorée familiale. *Revue Neurologique*, 9, 1152–62.

Langenbeck, K. 1913: Die akustisch-chromatischen Synopsien. *Zeitschrift für Sinnesphysiologie*, 47, 159–81.

Langfeld, H.S. 1914: Note on a case of chromaesthesia. *Psychological Bulletin*, 11, 113–14.

Lauret and Duchaussoy (sic). 1887: Un cas héréditaire d'audition colorée. *Revue Philosophique*, 23, 222–4.

Leibniz, G.W. von. 1896: On solidity. *New Essays Concerning Human Understanding*. New York: Macmillan; originally published, 1704.

Lemaitre, A. 1904: Un cas d'audition colorée hallucinatoire. *Archives de Psychologie*, 3, 164–77.

Lenzberg, K. 1923: Zur Theorie der Sekundärempfindungen und Bleulerschen Theorie im besonderen. *Zeitschrift für Angewandte Psychologie*, 21, 283–307.

Leuda, C. 1940: Images as conditioned sensations. *Journal of Experimental Psychology*, 26, 345–51.

Leuba, C. and Dunlap, R. 1951: Conditioning imagery. *Journal of Experimental Psychology*, 41, 352–5.

Locke, J. 1690: *An Essay Concerning Humane Understanding, Book III*. London: Basset.

Lomer, G. 1905: Beobachtungen über farbiges Hören (auditio colorata). *Archiv für Psychiatrie und Nervenkrankheiten*, 40, 593–601.

Lundlow, F. 1857: *The Hasheesh Eater*. New York: Harper.

Luria, A.R. 1968: *The Mind of a Mnemonist*. New York: Basic Books.

Mahling, F. 1926: Das Problem der 'Audition colorée.' *Archiv für die Gesamte Psychologie*, 57, 165–302.

Marinesco, G. 1912: Contribution à l'étude de synesthésies particulièrement de l'audition colorée. *Journal de Psychologie Normale et Pathologique*, 9, 385–422.

Marks, L.E. 1978: On associations of light and sound: the mediation of brightness, pitch, and loudness. *American Journal of Psychology*, 87, 173–88.

Marks, L.E. and Stevens, J.C. 1966: Individual brightness functions. *Perception and Psychophysics*, 1, 17–24.

Masson, D.I. 1952: Synesthesia and sound spectra. *Word*, 8, 39–41.

Modell, J.D. and Rich, G.J. 1915: A preliminary study of vowel qualities. *American Journal of Psychology*, 26, 453–6.

Mudge, E.L. 1920: The common synaesthesia of music. *Journal of Applied Psychology*, 4, 342–5.

Myers, C.S. 1911: A case of synaesthesia. *British Journal of Psychology*, 4, 228–38.

Nahlowsky, J.W. 1826: *Das Gefühlsleben. Dargestellt aus praktischen Gesichtspunkten nebst einer kritischen Einleitung*. Leipzig: Louis Pernitzsch.

Newman, S.S. 1933: Further experiments in phonetic symbolism. *American Journal of Psychology*, 45, 53–75.

Newton, I. 1704: *Opticks*. London: Smith & Walford.

Odbert, H.S., Karwoski, T.F. and Eckerson, A.B. 1942: Studies in synesthetic thinking: I. Musical and verbal association of color and mood. *Journal of General Psychology*, 26, 153–73.

Ortmann, O. 1933: Theories of synesthesia in the light of a case of color-hearing. *Human Biology*, 51, 155–211.

Osgood, C.E. 1960: The cross-cultural generality of visual–verbal synesthetic tendencies. *Behavioral Science*, 5, 146–69.

Osgood, C.E. 1969: On the whys and wherefores of E, P, and A. *Journal of Personality and Social Psychology*, 12, 194–9.

Osgood, C.E. 1971: Exploration of semantic space: a personal diary. *Journal of Social Issues*, 27, 5–64.

Osgood, C.E., Suci, G.J. and Tannenbaum, P.H. 1957: *The Measurement of Meaning*. Urbana: University of Illinois Press.

Paivio, A. 1971: *Imagery and Verbal Processes*. New York: Holt, Rinehart & Winston.

Pedrono (sic). 1882: De l'audition colorée. *Annales d'Oculistique*, 88, 224–37.

Perky, C.W. 1910: An experimental study of imagination. *American Journal of Psychology*, 21, 422–52.

Philippe, J. 1893a: L'audition colorée des aveugles. *Revue Scientifique*, 1, 806–9.

Philippe, J. 1893b: Résumé d'une observation d'audition colorée. *Revue Philosphique*, 36, 330–4.

Plummer, H.C. 1915: Color music – a new art created with the aid of science. *Scientific American*, 112, 343, 350–1.

Quincke, H. 1890: Ueber Mitempfindungen und verwandte Vorgänge. *Zeitschrift für Klinische Medizin*, 17, 429–51.

Raines, T.H. 1909: Report of a case of psychochromesthesia. *Journal of Abnormal Psychology*, 4, 249–52.

Reichard, G., Jakobson, R. and Werth, E. 1949: Language and synesthesia. *Word*, 5, 224–33.

Révész, G. 1923: Über audition colorée. *Zeitschrift für Angewandte Psychologie*, 21, 308–32.

Rich, G.J. 1919: A study of tonal attributes. *American Journal of Psychology*, 30, 121–64.

Riggs, L.A. and Karwoski, T. 1934: Synaesthesia. *British Journal of Psychology*, 25, 29–41.

Rimbaud, A. 1937a: Le sonnet des voyelles. (Originally published, 1871). In *Oeuvres de Arthur Rimbaud*. Paris: Mercure de France.

Rimbaud, A. 1937b: Alchimie du verbe. *Une Saison en Enfer* (Originally published, 1873). In *Oeuvres de Arthur Rimbaud*. Paris: Mercure de France.

Rose, K.B. 1909: Some statistics on synaesthesia. *American Journal of Psychology*, 20, 446.

Rossigneux, C. 1905: Essai sur l'audition colorée et sa valeur esthétique. *Journal de Psychologie Normale et Pathologique*, 2, 193–215.

Rousseau, J.-J. 1839: Essai sur l'origine des langues (Originally published, 1753). In G. Petitain (ed.), *Oeuvres complètes de J.J. Rousseau* (Tome 6). Paris: Lefèvre.

Sapir, E. 1929: A study of phonetic symbolism. *Journal of Experimental Psychology*, 12, 225–39.

Schultze, E. 1912: Krankafter Wandertrieb räumlich beschränkte Taubheit für bestimmte Töne und 'tertiäre' Empfindungen bei einem Psychopathen. *Zeitschrift für die Gesamte Neurologie und Psychiatrie*, 10, 399–419.

Scriabin, A. 1911: *Prométhée, le Poème du feu, pour grand orchestre et piano avec orgue, choeurs et chavier à lumières*. Berlin: Breitkopf Hartel (musical composition).

Segal, S.J. and Fusella, V. 1970: Influence of imaged pictures and sounds on detection of visual and auditory signals. *Journal of Experimental Psychology*, 83, 458–64.

Segal, S.J. and Nathan, S. 1964: The Perky effect: Incorporation of an external stimulus into an imagery experience under placebo and control conditions. *Perceptual and Motor Skills*, 18, 385–95.

Sherrick, C.E. Jr. 1953: Variables affecting sensitivity of the human skin to mechanical vibration. *Journal of Experimental Psychology*, 45, 273–82.

Simpson, R.H., Quinn, M. and Ausubel, D.P. 1956: Synesthesia in children: association of colors with pure tone frequencies. *Journal of Genetic Psychology*, 89, 95–103.

Slawson, A.W. 1968: Vowel quality and musical timbre as functions of spectrum envelope and fundamental frequency. *Journal of the Acoustical Society of America*, 43, 87–101.

Smith, H.L. 1903: Synaesthesia. *Bulletin of The Johns Hopkins Hospital*, 16, 258–63.

Starkie, E. 1961: *Arthur Rimbaud*. Norfolk, Conn.: New Directions.

Starr, F. 1893: Note on color-hearing. *American Journal of Psychology*, 51, 416–18.

Stevens, J.C. and Marks, L.E. 1965: Cross-modality matching of brightness and loudness. *Proceedings of the National Academy of Sciences*, 54, 407–11.

Stevens, S.S. 1934: Are tones spatial? *American Journal of Psychology*, 46, 145–7.

Stevens, S.S. 1935: The relation of pitch to intensity. *Journal of the Acoustical Society of America*, 6, 150–4.

Stevens, S.S., Guirao, M. and Slawson, A.W. 1965: Loudnes, a product of volume times density. *Journal of Experimental Psychology*, 69, 503–10.

Stelzner, H.-F. 1903: Ein Fall von akustisch-optischer Synästhesie. *Albrecht von Graefes Archiv für Ophthalmologie*, 55, 549–63.

Stelzner, H.-F. 1904: Un cas de synesthésie audito-visuelle. *Annales d'Oculistique*, 131, 137.

Suarez de Mendoza, F. 1890: *L'Audition colorée*. Paris: Octave Doin.

Sullivan, J.W.N. 1914: An organ on which color compositions are played. *Scientific American*, 110, 163, 170.

Sully, J. 1879: Harmony of colours. *Mind*, 4, 172–91.

Terrace, H.S. and Stevens, S.S. 1962: The quantification of tonal volume. *American Journal of Psychology*, 75, 596–604.

Tieck, J.L. 1828: *Schriften*, vol. 10. Berlin: Reimer.

Troland, L.T. 1930: *Principles of psychophysiology*, vol 2.: *Sensation*. New York: Van Nostrand.

Ulrich, A. 1903: Phénomènes de synesthésies chez un épileptique. *Revue Philosophique*, 56, 181–7.

Vernon, P.E. 1930: Synaesthesia in music. *Psyche*, 10, 22–40.

Voss, W. 1929: Das Farbenhören bei Erblindeten. *Archiv für die Gesamte Psychologie*, 73, 407–524.

Wehofer, F. 1913: 'Farbenhören' (chromatische Phonopsien) bei Musik. *Zeitschrift für Angewandte Psychologie*, 7, 1–54.

Werner, H. 1934: L'unité des sens. *Journal de Psychologie Normale et Pathologique*, 31, 190–205.

Werner, H. 1940: *Comparative Psychology of Mental Development*. New York: Harper.

Werner, H. and Wapner, S. 1949: Sensory-tonic field theory of perception. *Journal of Personality*, 18, 88–107.

Wheeler, R.H. 1920: The synaesthesia of a blind subject. *University of Oregon Publications*, no. 5.

Wheeler, R.H. and Cutsforth, T.D. 1922: The synaesthesia of a blind subject with comparative data from an asynaesthetic blind subject. *University of Oregon Publications*, no. 10.

Whipple, G.M. 1900: Two cases of synaesthesia. *American Journal of Psychology*, 11, 377–404.

Whorf, B.L. 1956: *Language, Thought, and Reality*. Cambridge, Mass.: Technology Press.

Wicker, F.W. 1968: Mapping the intersensory regions of perceptual space. *American Journal of Psychology*, 81, 178–88.

Willis, R. 1830: On the vowel sounds, and on reed organpipes. *Transactions of the Cambridge Philosophical Society*, 3, 231–68.

Wissemann, H. 1954: *Untersuchungen zur Onomatopoiie*. Heidelberg: Winter.

Wundt, W. 1874: *Grundzüge der physiologischen Psychologie*. Leipzig: Engelmann.

Zigler, M.J. 1930: Tone shapes: a novel type of synaesthesia. *Journal of General Psychology*, 3, 277–87.

5

*'Correspondances'**

Charles Baudelaire

La Nature est un temple où de vivants piliers
Laissent parfois sortir de confuses paroles;
L'homme y passe à travers des forêts de symboles
Qui l'observent avec des regards familiers.

Comme de longs échos qui de loin se confondent
Dans une ténébreuse et profonde unité,
Vaste comme la nuit et comme la clarté,
Les parfums, les couleurs et les sons se répondent.

Il est des parfums frais comme des chairs d'enfants,
Doux comme les hautbois, verts comme les prairies,
Et d'autres, corrompus, riches et triomphants,

Ayant l'expansion des choses infinies,
Comme l'ambre, le musc, le benjoin et l'encens,
Qui chantent les transports de l'esprit et des sens.

*Reprinted from Christopher Robinson, *French Literature in the Nineteenth Century*. London: David & Charles; New York: Barnes & Noble, 1978, pp. 129–30. Translation appears overleaf.

[Nature is a temple where living pillars sometimes let forth confused words; in it man goes through forests of symbols which watch him with familiar looks.

Like long echoes which from a distance mingle into a shadowy and deep unity, as vast as night and light, perfumes, colours and sounds reply to one another.

There are perfumes fresh as children's flesh, sweet as oboes, green as meadows, and others corrupt, rich and triumphant,

Sharing the capacity of expansion that infinite things have, such as amber, musk, balsam and incense, which hymn the transports of the mind and the senses.]

6

*Synaesthesia**

Alexander Luria

Our curiosity had been aroused by a small and seemingly unimportant observation. S had remarked on a number of occasions that if the examiner said something during the experiment – if, for example, he said 'yes' to confirm that S had reproduced the material correctly or 'no' to indicate he had made a mistake – a blur would appear on the table and would spread and block off the numbers, so that S in his mind would be forced to 'shift' the table over, away from the blurred section that was covering it. The same thing happened if he heard noise in the auditorium; this was immediately converted into 'puffs of steam' or 'splashes' which made it more difficult for him to read the table.

This led us to believe that the process by which he retained material did not consist merely of his having preserved spontaneous traces of visual impressions; there were certain additional elements at work. I suggested that S possessed a marked degree of *synaesthesia*. If we can trust S's recollections of his early childhood . . . , these synaesthetic reactions could be traced back to a very early age. As he described it:

> When I was about two or three years old I was taught the words of a Hebrew prayer. I didn't understand them, and what happened was that the words settled in my mind as puffs of steam or splashes . . . Even now I *see* these puffs or splashes when I hear certain sounds.

Synaesthetic reactions of this type occurred whenever S was asked to listen to *tones*. The same reactions, though somewhat more

*Reprinted from A.R. Luria, *The Mind of a Mnemonist*. New York: Basic Books, 1968, pp. 23–9.

complicated, occurred with his perception of *voices* and with speech sounds.

The following is the record of experiments that were carried out with S in the Laboratory on the Physiology of Hearing at the Neurological Institute, Academy of Medical Sciences.

Presented with a tone pitched at 30 hertz and having an amplitude of 100 decibels, S stated that at first he saw a strip of 12–15 centimetres in width the colour of old, tarnished silver. Gradually this strip narrowed and seemed to recede; then it was converted into an object that glistened like steel. Then the tone gradually took on a colour one associates with twilight, the sound continuing to dazzle because of the silvery gleam it shed.

Presented with a tone pitched at 50 hertz and an amplitude of 100 decibels, S saw a brown strip against a dark background that had red, tongue-like edges. The sense of taste he experienced was like that of sweet and sour borscht, a sensation that gripped his entire tongue.

Presented with a tone pitched at 100 hertz and having an amplitude of 86 decibels, he saw a wide strip that appeared to have a reddish-orange hue in the centre; from the centre outwards the brightness faded with light gradations so that the edges of the strip appeared pink.

Presented with a tone pitched at 250 hertz and having an amplitude of 64 decibels, S saw a velvet cord with fibres jutting out on all sides. The cord was tinged with a delicate, pleasant pink-orange hue.

Presented with a tone pitched at 500 hertz and having an amplitude of 100 decibels, he saw a streak of lightning splitting the heavens in two. When the intensity of the sound was lowered to 74 decibels, he saw a dense orange colour which made him feel as though a needle had been thrust into his spine. Gradually this sensation diminished.

Presented with a tone pitched at 2000 hertz and having an amplitude of 113 decibels, S said: 'It looks something like fireworks tinged with a pink-red hue. The strip of colour feels rough and unpleasant, and it has an ugly taste – rather like that of a briny pickle . . . You could hurt your hand on this.'

Presented with a tone pitched at 3000 hertz and having an amplitude of 128 decibels, he saw a whisk broom that was of a fiery colour, while the rod attached to the whisks seemed to be scattering off into fiery points.

The experiments were repeated during several days and invariably the same stimuli produced identical experiences.

What this meant was that S was one of a remarkable group of people, among them the composer Scriabin, who have retained in an especially vivid form a 'complex' synaesthetic type of sensitivity. In S's case every sound he heard immediately produced an experience of light and colour and, as we shall see later in this account, a sense of taste and touch as well.

S also experienced synaesthetic reactions when he listened to someone's *voice*. 'What a crumbly, yellow voice you have,' he once told L.S. Vygotsky[1] while conversing with him. At a later date he elaborated on the subject of voices as follows:

> You know there are people who seem to have many voices, whose voices seem to be an entire composition, a bouquet. The late S.M. Eisenstein[2] had just such a voice: listening to him, it was as though a flame with fibres protruding from it was advancing right toward me. I got so interested in his voice, I couldn't follow what he was saying . . .
>
> But there are people whose voices change constantly. I frequently have trouble recognizing someone's voice over the phone, and it isn't merely because of a bad connection. It's because the person happens to be someone whose voice changes twenty to thirty times in the course of a day. Other people don't notice this, but I do. (*Record* of November 1951)

> To this day I can't escape from seeing colours when I hear sounds. What first strikes me is the colour of someone's voice. Then it fades off . . . for it does interfere. If, say, a person says something, I see the word; but should another person's voice break in, blurs appear. These creep into the syllables of the words and I can't make out what is being said. (Record of June 1953)

'Lines', 'blurs', and 'splashes' would emerge not only when he heard tones, noises or voices. Every speech sound immediately summoned up for S a striking visual image, for it had its own distinct form, colour and taste. Vowels appeared to him as simple figures, consonants as splashes, some of them solid configurations, others more scattered – but all of them retained some distinct form. As he described it:

> A [a] is something white and long; **И** [ε] moves off somewhere ahead so that you just can't sketch it, whereas **й** [j'ɪ] is pointed in form. Ю [j'u] is also pointed and sharper than е [j'ε], whereas **Я** [j'a] is big, so big that you can actually roll right over it. O [ɔ] is a sound that comes from your chest . . . it's broad, though the sound itself tends to fall. Эй [j'ɔ] moves off somewhere to the side. I also experience a sense of taste from each sound. And when I see lines, some configuration that has been drawn, these produce sounds. Take the figure ⌊___. This is somewhere in

> between e, Ю, and й; 〰 is a vowel sound, but it also resembles the sound *r* – not a pure *r* though . . . But one thing still isn't clear to me: if the line goes up, I experience a sound, but if it moves in the reverse direction, it no longer comes through as a sound but as some sort of wooden hook for a yoke. The configuration ⌣ appears to be something dark, but if it had been drawn slower, it would have seemed different. Had you say, drawn it like this ⌣, then it would have been the sound e.

S had similar experiences with numbers:

> For me 2, 4, 6, 5 are not just numbers. They have forms. 1 is a pointed number – which has nothing to do with the way it's written. It's because it's somehow firm and complete. 2 is flatter, rectangular, whitish in colour, sometimes almost a grey. 3 is a pointed segment which rotates. 4 is also square and dull; it looks like 2 but has more substance to it, it's thicker. 5 is absolutely complete and takes the form of a cone or a tower – something substantial. 6, the first number after 5, has a whitish hue; 8 somehow has a naïve quality, it's milky blue like lime . . .

What this indicates is that for S there was no distinct line, as there is for most of us, separating vision from hearing, or hearing from a sense of touch or taste. The remnants of synaesthesia that many ordinary people have, which are of a very rudimentary sort (experiencing lower and higher tones as having different colorations: regarding some tones as 'warm', others as 'cold'; 'seeing' Friday and Monday as having different colours), were central to S's psychic life. These synaesthetic experiences not only appeared very early in his life but persisted right to his death. And, as we shall have occasion to see, they left their mark on his habits of perception, understanding and thought, and were a vital feature of his memory.

S's tendency to recall material in terms of 'lines' or 'splashes' came into play whenever he had to deal with isolated sounds, nonsense syllables or words he was not familiar with. He pointed out that in these circumstances sounds, voices, or words evoked some visual impression such as 'puffs of steam', 'splashes', 'smooth or broken lines'; sometimes they also produced a sensation of taste, at other times a sensation of touch, of having come into contact with something he would describe as 'prickly', 'smooth' or 'rough'.

These synaesthetic components of each visual and particularly of each auditory stimulus had been an inherent part of S's recall at a very early age; it was only later, after his faculty for logical and figurative memory had developed, that these tended to fade into the background, though they continued to play some part in his recall.

From an objective standpoint these synaesthetic components were important to his recall, for they created, as it were, a background for each recollection, furnishing him with additional, 'extra' information that would guarantee accurate recall. If, as we shall see later, S was prompted to reproduce a word inaccurately, the additional synaesthetic sensations he experienced would fail to coincide with the word he produced, leaving him with the sense that something was wrong with his response and forcing him to correct the error:

> I recognize a word not only by the images it evokes but by a whole complex of feelings that image arouses. It's hard to express . . . it's not a matter of vision or hearing but some overall sense I get. Usually I experience a word's taste and weight, and I don't have to make an effort to remember it – the word seems to recall itself. But it's difficult to describe. What I sense is something oily slipping through my hand . . . or I'm aware of a slight tickling in my left hand caused by a mass of tiny, lightweight points. When that happens I simply remember, without having to make the attempt . . . (Record of 22 May 1939)

Hence, the synaesthetic experiences that clearly made themselves felt when he recalled a voice, individual sounds or complexes of sound, were not of major importance but served merely as information that was secondary in *his recall of words*.

Notes

1 The well-known Russian psychologist [trans.].
2 The famous film producer [trans.].

Part III
Neuroscientific Perspectives

7

Synaesthesia: a Review of Psychological Theories

John E. Harrison and Simon Baron-Cohen

7.1 Introduction

Studies that have used the classical paradigms of experimental psychology to understand synaesthesia are remarkably few and far between. In fact, presumably due to the lack of availability of synaesthetic subjects, many studies have studied cross-modal transfer in normal subjects, i.e. individuals who are not synaesthetic. In contrast, our own work has been aimed at verifying the existence of the condition and investigating the nature of the synaesthetic experience.

Almost all studies of synaesthesia, be they psychological or physiological, have sought to answer the question: what causes synaesthesia? Given the varieties and degrees of synaesthesia that appear to exist, as well as the evidence for cross-modal transfer in normal people, an important question to address is: are people with synaesthesia qualitatively or simply quantitatively different? Expressed another way: are synaesthetes categorically different from non-synaesthetes, or do they simply reflect one end of a distribution? A final issue concerns the varieties of synaesthesia. As mentioned in chapter 1, the vast majority of individuals contacted and tested by our group have 'coloured-hearing' synaesthesia. Even in acquired forms of synaesthesia, the vast majority of reported cases involve visual experience triggered by auditory stimulation. Why should this be the most common form? In this chapter we explore these issues.

7.1.1 *What causes synaesthesia?*

Over the past 200 years a number of hypotheses have been put forward to explain the cause of synaesthesia. A number of the early theories are reviewed by Marks (chapter 4 in this volume), so in what follows here we shall concentrate on later theories. However, before doing so it is worth pointing out Marks's dismissal of neurobiological accounts. His stance should be seen in the context of the time in which he was writing and in the following section we shall review a number of recent findings suggesting plausible neurological causes of the condition.

7.2 Preserved Neural Connectivity Theory

The normal adult human brain does not contain direct neural connections between auditory and visual areas. However, the early developing brain in many species does. This first theory holds that, probably for genetic reasons, in individuals with synaesthesia pathways between auditory and visual areas in the brain continue to exist beyond neoteny, such that when words, or sounds, give rise to activation in auditory areas, the visual cortex is also stimulated. What is the evidence for this theory?

One method of investigation would be to look at the brains of people with synaesthesia to establish whether such pathways are present. This is currently impossible to do either in living individuals or post-mortem. The potential for doing such post-mortem studies does however exist and two tracers, DiI and DiO, have been used to trace such pathways (Buhl and Lubke 1989). Unfortunately, these tracers are lipid soluble dyes and therefore only effective in tracing pathways in relatively unmyelinated neurons (i.e. in foetal tissue). Consequently, in order to establish that such pathways exist, we must await further technological developments in the field of neuroanatomy.

However, there is evidence for the presence of such connective pathways in other species (see Kennedy et al.: chapter 14 in this volume). Kennedy and others in a number of studies (Dehay, Bullier and Kennedy 1984; Kennedy, Bullier and Dehay 1989) have found that connections between auditory and visual areas exist in the brain structure of species such as the macaque monkey (*Macaca irus*) and the domestic cat (*Felis domesticus*). These projections appear to be transient, typically disappearing approximately three months *post partum*. There is also some evidence that these transitory pathways exist in human neonates, and may, as in cats and macaques, get 'pruned' as part of the biological maturation of the brain. Much of this evidence is reviewed by Maurer (see chapter 13 in this volume).

Maurer's hypothesis is that human babies mix the input from different senses and that this gives rise to 'normal synaesthesia'. We know from the work by Meltzoff and Borton (1979) that babies who suck on either a 'nubby' or a 'smooth' pacifier (dummy) will prefer to look at a picture of the pacifier they sucked on, thereby showing a match between touch and vision. The Meltzoff and Borton study is usually taken as evidence for cross-modal transfer. Maurer goes one step further in suggesting that synaesthesia might be a normal stage of perceptual experience in addition to cross-modal transfer.

Maurer's evidence in support of this view comes from other studies of neonates. One such study is that reported by Lewkowicz and Turkewicz (1980). In this experiment one-month-old children, who had seen a patch of white light for 20 trials, were presented with bursts of white noise presented at different intensities. During the noise presentation, the patch of light that they had been trained on was interspersed repeatedly and the children's heart rate was measured. Normally heart rate increases as a function of noise intensity, but Lewkowicz and Turkewicz found that the heart rate recorded at a noise intensity of 74dB showed the lowest heart rate change and that for values greater or less than this value heart rate increased. Lewkowicz and Turkewicz's interpretation of this finding was that 'infants were responding to the auditory stimuli in terms of their similarity to the previously presented visual stimulus' (1980: 597), or, as Maurer (1993: 110) put it, 'the children responded least to the "familiar" intensity'. Maurer also cites evidence from electrophysiological studies of neonates showing that the amplitude of somatosensory evoked potentials (SEPs) increases when white noise is played to them. Normally, SEPs only increase as a consequence of tactile stimulation. Finally, she cites the work of Neville that in early infancy auditorily evoked potentials (AEPs) to language evoke a potential in the occipital cortex whereas in older individuals AEPs yield potentials only in auditory areas such as the temporal lobes.

The evidence in the previous paragraph is consistent with the theory that synaesthesia might be due to the persistence of neural information passing from auditory to visual brain areas, beyond the neonatal stage. Taken in the context of development, it also suggests the intriguing possibility that we might *all* be coloured-hearing synaesthetes until we lose connections between these two areas somewhere about three months of age, at which point cortical maturation gives rise to sensory differentiation. This is consistent with Cytowic's (1989) view of synaesthetes being 'cognitive fossils'.

7.3 Sensory Leakage Theory

Jacobs et al. (1981) proposed what we shall call the 'Sensory Leakage Theory'. This is an account of how simple photisms arise in cases of acquired synaesthesia, though it could in principle be extended to account for idiopathic (developmental) synaesthesia. As we mentioned in chapter 1, most cases of *acquired* synaesthesia appear to arise in individuals who suffer damage to anterior portions of the brain, often the optic nerve. We suggested in our review of this work that the simple photisms experienced by these individuals were markedly different from the percepts reported by synaesthetes and almost certainly different in kind. Close examination of the nine patients reported in Jacobs et al. reveals that four of these patients (cases 1, 2, 4 and 7) also experienced photisms in the *absence* of auditory stimulation, casting doubt on whether these instances should be described as cases of auditory visual synaesthesia at all. It is also worth observing that seven patients always experienced their photisms when they were 'relaxed, drowsy or dozing' (p. 214), circumstances in which hypnagogic hallucinations are possible.

The essence of Jacobs et al.'s theory is that auditory information 'leaks' into pathways and areas in the brain that ordinarily deal with visual information. Jacobs et al. expand this 'leakage' theory by suggesting that there are 'numerous regions of the brain where visual and auditory pathways lie in close anatomic proximity' (p. 216) and that at these points post-synaptic fibres might converge to cause the synaesthesia seen in a range of pathological states such as congenital blindness and drug intoxication.

Evidence to support leakage between areas subserving different forms of sensory information is sparse, causing some difficulties for Jacobs et al.'s theory. However, recent work has suggested that, rather than posit the need for leakage, it is possible to find at certain locations in the brain classes of neurons that are responsive to stimulation from more than one sensory modality. For example, in a study carried out by Graziano, Yap and Gross (1994), recordings were made from neurons ($N = 141$) in the ventral portion of the premotor cortex. Of these neurons, 27–31 per cent were found to be bimodally responsive, firing as a result of either, or both, visual and somasthetic stimulation.

The existence of bimodally responsive neurons means that other brain areas could produce ambiguous interpretations of the firing of these neurons. Presumably, under normal circumstances, areas that deal with afferent sensory information provide details of the *source* of these data. However, as Halligan et al. (in press) have recently suggested, when normal brain function is disrupted access to other sources of information regarding the nature of these data might be lost. The patient DN reported by Halligan et al. might provide an example of this, in that as a result of brain damage causing hemianaesthesia, he is unable to feel tactile stimuli administered to his left side. However, when permitted to observe the application of the stimulus he reports tactile sensation. If Halligan et al.'s theory turns out to be an accurate account of DN's condition, then this provides an example of how the brain seeks to provide a meaningful interpretation of incoming sensory stimulation when deprived of a full complement of information.

7.4 Cytowic's Theory of Synaesthesia

Perhaps the most controversial theoretical account of the cause of synaesthesia is that most recently advanced by Cytowic (1993) in his book *The Man Who Tasted Shapes*. Cytowic proposes that synaesthesia occurs because 'parts of the brain get disconnected from one another . . . causing the normal processes of the limbic system to be released, bared to consciousness, and experienced as synaesthesia' (p. 163). An analogy is drawn with migraine, based upon the notion that in both conditions 'a stimulus causes a rebalancing of regional metabolism' (ibid.). Cytowic maps the analogy by pointing out that both synaesthesia and migraine (of some kinds) are evoked by a stimulus, and, consequently, just as the migraine stimulus causes metabolic and circulatory changes, so too does the stimulus in synaesthesia. This theory might be true, though as the product of a new view of brain function it is not readily testable. However, his assertion that the limbic system is the critical brain locus can and has been tested.

In the final chapter of *The Man Who Tasted Shapes*, Cytowic concedes that whilst he has no direct evidence to implicate a particular neural structure, given the 'stunning shut-down of the cortex' (p. 152) observed in the ^{133}Xenon studies of rCBF in MW's brain, he points to the limbic areas as being 'the seat of synaesthesia'. Direct evidence of the involvement of the limbic system would have been provided by evidence of blood flow changes in this brain region, though unfortunately neuroimaging using ^{133}Xenon inhalation does not permit such deep structures to be imaged.

Fortunately, this is not a limitation shared by PET, so the importance of the limbic system in synaesthesia can be evaluated using this technique. As discussed by Paulesu and Frith (see chapter 8 in this volume), whilst considerable differences in rCBF were found in the comparison of control subjects with synaesthetes and in the within subjects' comparison of words with tones in synaesthetes, none of these differences were reported to be in the limbic system. Of course, it might be that Cytowic's subject MW is different in *kind* from the subjects scanned by Paulesu et al. (1995). Given MW's grossly abnormal resting blood flow levels, together with his polymodal synaesthesia, this remains a strong possibility. It would be interesting to know if any of the other synaesthetes examined by Cytowic exhibit similar blood flow characteristics as those described for MW.

7.5 The Learned Association Theory

This theory was originally suggested by Calkins (1893); it holds that in coloured-hearing synaesthesia, the colour–word and/or sound correspondences reported are due entirely to learned association. An explanation put forward by some commentators (J. Mollon, personal communication), including some of the synaesthetes we have met, is that the colour–letter associations are derived from coloured alphabet books or from coloured letters that the individual saw as a child. Whilst we regard this as a plausible account of the acquisition of pseudosynaesthesia, we suspect, for a number of reasons, that it is an unsatisfactory account of developmental synaesthesia. Our reasons include the following:

1 *The gender ratio* If all coloured-hearing synaesthesia was explicable in the same terms as pseudosynaesthesia, why would so many more women, as compared to men, form such associations? A socialization account which would lead to this gender ratio is not immediately obvious, though transmission from mothers to daughters via modelling may be a possibility (though a tenuous one).
2 *Consecutive letters* We have examined the 'coloured alphabets' of many of the subjects who have contacted us. Careful scrutiny yields the finding that often consecutive letters are closely described in colour terms (e.g. M = olive green, N = emerald green, O = washed-out pale green). We have compared this with contemporary coloured alphabet books and have found, in contrast, that publishers logically go to great lengths to ensure that consecutive letters are printed in very different colours. Learned association therefore cannot account for the specific colours of particular letters or phonemes.
3 *Synaesthesic twins* A comparison of the coloured alphabets of twins has so far yielded substantial variation in the colour–letter

correspondences made by each of the pair. The same variation is given by siblings and by mothers and daughters in the same family. We regard it as surprising that there is not greater similarity in the colour–letter correspondences of family members if coloured alphabets are acquired as learned associations.

4 *Lack of recollection* We have yet to meet a person with synaesthesia who is able to report *knowing* that their letter–colour associations were learnt either purposefully or incidentally are a result of exposure to coloured alphabet letters or books.

The learned association theory of synaesthesia has not yet provided satisfactory explanations of these anomalies.

7.6 The Genetic Theory of Synaesthesia

The possibility that synaesthesia might be an inherited trait seems to have first been put forward by Galton (1883: see chapter 4 in this volume). We share this view and suspect that genetic mechanisms might cause the preserved neural connectivity described above. Earlier we reviewed the evidence for transitory connections between auditory and visual brain areas in other mammalian species. Assuming that such connections are also to be found in our species, the most parsimonious explanation for synaesthesia is that in individuals with the condition these neonatal pathways persist due to inherited mechanisms.

A recent study (Baron-Cohen, Burt, Laittan-Smith, Harrison and Bolton 1995) has provided evidence to support the notion that synaesthesia might be an inherited trait. In that study, the pedigrees of seven families of probands suggested that the condition is transmitted as an autosomal dominant X chromosome-linked condition (see figure 7.1). We are currently testing this theory by extending the number of pedigrees tested and by taking blood for linkage analysis (see also Bailey and Johnson, chapter 11 in this volume).

If the genetic theory is supported, this begs the question of the mechanism by which such a biological inheritance has its effect. A candidate mechanism would be the expression of genes that regulate the migration and maturation of neurons within the developing brain. A second candidate mechanism is 'neuronal pruning'. On this account, synaesthesia can be best explained, not by positive forces creating neural pathways that in non-synaesthetes do not exist, but by maturational effects that lead to neonatal pathways being left active.

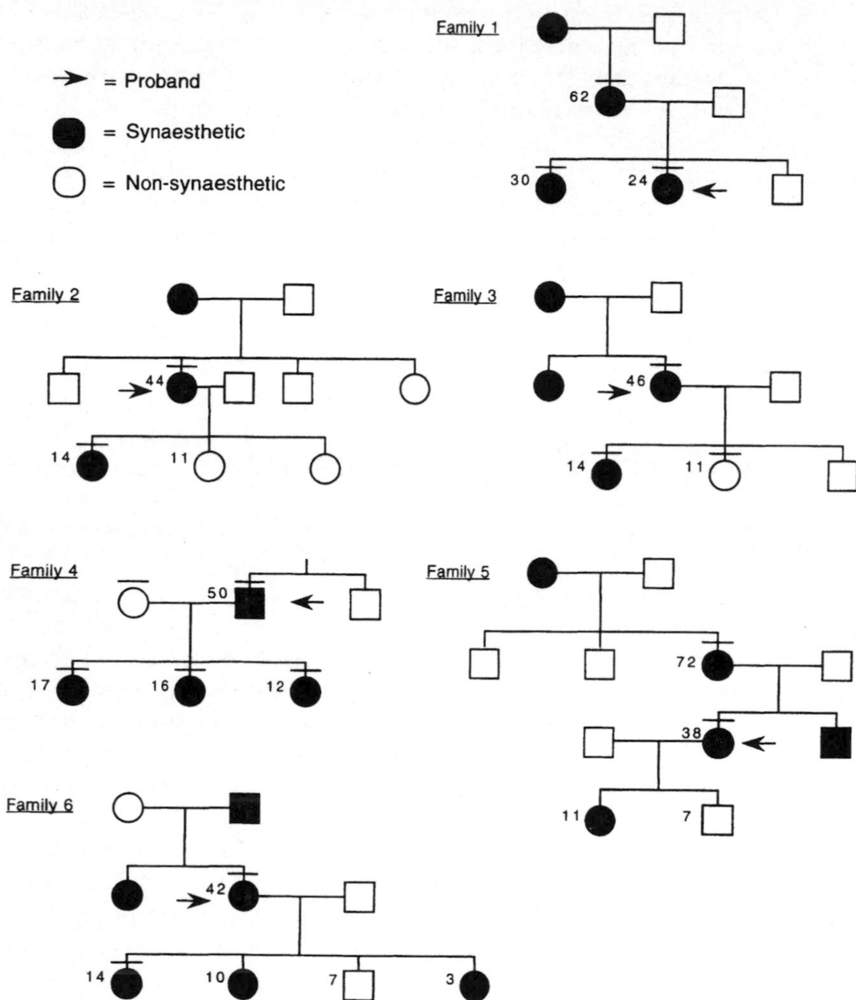

Figure 7.1 Patterns of inheritance in families where synaesthesia occurs
Note: Squares represent males; circles, females. (Reproduced from Baron-Cohen et al. 1995.)

7.7 Environmentally Shaped Brain Maturation Theory

It seems to us at least possible that environmental factors might shape brain structure through the selective reinforcement of specific neural connections. It might be that the brains of individuals with synaesthesia are 'shaped' by environmental factors such that the normally transient connections between auditory and visual areas are reinforced through use and lead to the maintenance of these pathways. It is well recognized that brain experience plays a role in shaping the structure of the brain, as work by visual scientists has shown (Hubel and Wiesel 1963). For example, animals deprived of visual stimulation during sensitive periods exhibit marked changes in areas of visual cortex (Levay, Wiesel and Hubel 1980). The importance of this work for our considerations of the possible causes of synaesthesia is that it shows how early visual experience, acquired whilst the brain is relatively 'plastic', has a lasting impact upon neural structure.

The circumstances by which such stimulation may occur are necessarily speculative. One means by which this might occur has been suggested by Francis Crick (personal communication). He suggests that individuals who in later life test positive for synaesthesia are those who may have been given coloured letters to play with when neonates, and that it is exposure to this stimulation that accounts for their synaesthesia. This theory of synaesthesia superficially appears to share much in common with the learned association theory discussed earlier. Whilst both theories view synaesthesia as the consequence of environmentally mediated mechanisms, they are not necessarily synonymous with one another. Learned associations do not necessarily require direct connections between auditory and visual areas of the brain. Associations of this kind could be made at the level of semantics and therefore stored as engrams, possibly in areas of temporal cortex. By contrast, environmentally shaped pathways require direct connections between auditory and visual areas of the brain.

The environmental shaping theory of synaesthesia suggests that within us all is the potential to remain a synaesthete, whereas the genetic theory suggests that only those biologically disposed to synaesthesia will develop the condition.

7.8 The Cross-modal Matching Theory

This is based on evidence of cross-modal matching in normal subjects, in addition to the evidence from Lewkowicz and Turkewicz described earlier. Do the presence of such abilities in normal subjects represent a *'forme fruste'* of the condition? Much of the work looking at cross-modal analogues of characteristics such as brightness/loudness, and so on, has been carried out by Marks (1982a, 1982b, 1987). In the following review of whether mild synaesthesia is found in 'normal' subjects we draw on both his work and that of Zellner and Kautz (1990).

Research designed to test whether synaesthesia is found in all normal subjects shares some of the obstacles that exist in work with the profoundly synaesthetic; that is, if normal subjects equate bright visual phenomena with high-pitched sounds, is this a result of learning culturally inherited metaphors or via residual synaesthesia? Marks (1975: chapter 4 of this volume) suggests that 'cross-modal correspondences between and among the senses serve to highlight, in a convenient manner, important dimensions held in common (brightness, size, affect, etc.)'. Later work by Marks (1982a) yielded evidence in support of this, showing that normal subjects exhibited remarkable consistency when asked to rate a selection of auditory–visual synaesthetic metaphors using scaled ratings of loudness, pitch and brightness. For example, 'sunlight' was rated as louder than 'glow', which was in turn rated as louder than 'moonlight'. A second study reported by Marks (1982b) required subjects to set the loudness of a 1,000 Hz tone and the brightness of white light for 15 cases of visual–auditory metaphor taken from works of poetry (e.g. Poe's 'The murmur of coming twilight', and Swinburne's 'Bright sound of battle, loud light of thunder'). Again, marked consistency characterized the performance of these subjects, leading Marks to propose that intensity might be a common sensory dimension.

Just as Marks has shown that auditory and visual judgements can interact with one another, so Zellner and Kautz (1990) have found that perceived odour intensity can be affected by the colour of the smelled substance. A parsimonious explanation for this finding would be that when substances are presented in a form that reflects their traditional colouring (e.g. orange-flavoured drinks of an orange colour – a trick known to soft-drinks manufacturers the world over), consumers are set to expect a specific flavour and intensity. However, Zellner and Kautz also showed that colour-induced changes in intensity occurred with novel colour–odour combinations. In their discussion section, Zellner and Kautz (1990: 391) suggest that their effect may be due to conditioned association, or, that it might be 'the result of residual intersensory neural connections'. With respect to the first hypothesis, they point out that clear, colourless solutions are generally lacking in odour, whereas coloured solutions are generally expected to be aromatic. In fact, so strong is this expectation that subjects in Zellner and Kautz's experiment when asked to judge coloured and uncoloured solutions of equal odour intensity refused to believe the equality when debriefed!

7.9 The Modularity Theory

In order for us to 'know' that a percept is visual, auditory, olfactory, and so on, we must have developed a method of identifying information as being of one sensory kind or another. There is therefore likely to be a modular structure to sensation which allows for discrete identification of information as specific to a sensory system (Fodor 1983). The structural modularity expressed in the preserved neural connectivity theory outlined above has its functional correlate cast in the language of functional modularity (see Segal, chapter 12 in this volume). Our modularity theory holds that, whereas in non-synaesthetes audition and vision are functionally discrete, in individuals with synaesthesia a breakdown in modularity has occurred. The consequence of this, in the case of coloured–hearing synaesthesia, is that sounds have visual attributes.

7.9.1 A summary of theory

Marks (1975, chapter 4 in this volume) suggests that the hypotheses posited as explanations 'for synaesthesia in all its sundry forms' seem insufficient. We concur with this view and suggest that we would be best off referring to the pseudosynaesthetic cross-modal matching reported by various authors as metaphoric reference acquired by learning associations and the internalizing of cultural convention.

Over the course of the last decade we have received correspondence from over 900 individuals world-wide, many of whom report having synaesthesia. Two things characterize the vast majority of these correspondents: (a) the vast majority (.90 per cent) are female; and (b) of those reporting forms of synaesthesia, the vast majority report only forms of coloured-hearing. Of the latter group, a substantial number of the accounts we receive show colour associations (probably learned) for only a limited set of word categories, such as for days of the week, months of the year, etc. A sub-group of these individuals with colour–word associations have correspondences for all words. We suspect that these are synaesthetes of the kind reported in Baron-Cohen et al. (1993) and Paulesu et al. (1995), whose synaesthesia is based upon coloured letter correspondences. Markedly different from these subjects is EP, the synaesthete reported by Baron-Cohen, Wyke and Binnie (1987).

From these observations it follows that the literature dealing with cases of synaesthesia almost certainly includes studies of individuals who have limited repertoires of learned colour–auditory associations, those with colour–letter correspondences, and those with the form of synaesthesia exhibited by EP. If we include the apparently extremely rare examples of those with sensory matches that are not auditory–visual (such as Cytowic's MW) and those who suffer photisms as a consequence of damage to visual pathways, it can be seen that the term 'synaesthesia' covers a number of very different examples. It is also likely that no single theory is likely to account successfully for this variety of forms.

We have enumerated the various theories of the cause of synaesthesia and recognize that they are not necessarily mutually exclusive accounts. Implicit in most neuroscientific research is the idea that complete accounts of human behaviour require theories couched at both the functional and the structural level. This implies a hierarchy of science in which theories of the same concept can be phrased in different language and so do not compete as theoretical models of brain function but, rather, provide explanations couched in vocabulary appropriate to each discipline.

7.9.2 *Current work and future studies*

Recent work has strongly suggested that synaesthesia is an inherited condition. Furthermore, as discussed by Bailey and Johnson (chapter 11 in this volume), the pattern of inheritance narrows the number of locations in the genome at which candidate genes for synaesthesia may be found. We are currently testing the families of probands for evidence of synaesthesia and taking blood for genetic analysis. We are also testing, using a number of neuropsychological measures, Cytowic's view that synaesthetes have left–right confusion, difficulty with mental arithmetic and poor navigational skills.

As we discussed, a number of commentators have suggested that synaesthesia is due 'simply' to learned association. We suspect that in a number of cases this may be true, but also suspect that such an account cannot explain all incidences of synaesthesia. One way in which we can address the question of learned association is to functionally image the brains of synaesthetes while they listen to words and compare their patterns of regional cerebral blood flow to those of normal subjects who have been taught to associate words with colours. We are currently engaged in such a study with colleagues at the Institute of Psychiatry.

Finally, a planned study will monitor any changes in synaesthesia that occur with the acquisition of reading skills. We suspect that such a shift may occur, as it seems to us that colour correspondences for words in pre-literate children would be based on phonology.

Synaesthetes in the Baron-Cohen et al. (1993) and Paulesu et al. (1995) studies showed correspondences that were based on orthographic forms. So, for example, a subject for whom the letter P is blue would tend to respond with this colour for 'photograph' but not for 'fish', though both words begin with the same phoneme. Evidence suggests that fundamental changes in thinking occur with the acquisition of reading (Karmiloff-Smith 1992), and so testing synaesthetic individuals before and after the acquisition of literacy may well show a shift from phonemic to written colour correspondences.

References

Baron-Cohen, S., Wyke, M. and Binnie, C. 1987: Hearing words and seeing colours: an experimental investigation of synaesthesia. *Perception*, 16: 761–7.

Baron-Cohen, S., Burt, L., Laittan-Smith, F., Harrison, J.E. and Bolton, P. 1995: Synaesthesia: prevalence and familiality. Unpublished manuscript, University of Cambridge.

Baron-Cohen, S., Harrison, J., Goldstein, L. and Wyke, M. 1993: Coloured speech perception: is synaesthesia what happens when modularity breaks down? *Perception*, 22, 419–26.

Buhl, E.H. and Lubke, J. 1989: Intracellular lucifer yellow injection in fixed brainslices combined with retrograde tracing, light and electron microscopy. *Neuroscience*, 28(1), 3–16.

Calkins, M.W. 1893: A statistical study of pseudo-chromesthesia and of mental-forms. *American Journal of Psychology*, 5, 439–66.

Cytowic, R.E. 1989: *Synaesthesia: a union of the senses*. New York: Springer-Verlag.

Cytowic, R.E. 1993: *The Man Who Tasted Shapes*. New York: Putnam.

Cytowic, R.E. and Wood, F.B. 1982: Synaesthesia. I: A review of theories and their brain basis. *Brain and Cognition*, 1, 23–35.

Dehay, C., Bullier J. and Kennedy, H. 1984: Transient projections from the fronto-parietal and temporal cortex to areas 17, 18 and 19 in the kitten. *Experimental Brain Research*, 57, 208–12.

Fodor, J.A. 1983: *The Modularity of Mind: An Essay on Faculty Psychology*. Cambridge, Mass.: MIT Press.

Graziano, M.S.A., Yap, G.S. and Gross, C.G. 1994: Coding of visual space by premotor neurons. *Science*, 266(5187), 1054–7.

Halligan, P., Hunt, M., Marshall, J. and Wade, D.T. In press: When seeing is feeling: acquired synaesthesia or phantom touch? *Neurocase*.

Hubel, D.H. and Wiesel, T.N. 1963: Receptive fields of cells in striate cortex of very young, visually unexperienced kittens. *Journal of Neurophysiology*, 26, 994–1002.

Jacobs, L., Karpik A., Bozian, D. and Gothgen, S. 1981: Auditory–visual synaesthesia: sound induced photisms. *Archives of Neurology*, 38, 211–16.

Karmiloff-Smith, A. 1992: *Beyond Modularity*. Cambridge, Mass.: MIT Press/ Bradford Books.

Kennedy, H., Bullier, J. and Dehay, C. 1989: Transient projection from the superior temporal sulcus to area 17 in the newborn macaque monkey. *Proceedings of the National Academy of Sciences*, 86, 8093–7.

Levay, S., Wiesel, T.N. and Hubel, D.H. 1980: The development of ocular dominance columns in normal and visually deprived monkeys. *Journal of Computational Neurology*, 191: 1–51.

Lewkowicz, D.J. and Turkewicz, G. 1980: Cross-modal equivalence in early infancy: auditory–visual intensity matching. *Developmental Psychology*, 16(6), 597–607.

Marks, L.E. 1982a: Bright sneezes and dark coughs, loud sunlight and soft moonlight. *Journal of Experimental Psychology: Human Perception and Performance*, 8(2), 177–93.

Marks, L.E. 1982b: Synaesthetic perception and poetic metaphor. *Journal of Experimental Psychology: Human Perception and Performance*, 8(1), 15–23.

Marks, L.E. 1987: On cross-modal similarity: auditory–visual interactions in speeded discrimination. *Journal of Experimental Psychology*, 13(3), 384–94.

Maurer, D. 1993: Neonatal synaesthesia: implications for the processing of speech and faces. In B. de Boysson-Bardies, S. de Schonen, P. Jusczyk, P. McNeilage and J. Morton (eds), *Developmental Neurocognition: speech and face processing in the first year of life*, Dordrecht: Kluwer.

Meltzoff, A.N. and Borton, R.W. 1979: Intermodal matching by human neonates. *Nature*, 282, 403–4.

Paulesu, E., Harrison, J., Baron-Cohen, S., Watson, J., Goldstein, L., Heather, J., Frackowiak, R.S.J. and Frith, C.D. 1995: The physiology of coloured hearing. *Brain*, 118, 661–76.

Wise, R., Chollet, F., Hadar, U., Friston, K. and Frackowiak, R. 1991: Distribution of cortical neural networks involved in word comprehension and word retrieval. *Brain*, 114, 1803–17.

Zeki, S. 1993: *A Vision of the Brain*. Oxford: Blackwell Scientific.

Zellner, D.A. and Kautz M.A. 1990: Color affects perceived odor intensity. *Journal of Experimental Psychology*, 16(2), 391–7.

8

The Physiological Basis of Synaesthesia

Christopher D. Frith and Eraldo Paulesu

8.1 Consciousness and the Brain

Synaesthesia is a special form of conscious experience. Like all conscious experience it cannot be observed by an outsider. I know what I am experiencing, but I only know about your experience because you tell me about it. I have to take what you say on trust and assume that you are not lying or misguided or using words in an unusual way. In most cases it is easy for me to believe you because the experience you describe is very similar to mine. But when your experience is different I may begin to have doubts. You tell me that when you hear words you see colours. I don't see colours when I hear words. Some special words, like sky, are associated with colours for me, but you insist that such associations do not underlie the experiences you are describing. We seem to have reached an impasse for there is no way I can obtain independent, 'objective' evidence about your unusual experiences.

Of course, this last statement is an exaggeration. In earlier chapters in this book ingenious behavioural paradigms have been presented which give strong confirmation of the subjective reports of synaesthetic experiences. In particular, the extremely high consistency of the experiences elicited by particular stimuli resembles perception rather than memory or association. Synaesthetes who see colours when hearing words showed a consistency of over 90 per cent in their experiences, while controls showed a consistency of less than 50 per cent for the colour associations elicited by these words (Baron-Cohen et al. 1993). Nevertheless, an extreme sceptic might rightly claim that anyone could achieve the same level of consistency with sufficient practice. However, as we know from phenomena such as blind-sight (Weiskrantz 1986), there is not a one-to-one relationship between behaviour and conscious experience. With sufficient practice a 'control' subject might imitate the behaviour of the synaesthete without having the experience.

The new brain-imaging techniques provide a more direct index of conscious experience than does behaviour. There are a number of things brain activity can reveal about consciousness. First, we believe that each conscious experience is associated with a specific pattern of brain activity. If the experience of the synaesthete is genuinely different from that of other people, then the associated pattern of brain activity should be different also. Thus brain imaging can confirm that synaesthetes are having a different experience (rather than, for example, describing the same experience in different words). Secondly, we believe in the principle of functional segregation: that different kinds of information are localized in different brain areas (Zeki 1978). Thus the location of brain activity tells us something about the content of the associated experience. Visual experiences will be associated with activity in visual areas, auditory experiences in auditory areas. In principle, once the human cortex has been 'mapped' with sufficient accuracy, the location of the activity associated with synaesthesia should provide independent evidence about what the experience is like. Thirdly, we believe that brain imaging will eventually be able to uncover the mechanism by which stimulation in one modality can lead to experience in another. Ultimately we should be able to discover the differences in brain stucture that lead to the phenomenon of synaesthesia.

Synaesthesia can be seen as a special case of integrated cross-modal perception, one of the least understood physiological properties of the brain. A typical (normal) example of such cross-modal perception is the appreciation of our body in space, where visual, somaesthetic and vestibular signals, recorded by anatomically separated sensory systems, are combined into a unitary non-ambiguous representation (Ventre, Flandrin and Jeannerot 1984). A similar integration must occur also within single systems: e.g. in the visual system, where the various attributes of the visual world (shapes, colours, movement, etc.) are processed in a segregated fashion and then recombined (Zeki and Shipp 1988). Understanding synaesthesia should increase our understanding of these kinds of sensory integration.

So far there have been very few studies of the physiological basis of synaesthesia. There has been a functional imaging experiment on a single subject with taste–shape synaesthesia (Cytowic and Wood 1982; Cytowic 1989). Measurements of cerebral blood flow with the non-tomographic ^{133}Xenon inhalation technique showed widespread decreases in the neocortex during the synaesthetic experience. Partly on the basis of this result, Cytowic and Wood (1982) have suggested that, in all form of synaesthesia, sensory integration is likely to occur in the limbic system, in conjunction with neocortical inhibition. However, the technical limitations of the ^{133}Xenon inhalation technique did not allow testing of this role of the limbic system.

A correlation between specific perceptual abilities in the neocortex and synaesthesia would be suggested by the description of a patient who became colour-blind after a car accident (Sacks and Wasserman 1987; Sacks et al. 1988). Before the car accident this patient was a coloured-hearing synaesthete. This condition vanished in conjunction with the loss of colour perception. Unfortunately, no reliable information is available about the anatomical location of the damage in this patient, who died three years after the accident (S. Zeki, personal communication).

In the remainder of this chapter we shall describe a brain imaging study of six volunteers with synaesthesia (Paulesu et al. 1995). We used the technique of positron emission tomography (PET) to measure changes in relative regional cerebral blood flow (rCBF) as an index of altered synaptic activity across the entire brain volume simultaneously (Raichle 1987).

From the several types of synaesthesia, we chose to study people whose synaesthesia consisted of seeing colours when they heard a word, a phenomenon we call colour–word synaesthesia (see chapter 1). We hypothesized that when these synaesthetes heard words we might see unusual levels of activity in extrastriate brain areas responsible, under normal circumstances, for colour perception (e.g. the fusiform gyrus) (Lueck et al. 1989; Zeki et al. 1991). Alternatively, synaesthesia could be associated with the simultaneous activity of auditory verbal cortex with some associative visual area responsible for a conjoint representation of letter shapes and colours. A suitable candidate for such an area would be the inferior temporal region, which is active when subjects have to detect objects on the basis of conjoint features such as shape and colour (Corbetta et al. 1991a). Finally, we were also interested to observe whether primary visual cortex (areas V1 and V2) was active during colour–word synaesthesia. There are feedback connections between associative and primary visual areas (Shipp and Zeki 1989a and b). Activation of V1 and V2 during synaesthesia would provide strong evidence for a role for such modulatory feedback in visual experience since no direct visual stimulation would be occurring. On the other hand, a lack of activity in V1 and V2 would suggest that the brain is capable of generating conscious percepts without a contribution from primary sensory areas (Zeki, Watson and Frackowiak 1993; Barbur et al. 1993).

8.2 The PET Activation Technique

Before describing our experiment in detail it might be useful to give the non-specialist reader a brief presentation of the PET activation technique and the data analysis procedures involved in it.

PET is the most versatile and complex of the nuclear medicine functional imaging techniques. It can be used to measure a number of physiological parameters, depending on the radiotracer used, for example, regional cerebral blood flow, brain glucose and oxygen consumption and extraction, regional neurotransmission at the pre- and post-synaptic level, to name a few. All these variables are calculated from measurements of the distribution of brain radioactivity by a PET scanner. The brain distribution of a positron-emitting isotope incorporated into a tracer molecule is monitored in space and in time. The tracer used determines the function to be investigated.

The physiological parameter measured for PET activation studies is in the large majority of cases regional cerebral blood flow. The most widely used radiotracers for rCBF measurements are 150-water or 150-butanol. The brain distribution in these freely diffusible substances reflects tissue perfusion.

After the injection of radio-labelled water, the relationship between recorded counts and blood flow is linear in any region of brain. This linear dependence suggests that even non-quantitative maps of the distribution of radioactivity (as opposed to the derived quantitative blood flow maps) will provide information about the relative functional state of given brain regions. This key observation has resulted in a wide application of relative regional CBF measurement in activation studies because in this way the arterial cannulation that is required for quantitation can be completely avoided (Mazziotta et al. 1985; Fox and Mintun 1989).

Modern PET activation studies in normal subjects are therefore based on the measurement of relative regional cerebral blood flow (rCBF) during control and experimental conditions. Changes in rCBF between an experimental and a control condition are used as an index of altered synaptic activity to identify brain activation associated with the physiological or cognitive component isolated on the basis of the experimental design. Instrumentation and knowledge about the kinetics of such radiotracers have reached a stage of development such that no major ambiguities remain about the origin of the signal measured with perfusion PET scans. This is still an advantage over other functional imaging techniques, such as functional MRI, for which a full understanding of the nature of the signal sampled in activation studies is still to be ascertained.

As recent advances in PET scanner technology have resulted in a five-fold increase in sensitivity, it is now possible to collect between 12 and 16 rCBF scans in the same subject in the same scanning session with a much-reduced radiation dose. If the number of experimental and control conditions is kept at a reasonably low level (two or three, including control conditions), the number of replications per condition are sufficient for the determination of meaningful activation maps in single subjects (Watson et al. 1993; Bottini et al. 1995; Paulesu et al. 1995; Silbersweig et al. 1995).

PET activation studies can be designed and analysed as group studies or on a single-subject basis. Group analyses require the normalization of PET brain images into a standard (stereotactic) anatomical space before statistical assessment of rCBF differences across conditions at each and every voxel in the brain images (Friston et al. 1991a). These comparisons are usually performed using the t-statistic, after removal of confounding global CBF differences across conditions and subjects with analysis of covariance (Friston et al. 1990, 1991b). Given that thousands of voxels are interrogated during these analyses, appropriate analytically derived corrections for multiple comparisons have had to be developed to determine appropriate confidence thresholds for interpretation of the results (Friston et al. 1991b, 1995).

Group analyses retain biological validity in that they magnify functional anatomical commonalities across subjects and minimize idiosyncratic intersubject variability. On the other hand, it has now become possible to study patterns of cerebral activity in single subjects with PET and to identify the variability in functional anatomy or processing strategy during the performance of cognitive or perceptuomotor tasks. The individual activation maps determined by PET can be readily, automatically and accurately superimposed on to individual MRI images to give accurate integrated anatomical and functional information.

8.2.1 Experimental designs used in PET activation experiments

The earliest activation experiments were based on comparisons of perfusion maps from pairs of experimental conditions; for example, a specific physiological stimulation and its appropriate stimulus-deficient control. This technique is known as the (cognitive) subtraction method. The tenet of this approach is that, in well-constructed experiments, the difference between two sets of blood flow maps should isolate anatomical counterparts of the physiological or cognitive components that distinguish the two tasks or conditions under which scanning was performed. A powerful example of the use of this approach has been in studies of functional segregation in prestriate visual cortex (Lueck et al. 1989; Zeki et al. 1991; Watson et al. 1993). This neuro-reductionist approach has resulted in identification of human homologues of visual prestriate cortical areas such as areas V4 and V5 that have been well characterized physiologically and anatomically in monkeys.

The cognitive subtraction technique is conceptually simple and powerful but depends on a major assumption, which is that cognitive components can be added or subtracted from tasks without any resultant interaction between any of the remaining components. Alternative approaches have been developed to go beyond the simplistic view of pure insertion. For example, parametric experimental designs in which regional perfusion is correlated with a variable of interest that is manipulated linearly (for example, the rate of presentation of auditorially presented words; Price et al. 1992). Another powerful experimental design is factorial, in which two treatments are combined and the anatomical correlates of an interaction, or modulation, of one treatment by another are identified. This is the experimental design that was used for the study in synaesthesia. The physiology of coloured hearing was characterized by asking the question of how activation patterns associated with hearing words are altered by synaesthesia (see sub-section 8.3.2).

8.3 Subjects

The vast majority of people who report colour–word synaesthesia are female (see chapter 1). Therefore our synaesthetic subjects were five right-handed females and one left-handed female (mean age: 45 years ± 7). Our subjects were selected on the basis of the presence of colour–word synaesthesia exclusively, with no similar experiences for any other auditory stimuli (e.g. music). MRI scans were peformed to show that none of these subjects had macroscopic anatomical abnormalities. The control group consisted of five right-handed females and one left-handed female (mean age: 40 years ± 6) who had never experienced synaesthesia. All our subjects were neurologically normal, with no history of neurological or psychiatric disease, and none was taking psychoactive drugs. The IQs of all our subjects were in the superior range.

8.3.1 *Assessment of synaesthesia*

The exact nature of their experience when hearing words was examined in all our synaesthetic subjects. They were asked to described the colours triggered by hearing more than 100 words. Approximately six months later and without prior warning, they were tested again on the same word list and the two sets of responses were compared for consistency (Baron-Cohen et al. 1993).

In order to determine whether colour–word synaesthesias were triggered by the sounds of the words or by their letters, we administered another test in which words were chosen so that they shared the first phoneme, but not the first letter (e.g. *photograph* and *fish*) or had a different first phoneme, but shared the same first letter (e.g. *apple* and *art*). If the synaesthesias were based on a phonological code, then paired items such as *photograph* and *fish* would elicit the same colour. On the other hand, if the same colours were triggered by pairs such as *apple* and *art*, this would suggest that synaesthesias were based on letters. All our synaesthetes achieved at least 90 per cent consistency when retested on the 100-word list at six months. It was also clear that in all of them the chromatic quality of coloured hearing was predominantly based on the first letter of the word, not the first sound, even though the words were heard rather than seen. Thus *nice* and *knock* elicited different colours while *kind* and *knock* elicited the same colour. Examples from one subject's performance are shown in table 8.1.

For all our subjects, the synaesthetic perception consisted of seeing the words themselves in a colour which was dominated by the colour of the first letter in five cases, or by the first vowel in one case. In five out of six of our subjects numbers (from one to nine) also have their own colour which is not determined by the first letter of the number names. Interestingly, our subjects report synaesthesia also in conjunction with inner speech, whenever this is used explicitly, for instance when thinking. As during extrinsic stimulation, the perception is dominated by the first letter of each word. Our subjects do not have synaesthesia during reading, unless they sub-vocalize what they read. The colour percept is not localized in a particular part of the visual field except for subject AC, who localized synaesthetic percepts in the centre of her visual field. In addition, in no subject is there interference between synaesthesia and perception of the visual world.

8.3.2 *PET activation experiment*

Our subjects underwent 12 consecutive PET scans, during which relative regional cerebral blood flow (rCBF) was measured. There were two conditions which were each replicated six times:

Table 8.1 Performance of subject BJ on a colour–word association test designed to establish whether her synaesthesias are based on the first sound or the first letter of words.

Pair	*Word*	*Colour*	*Word*	*Colour*
1	Writer	silver grey	Rice	Oxford blue
2	Geoffrey	ginger brown	Judge	pink
3	Fish	grey	Photograph	blue
4	Kind	biscuit	Cut	green
5	Knock	biscuit	Kind	biscuit
6	Pharmacy	blue	Pill	blue
7	Water	silver grey	Writer	silver grey
8	Geoffrey	ginger brown	Goggle	mid-brown

Note: Examples 1 to 4 (e.g. *photograph* and *fish*) start with the same sound, but a different letter, while examples 5 to 8 (e.g. apple and art) start with the same letter, but a different sound. As the list shows, for subject BJ, the prevalent trigger to determine the colour of synaesthesias is the first letter of a word rather than its first sound. The same rule applied to other synaesthetes for the large majority of words. This indicates that in the synaesthetes reported in this paper, colour percepts are predominantly linked to letters rather than phonemes.

1 In the control condition tones were presented. These were pure tones which were delivered through earphones. The pitch of the tones varied randomly between 262 Hz and 523 Hz (the same range as the human voice). Subjects were blindfolded and instructed to listen to the tones and tap their left index finger each time they heard a tone. Stimulus duration was 0.5 seconds. To keep the level of attention high, interstimulus intervals were randomly varied from 0.5 to 1.5 seconds.
2 In the experimental condition spoken words were presented. Single words were delivered in the same fashion as tones, and subjects tapped their left index finger every time they heard a word. All stimuli were highly imaginable concrete words selected from the *Oxford Psycholinguistic Database* (Quinlan 1992).

The subjects with synaesthesia were asked to listen passively to the stimuli and to let the colour perception occur automatically. Controls were not informed that they were being compared with synaesthetes until after the scanning session was finished. They were also asked to listen to the words in a passive fashion. The experience of the synaesthetes when listening to tones was the same as for the controls. However, when listening to words, the synaesthetes had the additional experience of colour. We would therefore expect to see a difference in brain activity between the groups for words, but not for tones. Therefore the brain activity associated with colour–word synaesthesia could be examined statistically by looking at the interaction between groups (synaesthetics vs. controls) and conditions (words vs. tones).

8.4 PET Data Analysis

Details of the PET data acquisition procedures and image analysis have been published elsewhere (Paulesu et al. 1995). We summarize here the most important aspects of it.

The PET data were analysed on a group basis and on a single-subject basis. The group data analysis involves preliminary normalization of the brain images into a stereotactic space. All subsequent procedures were identical for both analyses.

8.4.1 Smoothing

In order to increase signal-to-noise ratio and accommodate normal variability in functional gyral anatomy, each PET image was smoothed in three dimensions with a low-pass Gaussian filter (FWHM $5 \times 5 \times 3$ pixels, $10 \times 10 \times 6$ mm) (Friston et al. 1991a).

8.4.2 Normalization of global CBF changes and statistical computations

Differences in global activity were removed following an analysis of covariance with global counts as covariate and activation condition as treatment (Friston et al. 1990). This analysis generated 12 mean values across subjects for each treatment (condition) and the associated error variance estimates for every voxel, allowing a comprehensive *post hoc* interrogation of the data. This was made with appropriately weighted comparisons of means for all voxels using the t-statistic. This procedure allows generation of images of t-values that constituted statistical parametric maps (SPM(t)) (Friston et al. 1990, 1991b; Frackowiak and Friston 1994) which were transformed to Z-distribution maps.

8.4.3 Statistical comparisons

The main effects of rCBF changes induced by our experiment (words minus tones and vice versa) were first computed in each group of subjects (synaesthetes and controls). Significant changes were identified by applying a statistical threshold of 0.05 corrected for multiple non-independent comparisons (Friston et al. 1991b). In addition, because some of our hypotheses regarding brain activations during synaesthesia were constrained to a few locations (see section 8.1), a less-conservative analysis was also performed where the level of significance was thresholded at the omnibus significance level $p < 0.01$ (Z score threshold: 2.4). This approach is justified in hypothesis-led experiments (Friston et al. 1991b). Finally, differences in rCBF changes for subjects with synaesthesia compared to controls were assessed as interactions between treatments. As before, the omnibus significance threshold corresponding to $p < 0.01$ was chosen, as the sites of interactions were predicted from the results obtained in the main effects analysis of the data from the synaesthetes. Individual patterns of rCBF changes were assessed in the same way as the group main effect analysis ($p < 0.01$).

8.5 Results

As expected, hearing words compared to hearing tones led, in both groups, to greater activation of a series of perisylvian brain areas implicated in language. These included the superior and middle temporal gyri bilaterally and also the inferior frontal gyrus on the left.

However, in the group with synaesthesia we saw additional foci of activation which included the middle frontal gyrus and the insula on the right and the posterior inferior temporal (PIT) cortex on the left. All these activation foci survived a correction for multiple non-independent comparisons (Z score >3.7). At a lower threshold an additional activation focus was detected in the homologous right PIT cortex and there were also bilateral activation foci in the parieto/occipital junctions that were not seen in control subjects. We specifically tested for rCBF increases in the region of putative human colour area (V4) described by Zeki et al. (1991). This area, however, did not reach our *a priori* criterion for significance set at $p < 0.01$ (stereotactic co-ordinates: $x = -22$; $y = -72$; $z = -8$; Z score: 2.1).

The differences of activation between synaesthete and control groups were tested formally as interactions between groups and conditions by using the appropriate linear contrasts. All the areas described above that were not readily related to word perception were significantly more active in subjects with synaesthesia than in controls. In addition, activation in the right superior temporal gyrus and insula was also significantly greater than in control subjects.

Table 8.2 Cerebral structures activated by word perception

(a) In controls

	Left				*Right*			
Brain structure	*x*	*y*	*z*	*Z score*	*x*	*y*	*z*	*Z score*
Inferior frontal gyrus (BA 44/45)	–48	16	16	4.4	–	–	–	–
Superior temporal gyrus (BA 21/22)	–52	–14	0	6.1	52	–12	0	3.6
Middle temporal gyrus (BA 21)	–54	–42	4	4.0	46	–26	0	4.4

(b) In synaesthetes

	Left				*Right*			
Brain structure	*x*	*y*	*z*	*Z score*	*x*	*y*	*z*	*Z score*
Middle frontal gyrus (BA 46/10)	–	–	–	–	30	48	8	3.7
Inferior frontal gyrus (BA 44/9)	–42	12	28	4.3	–	–	–	–
Insula	–	–	–	–	**44**	**8**	**0**	**4.5**
Superior temporal gyrus (BA 22)	–52	–10	0	7.6	56	–10	4	6.8
Middle temporal gyrus (BA 21)	–54	–30	4	5.2	–	–	–	–
Posterior inferior temporal cortex (BA 20/37)	**–50** **–50**	**–42** **–44**	**–12** **–16**	**4.1** **3.8**	**40**	**–46**	**–16**	**2.6**
Superior occipital gyrus/superior parietal lobule (BA 19/7)	**–26** **–26**	**–78** **–68**	**40** **44**	**2.5** **2.7**	**32**	**–68**	**40**	**2.5**

Note: Areas in bold type were not activated in controls.

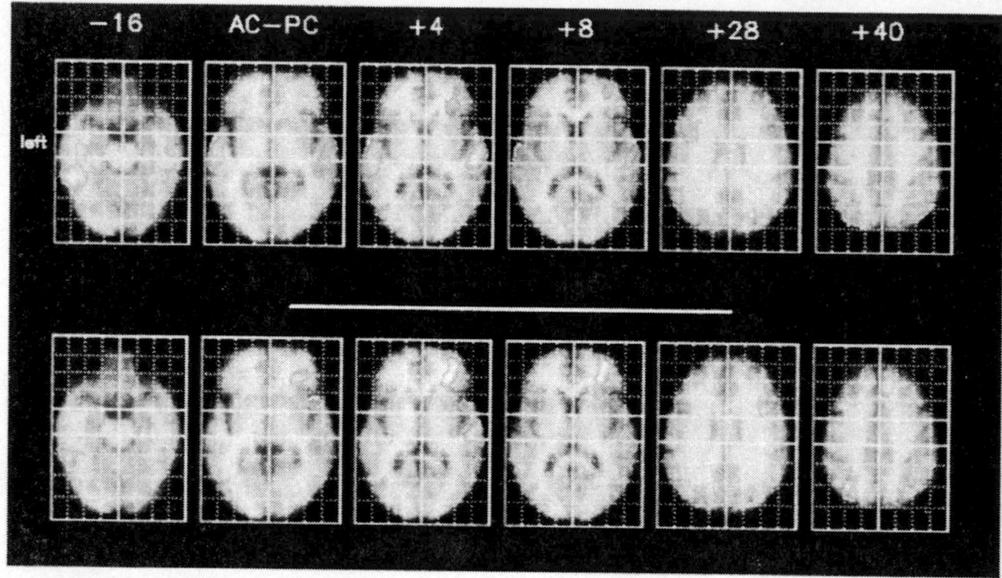

Figure 8.1 Activations during colour–word synaesthesia

Note

1 The *top row* displays the increases in activity which occur when synaesthetes hear words (in comparison with tones). Areas of significant increase are plotted on averaged MRI images in the stereotactic space of Talairach and Tournoux (1988).

2 The *lower row* displays the subset of areas where there was activity in the synaesthetes, but not in the controls. These areas include the inferior temporal cortex, the parietal-occipital junction and the right prefrontal cortex. We presume that the activity in these areas is associated with the colour experience (see also table 8.2).

3 Each image is a horizontal slice through the brain. AC–PC = the plane containing the line joining the anterior and posterior commissures. The numbers (in mm) refer to the height of the slice above or below the AC–PC plane.

The comparison of rCBF between tasks also showed a rich pattern of deactivation. The formal comparison of the rCBF decrease magnitudes between groups showed significantly greater deactivation of the left insula and of the left lingual gyrus in synaesthetes. The area of deactivation observed in the lingual gyrus spread into left primary visual cortex.

8.6 Discussion

The statistical analyses we have applied to our brain imaging data are very strict and err on the side of type II errors. In other words, we may well have missed some important activations, but we are unlikely to have made any false positive errors. Furthermore, activations reach an acceptable level of significance only if they are present in all subjects. Given this bias, our results provide strong evidence that the experience of colour–word synaesthesia is associated with a characteristic pattern of brain activity similar in all people who report this particular phenomenon. This result provides evidence at the level of physiology that people who report colour–word synaesthesia are indeed having a different experience from others when they hear words.

What clues does the location of this activity give us about the nature of this experience? Our central assumption is that colour–word synaesthesia is a visual experience. Therefore we expect associated activity to be located somewhere in the visual system and, in particular, in those parts of the visual system concerned with colour. The associative visual cortex is organized into a number of functionally specialized areas. Many specialized visual areas have been identified in the monkey: area V3 for dynamic form perception; area V5 for motion perception; and area V4 for colour and colour with form perception (for review, see Zeki 1978; Van Essen 1985; Livingstone and Hubel 1988). Functional imaging studies have provided evidence for the localization of putative human homologues of some of these monkey extrastriate visual areas. It has been proposed that human V4 lies in the fusiform gyrus (Lueck et al. 1989; Zeki et al. 1991), whereas human V5 is located ventrally on the lateral surface of the occipito-temporal junction (Zeki et al. 1991; Watson et al. 1993; Zeki, Watson and Frackowiak 1993).

This evidence is complemented by neuropathological data. For example, cerebral colour blindness (central achromatopsia) is usually associated with lingual-fusiform gyri lesions (Verrey 1888; Meadows 1974; Damasio et al. 1980; Rizzo et al. 1993; for review, see also Zeki 1990). Further evidence is provided by the fact that no cases of central colour-blindness have been reported for lesions that do not involve the lingual-fusiform gyri. However, other functional imaging studies have shown activation of additional areas (temporal and dorsal occipital cortex, Corbetta et al. 1991a and b; parietal cortex, Gulyas and Roland 1991) during tasks that involve colour discrimination. A possible reconciliation of pathological and functional imaging data from normal subjects is to assume that within the 'colour stream' there must be a hierarchy of areas. The lingual-fusiform gyri represent the minimum and indispensable neuronal substrate to permit colour perception, while additional areas (dorsal occipital, temporal and parietal cortex) may represent higher stages of visual information processing which make use of colour.

The most striking observation of our study is that, unlike

what happens with frank visual stimulation, there was no activity in classical visual areas. Among these we include area V1 and the surrounding V2 and V4. We have discounted the rCBF increase detected in area V4 because of its small statistical magnitude and because no significant difference was detectable in comparison with the control group.

We believe that this observation at the physiological level is consistent with the experiences described by our subjects. The coloured hearing of our colour–word synaesthetes does not usually interfere with vision, nor with colour perception due to stimulation in the conventional visual channel. Their colour experiences are also different from the colour perceptions (chromatophenes) induced in man by magnetic stimulation of area V4. According to Zeki (1993, from a personal communication from K. and G. Beckers), the spatial localization of chromatophenes within the optic field is reminiscent of the topographic organization of V4 in the monkey. In contrast, the colour percepts of our subjects could not be localized to any part of the visual field. The ambiguous spatial distribution of synaesthesias would point to the engagement of visual areas where neurons have a much looser representation of the visual field than in primary visual cortex or even than in area V4.

There were a number of areas involved in the particular phenomenon that we are investigating. Among these were: (a) the left (and to a lesser extent right) PIT cortex; (b) the parieto/occipital junctions; (c) the left lingual gyrus where rCBF decreases were observed. This pattern and the absence of consistent area V4 involvement raises the possibility that colour percepts triggered by a non-visual stimulus can be evoked by cortical areas other than area V4 in certain circumstances, even though they be aberrant or unusual, and that language stimulation can evoke such percepts. The potential relevance of these visual areas for synaesthesia is discussed below.

8.6.1 The posterior inferior temporal (PIT) cortex

In the macaque, the PIT cortex has a large proportion of colour-selective neurons (46 out of 65 neurons sampled = 71 per cent; Komatsu et al. 1992); this area is massively connected to area V4 (Desimone, Fleming and Gross 1980; Fries and Zeki 1983) and it is currently considered primarily a visual cortical area rather than 'polyfunctional' in nature (Van Essen 1985).

In man, Corbetta et al. (1991a) found activation of PIT cortex in a task where subjects were asked to discriminate visual stimuli on the basis of their colour (e.g. a red square was a target and distractors were squares of other colours). In a further experiment, Corbetta et al.

(1991a) found activation of PIT in a task where subjects attended targets defined by the colour and by the spatial orientation of a geometric object (a red vertical rectangle was a target; distractors varied for orientation, for colour or for both features). Taken together, these results suggest that human PIT cortex may be involved in complex aspects of colour perception and in linking colour to shape.

In the macaque, this structure has a further interesting property. It has a much more eroded topography than that of area V4 (Van Essen 1985; Komatsu et al. 1992), which is itself far less precise than that of area V1 (Van Essen and Zeki 1978). The involvement of a visual area such as area PIT in colour–word synaesthesia is therefore also consistent with the degraded topographic organization of the synaesthesias in most cases of coloured hearing.

It is of crucial importance that no activation has been found in PIT cortex in studies of single-word perception (Petersen et al. 1988; Wise et al. 1991), nor was this area significantly activated in our controls during auditory verbal stimulation. However, semantic judgements based, in part, on visual associations of words do engage this area. In the experiment by Démonet et al. (1992) subjects were invited to monitor pairs of words (an animal name and an adjective); target pairs were a positive adjective followed by the name of a small animal (e.g. kind mouse = target; kind elephant = distractor). Judging whether the animal is large or small involves visual imagery elicited by words, which may induce activation of PIT cortex.

To summarize, in both primates and humans the PIT region may contribute to both complex forms of colour perception or to higher-level cognitive processes involving colour, such as multimodal visual integration concerned with object recognition. The engagement of the PIT in synaesthesia may therefore have a great explanatory value as it is involved in both visual and language feature integration. This is precisely the level of integration necessary for synaesthesia (colour, shape, language).

8.6.2 *The parieto-occipital junctions*

The interpretation of the activations of these structures in synaesthesia is not simple as there is no agreement between the literature on primates, the neuropsychological literature on brain-damaged patients, and functional imaging data from normal subjects. In the macaque, the parietal cortex is consistently connected to visual areas concerned with colour processing (Zeki 1977; Seltzer and Pandya 1980), but single-cell recordings indicate no colour sensitivity in parietal neurons (Mountcastle et al. 1984) nor do lesions here cause colour imperception (Ecott and Gaffan 1991).

No cases of central achromatopsia due to parietal lesion have ever been reported in the human literature, although there are occasional reports of central dyschromatopsia (a milder form of central colour imperception) following parietal lesions (Capitani, Scotti and Spinnler 1978; Pirozzolo et al. 1980). In addition, a lesion of the left parietal cortex (documented by CT scan) has been associated with colour amnesia, a syndrome where affected patients have 'forgotten' previously learned associations between familiar objects and their colour (Varney and Digre 1983). This same patient, however, also showed upper-right quadrantanopia that could not be explained by the parietal lesion, suggesting additional undetected lesions in the left hemisphere.

Early PET experiments on passive colour perception or on attention to colour (Lueck et al. 1988; Corbetta et al. 1991b) did not show activation of the parietal cortex. On the other hand, PET experiments concerned with active colour discrimination or with perception of form-from-colour have shown activation of the parietal cortex (Gulyas and Roland 1991; Gulyas et al. 1994 a, 1994b). Given the disagreement between the different studies, we do not wish to over-interpret the functional relevance of the parieto-occipital cortex in synaesthesia. However, our findings seem to be corroborated by increasing evidence of a colour-sensitive cortical field in the human posterior parietal cortex.

8.6.3 Relevant features of the synaesthetic experience

Does the experience of our synaesthetes throw any further light on the role of these areas in colour perception? Their colour perceptions were related to the letters of the words rather than to phonology or meaning (see table 8.1). This could result from the following perceptual sequence: sound of word → visual form of word (orthography) → colour experience. There is evidence that at least part of this sequence occurs in normals. For a skilled reader, there is an automatic connection between the sound of a word and its visual appearance. For example, orthography can interfere with rhyme judgements even when words are presented aurally, so that it takes longer than expected to decide that *cough* and *bough* do not rhyme (Seidenberg and Tanenhaus 1979). Accordingly, the special feature of our synaesthetes is not that auditory verbal stimulation elicits a visual representation of words, rather that it is the link between orthography (or at least letters) and specific colours. However, the *auditory* component of verbal stimulation is a prerequisite for eliciting synaesthesia since, in our subjects, silent reading does not provoke synaesthesia.

It is interesting that, in most cases, numbers as well as letters have their own colour which is not determined by the letters that constitute the name of the number. This observation would emphasize the link between colours and specific language symbols. These associations are reminiscent of those links between some objects and a particular colour (e.g. banana–yellow, carrot–orange, and so on). If we accept that letters and numbers are special instances of coloured objects for synaesthetes, it is possible that these representations are evoked via auditory stimulation.

A recent PET study provides support for these speculations. Martin et al. (1995) asked people to name the colours of objects represented in black and white drawings (for example, the response to a picture of a banana would be 'yellow'). In comparison to a control task this colour generation task elicited activity in a number of areas, some close to those observed in colour–word synaesthesia. One area is referred to as fusiform gyrus (−46, −46, −12; 44, −48, −12), but the co-ordinates are almost indentical to the area we have referred to as PIT (−50, −42, −12; 40, −46, −16). Martin et al. note that this region is in the 'object' stream', 2–3 cm anterior to the 'colour' area (human V4) identified in previous PET studies. They suggest that PIT has a role in the representation of knowledge about object colour rather than object form. They also comment that most of their volunteers reported colour imagery while generating colour words for objects.

The other area is referred to as inferior parietal gyrus (−34, −62, 40), but is close to what we have called parietal–occipital junction (−26, −78, 40). Martin et al. (1995) do not comment on a possible role for this area. However, this result complements the observation of the parietal-lesioned patient who acquired 'colour amnesia', forgetting previously learned associations between familiar objects and their colours. This patient would therefore not have been able to perform the task studied by Martin et al.

The location of these regions of activity is consistent with the idea that in colour–word synaesthesia a major component of the experience is that graphic elements such as letters and digits are objects with a characteristic colour. We have yet to understand why the colour experience is only elicited when the object is presented auditorily.

8.6.4 *Cerebral deactivations: the left lingual gyrus and the insula*

In synaesthetes the left lingual gyrus, with the left insula, showed highly significant rCBF decreases during word stimulation. The area deactivated in the lingual gyrus may represent the ventral portion of area V2 (Clarke and Miklossy 1990) or part of area V3 (Horton and Hoyt 1991). The location of lingual gyrus' deactivation is very close to the area activated in the study of Corbetta et al. (1991a) when subjects passively viewed a set of coloured stimuli appearing on a display. Both the left lingual gyrus and insula have recently been implicated in brain imaging experiments in which normal volunteers had to convert visually presented letters into sounds (Paulesu, Frith and Frackowiak 1993). This result complements the observation that patients with lesions in the left lingual gyrus are often unable to read while other language abilities remain intact (Damasio and Damasio 1983; De Renzi, Zampolin and Crisi 1987). The functional relevance of our finding is, however, uncertain. Indeed, the interpretation of rCBF decreases is one of the most controversial issues in functional imaging. Jenkins et al. (1993) found large decreases of rCBF in associative visual areas during a motor learning task and interpreted these as a manifestation of a decrease in attentional resources allocated to brain structures irrelevant to their task. A similar interpretation of rCBF decreases was proposed by Kawashima, O'Sullivan and Roland (1993). rCBF decreases in these structures may therefore correspond to the 'switching off' of a part of the reading system in the absence of direct visual stimulation.

Frith et al. (1991) and Friston et al. (1991c) have proposed an alternative explanation for the deactivation that they detected in superior temporal gyri during a verbal fluency task. They suggest that the superior temporal gyri are activated or deactivated depending on whether access to word representations is by external stimulation (e.g. hearing words) or due to intrinsic generation (e.g. generating words). Accordingly and by analogy, the deactivation of the left lingual gyrus could be explained by anomalous (without specific visual input) access to colour and letter representations. The differences between these experiments and our paradigm are such, however, that it is premature to accept these explanations other than as hypotheses.

8.6.5 Synaesthesia and mechanisms of integration

We define integration in broad terms as the sensory combinations that underlie complex perception. Integration may depend on anatomical connectivity and/or on temporal synchronicity. Few aspects of the latter can be readily studied with PET, and therefore they will not be considered further here. Anatomical substrates for integration may include anatomical convergence in the form of feedforward (i.e. from primary to associative areas) and lateral connections, intrinsic connections within primary or associative areas, and feedback connections from associative areas to primary areas (Zeki and Shipp 1988). Forward connectivity implies convergence of inputs from multiple simple neurons on to more complex ones, whereas feedback connectivity is thought to be a basis for modulation of primary areas by associative areas (ibid.). The available anatomical evidence, however, is insufficient to provide unequivocal explanations as to how multimodal integration occurs, as in associative areas (e.g. the parietal cortex or the prefrontal cortex) the projections coming from different specialized areas remain segregated and their spatial overlap is limited (Goldman-Rakic 1984; Zeki and Shipp 1988).

To demonstrate any of these mechanisms using functional imaging with activation (cognitive subtraction) techniques has proved to be no easy task. Let us take as an example modulatory feedback from associative to primary areas, when stimuli are delivered via the usual sensory channel. Since brain activations are monitored as changes of rCBF, it remains ambiguous whether some of the activations observed in primary areas are simply due to more potent stimulation or to modulatory effects from associative areas (for a discussion of this issue, see Friston et al. 1991c; Watson et al. 1993; Zeki 1993: 333–4). In our experiment we circumvent this problem in a somewhat paradoxical way. We have studied a visual percept in the absence of direct visual stimulation. In this case we can legitimately speculate that changes in neural activity within the visual system must be due to some form of connectivity with the system directly stimulated (the auditory language system). Indeed, we observed in the synaesthetes a considerable perturbation of the visual cortex in the absence of any direct stimulation. This altered activity involved highly specialized visual areas (e.g. PIT cortex) which in both the macaque and in man may contribute to aspects of colour perception and integration between shape and colour. The activation of PIT cortex may well represent a form of forward convergence from basic perceptual language areas (e.g. the superior temporal cortex), as PIT is implicated in both colour perception and in lexical-semantic tasks (Corbetta et al. 1991b; Démonet et al. 1992; Martin et al. 1995). In addition, because coloured hearing is a one-way process (synaesthesia occurs from auditory language to colour but not vice versa) and because no direct visual stimulation occurred, we propose that the activity observed in at least some of the visual cortices (e.g. the lingual gyrus) might result from a form of modulatory (inhibitory) feedback.

8.6.6 *Synaesthesia and conscious visual perception*

We have proposed that the pattern brain activity detected in our synaesthetes is the neurophysiological counterpart of synaesthetic perception. This statement has at least one important implication, namely that a *conscious visual perception* can occur in the absence of activation in the primary visual area, V1. Such a possibility has been denied for a long time on the basis of evidence from *blindsight,* a syndrome associated with area V1 lesions (for review, see Cowey and Stoerig 1991; Zeki 1993). However, a recent experiment by Barbur et al. (1993) shows that associative visual areas, possibly stimulated via alternative pathways to the geniculo-striate connection, can promote a crude but *conscious* visual perception of motion even when area V1 is completely damaged. Indeed, Barbur and colleagues (1993) have been able to show that residual conscious motion perception in a 'blind' visual field was paralleled by activation of visual prestriate areas including the motion area V5. A further example of conscious visual perception in the absence of an explicit (additional) contribution of primary visual cortex is provided by the experiment on illusory visual motion perception in normal volunteers (Zeki, Watson and Frackowiak 1993) which, in the visual cortex, was associated with the activation of visual area V5 without additional activity in V1. Conscious visual perception without the engagement of area V1 has a cost of poor topographical definition. In synaesthesia this may turn out be an advantage since synaesthetic percepts are not confused with events in the outside visual world, while, in contrast, visual hallucinations are confused with reality by psychotic patients.

In conclusion, our thinking on colour–word synaesthesia and its neurophysiological implications can be summarized as follows. Colour–word synaesthesias are generated by an interaction between brain areas for language and higher vision. A key role in synaesthetic perception is played by associative areas, located at the boundary between the language and the visual systems. In man, some of these areas have been implicated in both attention for colour and complex language tasks based in part on imagery. Activation of some of these areas (e.g. PIT) may reflect a feedforward convergence mechanism for integration. Activity in the visual areas occurred in the absence of any direct visual stimulation, suggesting unusual anatomical connectivity between language and visual areas in synaesthesia.

We generalize our findings on colour–word synaesthesia and propose that the integration concerned with specific forms of synaesthesia is likely to occur where the two sensory dimensions implicated have a greater anatomical opportunity to be integrated, namely at their boundaries. Finally, the neurophysiology of synaesthesia supports recent evidence that a conscious visual perception can occur in the absence of activation of primary visual cortex, implying that high-level associative visual areas can contribute on their own to conscious visual perception.

References

Barbur, J.L., Watson, J.D.G., Frackowiak, R.S.J. and Zeki, S. 1993: Conscious visual perception without V1. *Brain*, 116, 1293–1302.

Baron-Cohen, S., Harrison, J., Goldstein, L.H. and Wyke, M. 1993: Coloured speech perception: is synaesthesia what happens when modularity breaks down? *Perception*, 22, 419–26.

Bottini, G., Paulesu, E., Sterzi, R., Warburton, E., Wise, R.J.S., Vallar, G., Frackowiak, R.S.J. and Frith, C.D. 1995: Modulation of conscious experience by peripheral sensory stimuli. *Nature*, 376, 778–81.

Capitani, E., Scotti, G. and Spinnler, H. 1978: Colour imperception in patients with focal excisions of the cerebral hemispheres. *Neuropsychologia*, 16: 491–6.

Clarke, S. and Miklossy, J. 1990: Occiptial cortex in man: organization of callosal connections, related myelo- and cytoarchitecture, and putative boundaries of functional visual areas. *Journal of Comparative Neurology*, 298, 188–214.

Corbetta, M., Miezin, F.M., Shulman, G.L. and Petersen, S.E. 1991a: Selective attention modulates extrastriate visual regions in humans during visual features discrimination and recognition. In D.J. Chadwick and J. Whelan (eds), *Exploring Brain Functional Anatomy with Positron Emission Tomography*, Ciba Foundation Symposium, vol. 163, Chichester: John Wiley, 165–80.

Corbetta, M., Miezin, F.M., Dobmeyer, S., Shulman, G.L. and Petersen, S.E. 1991b: Selective and divided attention during visual discrimination of shape, color and speed: functional anatomy by positron emission tomography. *Journal of Neuroscience*, 11, 2383–402.

Cowey, A. and Stoerig, P. 1991: Reflections on blindsight. In D. Milner and M. Rugg (eds), *The Neuropsychology of Consciousness*, London: Academic Press, 11–37.

Cytowic, R. 1989: *Synesthesia: a union of the senses.* Stuttgart: Springer-Verlag.

Cytowic, R.C. and Wood, F.B. 1982: Synesthesia. I: A review of major theories and their brain basis. *Brain and Cognition*, 1, 23–35.

Damasio, A. and Damasio, H. 1983: The anatomic basis of pure alexia. *Neurology*, 33, 1573–83.

Damasio, A., Yamada, T., Damasio, H., Corbett, J. and McKee, J. 1980: Central achromatopsia: behavioural, anatomic, and physiologic aspects. *Neurology*, 30, 1064–71.

Démonet, J.F., Chollet, F., Ramsay, S., Cardebat, D., Nespolous, J.L., Wise, R. et al. 1992: The anatomy of phonological and semantic processing in normal subjects. *Brain*, 115, 1753–68.

De Renzi, E., Zampolin, A. and Crisi, G. 1987: The pattern of neuropsychological impairment associated with left post posterior cerebral artery infarcts. *Brain*, 110, 1099–116.

Desimone, R., Fleming, J. and Gross, C.G. 1980: Prestriate afferents to inferior temporal cortex. *Brain Research*, 184, 41–55.

Ecott, M.J. and Gaffan, D. 1991: The role of monkey inferior parietal cortex in visual discrimination of identity and orientation of shapes. *Behavioural and Brain Research*, 46, 95–8.

Fox, P.T. and Mintun, M.A. 1989: Non-invasive functional brain mapping by change distribution analysis of averaged PET images of H215O tissue activity. *Journal of Nuclear Medicine*, 30, 141–9.

Frackowiak, R.S.J. and Friston, K.F. 1994: Functional neuroanatomy of the human brain: positron emission tomography – a new neuroanatomical technique. *Journal of Anatomy*, 184, 211–25.

Fries, W. and Zeki, S. 1983: The laminar origin of the cortical inputs to the fourth visual complex of macaque monkey. *Journal of Physiology*, 340, 51P.

Friston, K.J., Frith, C.D., Liddle, P.F., Dolan, R.J., Lammertsma, A.A. and Frackowiak, R.S.J. 1990: The relationship between global and local changes in PET scans. *Journal of Cerebral Blood Flow and Metabolism*, 10, 458–66.

Friston, K.J., Frith, C.D., Liddle, P.F. and Frackowiak, R.S.J. 1991a: Plastic transformation of PET images. *Journal of Computer Assisted Tomography*, 15, 634–7.

Friston, K.J., Frith, C.D., Liddle, P.F. and Frackowiak, R.S.J. 1991b: Comparing functional PET images: the assessment of significant change. *Journal of Cerebral Blood Flow and Metabolism*, 11, 458–66.

Friston, K.J., Frith, C.D., Liddle, P.F. and Frackowiak, R.S.J. 1991c: Investigating a network model of word generation with positron emission tomography. *Proceedings of the Royal Society of London, Series B*, 244, 101–6.

Friston, K.J., Frith, C.D., Liddle, P.F. and Frackowiak, R.S.J. 1993: Functional connectivity: the principal-component analysis of large PET data sets. *Journal of Cerebral Blood Flow and Metabolism*, 13, 5–14.

Friston, K.J., Holmes, A.P., Worsley, K.J., Poline, J.B., Frith, C.D. and Frackowiak, R.S.J. 1995: Statistical parametric maps in functional imaging: a general linear approach. *Human Brain Mapping*, 3, 189–210.

Frith, C.D., Friston, K.J., Liddle, P.F. and Frackowiak, R.S.J. 1991: A PET study of word finding. *Neuropsychologia*, 29, 1137–48.

Goldman-Rakic, P. 1984: Modular organization of the prefrontal cortex [review]. *Trends in Neuroscience*, 7, 419–29.

Gulyas, B. and Roland, P.E. 1991: Cortical fields participating in form and colour discrimination in the human brain. *Neuroreport*, 2, 585–8.

Gulyas, B. and Roland, P.E. 1994a: Processing and analysis of form, colour and binocular disparity in the human brain: functional anatomy by positron emission tomography. *European Journal of Neuroscience*, 6, 1811–28.

Gulyas, B., Heywood, C.A., Popplewell, D.A., Roland, P.E. and Cowey, A. 1994b: Visual form discrimination from color or motion cues: functional anatomy by positron emission tomography. *Proceedings of the National Academy of Sciences of the USA*, 91, 9965–9.

Horton, J.C. and Hoyt, W.F. 1991: Quadrantic visual field defect: a hallmark of lesions in extrastriate V2/V3 cortex. *Brain*, 144, 1703–18.

Jenkins, I.H., Brooks, D.J., Nixon, P.D., Frackowiak, R.S.J. and Passingham, R.E. 1993: The functional anatomy of motor sequence learning studied with positron emission tomography. *Journal of Neurosciences*, 14, 3775–90.

Kawashima, R., O'Sullivan, B.T. and Roland, P.E. 1993: A PET study of selective attention in man: cross-modality decreases in activity in somatosensory and visual tasks. *Journal of Cerebral Blood How and Metabolism*, 13, suppl. 1, S502.

Komatsu, H., Ideura, Y., Kaji, S. and Yamane, S. 1992: Color selectivity of the neurons in the inferior temporal cortex of the macaque awake monkey. *Journal of Neuroscience*, 12, 408–24.

Livingstone, M. and Hubel, D. 1988: Segregation of form, color, movement and depth: anatomy, physiology and perception [review]. *Science*, 240, 740–9.

Lueck, C.J., Zeki, S., Friston, K.J., Deiber, M.-P., Cope, P., Cunningham, V.J. et al. 1989: The colour centre in the cerebral cortex of man. *Nature*, 340, 386–9.

Martin, A., Haxby, J.V., Lalonde, F.M., Wiggs, C.L. and Ungerleide, L.G. 1995: Discrete cortical regions associated with knowledge of color and knowledge of action. *Science*, 270, 102–5.

Mazziotta, J.C., Huang, S.C., Phelps, M.E., Carson, R.E., MacDonald, N.S. and Mahoney, K. 1985: A non-invasive positron computed tomography technique using oxygen-15 labelled water for the evaluation of neurobehavioural task batteries. *Journal of Cerebral Blood Flow and Metabolism*, 5, 70–8.

Meadows, J.C. 1974: Disturbed perception of colours associated with localized cerebral lesions. *Brain*, 7, 615–32.

Mountcastle, W.B., Motter, B.C., Steinmetz, M.A. and Duffy, C.J. 1984: Looking and seing: the visual functions of the parietal lobe. In G.M. Edelman, W.E. Gall and W.M. Cowan (eds), *Dynamic aspects of neocortical function*, New York: John Wiley, 159–93.

Paulesu, E., Frith, C.D. and Frackowiak, R.S.J. 1993: The neural correlates of the verbal component of working memory. *Nature*, 362, 342–4.

Paulesu, E., Harrison, J., Baron-Cohen, S., Watson, J.D.G., Goldstein, L., Heather, J., Frackowiak, R.S.J. and Frith, C.D. 1995: The physiology of coloured hearing: a PET activation study of colour–word synaesthesia. *Brain*, 118, 661–76.

Petersen, S.E., Fox, P.T., Posner, M.I., Mintun, M. and Raichle, M.E. 1988: Positron emission tomographic studies of the cortical anatomy of single word processing. *Nature*, 331, 585–9.

Pirozzolo, F.J., Kerr, K.L., Obrzut, J.E., Morley, G.K., Haxby, J.V. and Lundgren, S. 1980: Neurolinguistic analysis of the language abilities of a patient with a 'double disconnection syndrome': a case of subangular alexia in the presence of mixed transcortical aphasia. *Journal of Neurology, Neurosurgery and Psychiatry*, 44, 152–5.

Price, C., Wise, R.J.S., Ramsay, S., Friston, K.J., Howard, D., Patterson, K. et al. 1992: Regional response differences within the human auditory cortex when listening to words. *Neuroscience Letters*, 146, 179–82.

Quinlan, P.T. 1992: *The Oxford Psycholinguistic Database*. Oxford: Oxford University Press.

Raichle, M. 1987: Circulatory and metabolic correlates of brain function in normal humans. In: V.B. Mouncastle, F. Plum and S.R. Geiger (eds), *Handbook of Physiology*, section 1, vol. 5, ch. 16. Bethesda, MD: American Physiological Society, 643–74.

Rizzo, M., Smith, V., Pokorny, J. and Damasio, A.R. 1993: Color perception profiles in central achromatopsia. *Neurology*, 43, 995–1001.

Robb, R.A. 1990: A software system for interactive and quantitative analysis of biomedical images. In K.H. Hohne, H. Fuchs and S.M. Pizer (eds), *3D Imaging in Medicine*, vol. F60. NATO ASI Series.

Sacks, O. and Wasserman, R.L. 1987: *The Painter Who Became Color Blind. New York Review of Books*, 34, 25–33.

Sacks, O., Wasserman, R.L., Zeki, S. and Siegel, R.M. 1988: Sudden color blindness of cerebral origin. *Society for Neuroscience Abstracts*, 14, 1251.

Seidenberg, M.S. and Tanenhaus, M.K. 1979: Orthographic effects on rhyme monitoring. *Journal of Experimental Psychology: Human Learning and Memory*, 6, 546–54.

Seltzer, B. and Pandya, D.N. 1980: Converging visual and somatic sensory cortical input to the intraparietal sulcus of the rhesus monkey. *Brain Research*, 192, 339–51.

Shipp, S. and Zeki, S. 1989a: The organization of connections between areas V5 and V1 in the macaque monkey visual cortex. *European Journal of Neuroscience*, 1, 309–32.

Shipp, S. and Zeki, S. 1989b: The organization of connections between areas V5 and V2 in the macaque monkey visual cortex. *European Journal of Neuroscience*, 1, 333–54.

Sibersweig, D.A., Stern, E., Frith, C., Cahill, C., Holmes, A., Grootoonk, S. et al. 1995: A functional neuroanatomy of hallucinations in schizophrenia. *Nature*, 378, 176–9.

Spinks, T.J., Jones, T., Bailey, D.L., Townsend, D.W., Grootoonk, S., Bloomfield, P.M. et al. 1992: Physical performance of a positron tomograph for brain imaging with retractable septa. *Physics in Medicine and Biology*, 8, 1637–55.

Talairach, J. and Tournoux, P. 1988: *A Co-planar Stereotactic Atlas of the Human Brain*. Stuttgart: Thieme.

Townsend, D.W., Geissbuhler, A., Defrise M., Hoffman, E.J., Spinks, T.J., Bailey, D.L. et al. 1991: Fully three-dimensional reconstruction for a PET camera with retractable septa. *IEEE Transaction: Medical Imaging*, 10, 505–12.

Van Essen, D.C. 1985: Functional organization of primate visual cortex. In A. Peters and E.G. Jones, *Cerebral Cortex*, vol. 4, New York: Plenum, 259–329.

Van Essen, D.C. and Zeki, S.M. 1978: The topographic organization of rhesus monkey prestriate cortex. *Journal of Physiology*, 277, 193–226.

Varney, N.R. and Digre, K. 1983: Color 'amnesia' without aphasia. *Cortex*, 19, 545–50.

Ventre, J., Flandrin, M. and Jeannerod, M. 1984: In search of the egocentric reference: a neurophysiological hypothesis. *Neuropsychologia*, 6, 797–806.

Verrey, L. 1888: Hémiachromatopsie droite absolue. *Archives d'ophtalmologie*, 8, 289–301.

Watson, J.D.G., Myers, R., Frackowiak, R.S.J., Hajnal, J.V., Woods, R.P., Mazziotta, J.C., Shipp, S. and Zeki, S. 1993: Area V5 of the human brain: evidence from a combined study using positron emission tomography and magnetic resonance imaging. *Cerebral Cortex*, 3, 79–94.

Weiskrantz, L. 1986: *Blindsight: A Case Study and Implications*. Oxford: Oxford University Press.

Wise, R., Chollet, F., Hadar, U., Friston, K., Hoffner, E. and Frackowiak, R.S.J. 1991: Distribution of cortical neural networks involved in word comprehension and word retrieval. *Brain*, 114, 1803–17.

Woods, R.P., Cherry, S.R. and Mazziotta, J.C. 1992: A rapid automated algorithm for accurately aligning and reslicing positron emission tomography images. *Journal of Computer Assisted Tomography*, 16, 620–33.

Zeki, S. 1977: Colour coding in the superior temporal sulcus of the rhesus monkey visual cortex. *Proceedings of the Royal Society of London B*, 197, 195–223.

Zeki, S. 1978: Functional specialization in the visual cortex of the rhesus monkey [review]. *Nature*, 274, 423–8.

Zeki, S. 1990: A century of cerebral achromatopsia [review]. *Brain*, 113, 1721–77.

Zeki, S. 1993: *A Vision of the Brain*. Oxford: Blackwell Scientific.

Zeki, S. and Shipp, S. 1988: The functional logic of cortical connections [review]. *Nature*, 335, 311–17.

Zeki, S., Watson, J.D.G. and Frackowiak, R.S.J. 1993: Going beyond the information given: the relation of illusory visual motion to brain activity. *Proceedings of the Royal Society of London B*, 252, 215–22.

Zeki, S., Watson, J.D.G., Lueck, C.J., Friston, K.J., Kennard, C. and Frackowiak, R.S.J. 1991: A direct demonstration of functional specialization in human visual cortex. *Journal of Neuroscience*, 11, 641–9.

9

Perception and Sensory Information in Synaesthetic Experience

Peter G. Grossenbacher

9.1 Introduction

We humans do not face the world with an empty mind. Our sensory experience is guided by a rich amalgam of biases, expectations, categories and concepts which constitutes each individual's perspective. Perceived reality is the continuous product of ongoing interplay between expectation and incoming sensory signals. A dynamically updated model of the world provides an ever-present context for each instance of perception. This mental modelling may be very idiosyncratic, depending on the experience and ensuing development unique to each individual. None the less, there are some important commonalities among the perceptual representations constructed by different individuals.

Consider a simple act of perception such as looking at the bottom of this page. As sophisticated perceivers, we have more than one method for avoiding serious misperception. A downward visual glance supplies information about the location and shape of the boundary between paper and air. This information can be validated through another sense modality simply by running a fingertip along the paper's edge. This crossmodal check can verify several aspects of the perceived page, including location, size, shape and object identity (e.g. as a page in this book). In addition to validation of sensory experience through multimodal agreement, perceptual verification can also be sought by communicating with another person: 'Look there; is that the moon or just another distant cloud?' We often resort to language or similar communication between individuals to confirm the perceptual qualities of objects, especially in situations which preclude cross-modal checking and only one sense modality supplies relevant information.

Perception is typically described and understood in terms of sense modalities. The classic concept of sense modality is a tripartite relation between some physical object (this page is a suitable visible *stimulus*), a receptor organ (at least one eye) and conscious phenomenology (what it is like to see). For perception to occur, the stimulus must be adequate (sufficiently near, big, opaque, illuminated, etc.) and the receptor organ must be oriented appropriately (eyes pointed at and focusing on the stimulus). Such conditions are necessary to yield the customary visual *percept* (that is, the content of conscious perceptual experience). Built into this tripartite model is a causal relationship in which the experience is *caused* by sensory stimulation in which physical energy from the stimulus impinges on the receptor organ. This relation between stimulus, receptor organ and conscious experience appears very reliable, and applies equally well to hearing, smelling, tasting and touching.

Is there more to perception than stimulus, receptor organ and percept? Consider a hypothetical driver whose open eyes are focused on the road ahead but who fails to see a looming pedestrian. For the sake of argument, this driver was thinking hard about possible repercussions from recent events and paying little attention to visual inputs. In agreement with modern cognitive research, this example indicates that, in addition to orientation of receptors, the *mind* must also be oriented and focused appropriately for conscious perception to occur (Poser and Rothbart 1991). Because perception can fail from lack of appropriately directed attention, the tripartite account of perception given above is incomplete, and must be amended to include a role for covert mental orienting (attention).

Attending to a perceived object entails extended processing of sensory information, resulting in elaborated awareness of that object. Attention is readily indexed by measures of behaviour in laboratory experiments (Greenwood, Parasuraman and Haxby 1993), and has been subjected to increasing scientific scrutiny in the last decade. As with other biological systems, attention does become fatigued with prolonged use (Godefroy, Cabaret and Rousseaux 1994). Attention has recently been linked to the activity of specific, localized brain areas which operate as an anatomically distributed system for control of information flow in the human brain (Posner, Grossenbacher and Compton 1994). Attention can be directed voluntarily, but can also be summoned by an irresistible stimulus (Posner 1980). With respect to different sense modalities, humans may be biased so as to attend to vision more than other senses (Colavita 1974; Posner, Nissen and Klein 1976).

9.2 Sensory Information in Synaesthetic Experience

Now that we have discussed so-called 'normal' perception, let us turn our attention to synaesthetic perception. By 'constitutional synaesthesia' I mean the condition experienced by those individuals who report a life-long history of perceptual experience in two sense modalities under conditions where sensory stimulation and overt orienting of receptor organs are adequate for perception in only one modality. Other, transient forms of synaesthetic experience which may arise from tumour (Vike, Jabbari and Maitland 1984) or drug ingestion (Hollister 1968; Simpson and McKellar 1955) are largely ignored in this chapter, so for convenience I shall use the term 'synaesthesia' to refer exclusively to constitutional synaesthesia. In a relatively common kind of synaesthesia, the synaesthete experiences vivid sensations of colour upon hearing sounds. This typical kind of synaesthesia (coloured hearing) will be used as an ongoing example throughout this chapter.

At the outset we should take note of three important features. First, the *sine qua non* aspect of synaesthesia consists in the unusual relation between sensory stimulation and conscious percepts. Thus, we can assess synaesthesia either by direct, subjective experience (accessible only to those who experience synaesthesia), or indirectly, by heeding the reports of those people who have synaesthetic experience. Secondly, it is appropriate to distinguish conceptually between synaesthetes and non-synaesthetes, because there exists something of a stable bifurcation in the human population between the small minority of individuals who typically do experience synaesthesia and the large majority of those who do not. And thirdly, for any synaesthete, the relations between auditory inputs and visual experience are qualitatively reliable; that is, when heard on different occasions, the same sound elicits much the same visual experience.

Synaesthesia links unimodal stimulation to bimodal experience in a very specific manner. In our coloured-hearing example, auditory stimulation *induces* a visual percept of colour which accompanies an otherwise normal hearing experience. With regard to this example of synaesthetic experience, let 'inducer' refer to the eliciting auditory stimulus, and let 'concurrent' signify the induced colour phenomenon. A diagnostic description of synaesthetic experience should delineate the exact set of inducers (inducer stimuli) and the associated concurrents (concurrent phenomena), and the rest of this section works toward this aim.

Unfortunately, many important aspects of synaesthetic perception are known only tentatively because synaesthesia has yet to be subjected to a great deal of psychophysical research. Gaps in scientific description provide a fundamental motivation for increased investigation into this intriguing variation of human experience. By focusing on the subjective content of reported synaesthetic experience and the relation between sensory stimulation and phenomenal experience, this section raises more questions than it answers. Ramifications concerning the neurocognitive basis for synaesthesia are mostly reserved for discussion later in this chapter.

Synaesthetes reportedly experience great confidence or certainty regarding their concurrent experience, exhibiting surprise when first encountering others who fail to share the synaesthetic portion of their perceptual experience. Of course, non-synaesthetes also place great credence on the information supplied by their senses, especially when sensory information coheres across more than modality. If you see and hear a dog, for example, you might be more confident about there being a dog nearby than if you had sensed it only in one modality. It seems difficult to judge whether the certainty reported by synaesthetes exceeds the normal degree of certainty associated with multimodal agreement.

Despite widespread reports of enjoyably positive feelings (and infrequent reports of discomfort) associated with synaesthetic experience, I have limited the scope of this chapter by ignoring these hedonic aspects of synaesthetic perception. It seems difficult to interpret the typical association between positive affect and synaesthetic perception, because sensual pleasure may merely be a natural consequence of multimodal agreement. After all, even in non-synaesthetes, rich sensory experience often elicits warm appreciation. Of course, a *complete* description of synaesthetic experience should cover all phenomenological aspects, including emotional tone. This chapter's somewhat exclusive emphasis on the *information content* of synaesthetic phenomenology is intended to flesh out the perceptual relations between sensory channels, but may miss other important dimensions of experience such as emotion.

9.2.1 *Inducers: eliciting stimuli*

Three inequalities are evident among the sensory stimuli reported to induce synaesthetic experience. First, most reported synaesthesia involves inducers which are external stimuli located outside the body.

Few if any reports of synaesthetic experience involve inducers internal to the body such as muscle stiffness, limb position, gut feelings, heart beating, etc. In contrast, sights, sounds, smells, tastes and touches have all been reported as synaesthetic inducers. This disparity in prevalence of exteroceptive and interoceptive inducers could be due in part to methodological artefact. Our vocabulary or language practices may favour description of external stimuli, which are subject to immediately shared experience, over stimuli internal to the body. It is possible that our classification of internal phenomenology may be so impoverished that some cases of interoceptively induced synaesthesia may have gone unnoticed. Give that stimuli internal to the body are rarely discernible to outside observers, investigators may feel hesitant to report cases in which they can observe neither inducer nor concurrent. But such cases are theoretically important and should not be overlooked. Indeed, it may be the case that internal stimuli only very seldom, if ever, induce synaesthetic experience. Why might this be so? There could be great survival value in avoiding confusion between sensory information about internal and external environments. Perhaps the central nervous system keeps interoceptive and exteroceptive signals anatomically segregated to a greater degree than it keeps exteroceptive sense modalities segregated from each other. For this reason, interoceptive stimuli might be more likely to induce synaesthetic concurrents in other interoceptive modalities than in any exteroceptive modality.

Among exteroceptive inducers, stimulation in some sense modalities induces synaesthetic experience more than others, another lopsided pattern which constitutes a second inequality among inducers. For example, across all reported cases of synaesthesia, sounds appear to induce synaesthetic experience more than stimuli in any other modality. A prepotency for auditory inducing could derive from the strong alerting effects customarily produced by auditory stimuli (Nickerson 1970). There are other special attributes of the auditory system which could account for the dominance of auditory stimuli among synaesthetic inducers, such as the very high rates of neural firing and cellular metabolism found in auditory brain structures such as the inferior colliculus (Kennedy et al. 1982).

The third inequality among synaesthetic inducers differs from the first two in that it does not relate to modality of sensory input, but instead relates to thinking: a majority of inducers are words or music, stimuli generated by fellow humans and designed to convey meaning. This point has been raised before (Glicksohn, Salinger and Roychman 1992; Paulesu et al. 1995), but can be elaborated here. Human brains contain an area located in the left occipital lobe of the neocortex which is metabolically active during perception of visually presented words, but activity in this area is so content-specific that it does not appear active during visual perception of non-word consonant strings (Posner et al. 1989). This localization of visual word representation in the occipital cortex, a region of the brain which contains many visual areas, suggests a possible neural mediator for linking linguistic stimuli with sensory visual attributes such as colour. This tentative account merely points to a likely anatomy by virtue of proximity, without specifying precise neural mechanisms. However, anatomical proximity between cortical areas known to process the sensory information pertaining to synaesthetic inducers and concurrents makes neural connectivity between these areas all the more likely.

The prevalence of linguistic tokens among synaesthetic inducers qualifies the previous point concerning unequal distribution of inducers across sense modalities. Many cases of hearing-induced synaesthesia selectively involve only spoken words or music, with a lack of synaesthetic experience when other sounds are heard. Perhaps the propensity for auditory inducing holds only for linguistic stimuli, suggesting that sensory modalities which involve language processing are especially well-suited for inducing synaesthetic concurrents. It is not clear whether auditory stimuli would still constitute a majority of synaesthetic inducers if linguistic stimuli were excluded from consideration. At any rate, this tendency for meaningful stimuli to induce synaesthetic experience reveals one high-level (cognitive) aspect of synaesthesia.

Another aspect of synaesthetic inducers seems consistent with the involvement of cognitive processes in synaesthesia: a synaesthetic concurrent can be induced without actual sensory exposure to the inducer stimulus. For example, 'thinking of the person so named' evoked visual phenomena in FKD, a coloured-hearing synaesthete (Cytowic 1989: 41). Whether or not imagery can induce the experience of a synaesthetic concurrent is a theoretically important point with respect to understanding the precise nature of how synaesthetic experience arises. Imagery involves activity in many of the same parts of the brain which are active during perception (Farah 1988), and may depend on the same neural mechanisms which support perceptual attention (Farah 1989). Imagery probably involves activation of sensory representations by feedbackward connections running opposite to afferent sensory streams. Only some synaesthetes report synaesthetic experience consequent to inducer imagery; others deny any experience of an imagery-induced synaesthetic concurrent. Does the ability for a synaesthete to voluntarily induce concurrent phenomena by imagining an inducer depend on the nature of inducer stimuli? Perhaps only relatively high-level inducers such as people, words or other familiar objects can induce synaesthetic concurrents via imagery.

9.2.2 *Concurrents: induced phenomena*

As was pointed out for inducers, synaesthetic concurrents do not distribute equally over the sense modalities. Visual phenomena comprise the most endorsed modality for synaesthetic concurrents, with documented cases of visual synaesthetic phenomena induced by hearing (Rizzo and Eslinger 1989), touch (Wheeler and Cutsforth 1922), smell (Cytowic and Wood 1982b), and taste (Simpson and McKellar 1955). Ordered in descending prevalence, the synaesthetic concurrent is typically seen, felt or heard. As with synaesthetic inducers, the vast majority of synaesthetic concurrents are phenomenal impressions which relate to apparent stimuli located outside the body.

Does synaesthesia never entail interoceptive concurrents? In contrast to sensations regarding external objects, internal sensations are not typically amenable to verification either through multimodal agreement or inter-individual discussion. For this reason it may be difficult for an individual to distinguish between synaesthetic concurrent or veridical perception. Inability to discern the existence of interoceptive concurrents would naturally result in the under-reporting of synaesthetically induced interoceptive sensations such as heartbeat or gastric motility. Moreover, induced internal sensations might be experienced as a familiar part of one's own reaction to the perception of an external stimulus, and therefore not appear anomalous from similar, non-synaesthetic experience.

Concurrent phenomena induced in synaesthesia do not range over all levels of perceptual processing within a sensory pathway. Typically, it is a *colour* which is induced, rather than a higher level percept such as the complete image of a face (several colours arrayed over a complex shape). On the other hand, the concurrent colour experienced by many synaesthetes often has some shape to it, and can appear more substantial than shapeless flecks of colour. This intermediate psychological level at which concurrents arise has been linked to particular neuroanatomical structures in non-synaesthetes. If synaesthetic experience were marked by concurrent phenomenology of faces or whole objects, this would implicate areas in the temporal lobe of cortex thought to represent entire objects (Perret et al. 1990; Ungerleider and Haxby 1994). But concurrent phenomena of colour suggest instead an earlier stage of visual processing closer to the primary visual area in the occipital lobe of cortex (Allison et al. 1993). Though not conclusive, this discussion exemplifies how the psychological nature of induced phenomena in synaesthesia can guide our thinking about its neurological basis, a topic to be pursued more fully later in this chapter.

As with other kinds of synaesthetic concurrents, colour is a stimulus feature which can have any of several values. The spectrum of colours is psychologically ordered into at least one sensory *dimension*. Psychological ordering along a dimension is evident in ratings of similarity between discrete colours. For example, a blue might be rated as more similar to green than to red. (In fact, colours are multidimensional with values of hue, saturation and brightness specifying points in colour space, but this complexity can be ignored for the purpose of this discussion.) For a synaesthete who experiences distinct colours upon hearing different sounds, the experienced colours arise within a dimension (or dimensional space) along which different colours are arranged in a particular way for that individual. The point here is that concurrent phenomena experienced in any given form of synaesthesia arise within a psychological dimension (or dimensional space) within the bounds of a single psychological category. Typically, sounds do not induce colours on some occasions and induce smells on other occasions in the same synaesthete.

It would be premature to compare the incidence of synaesthetic concurrents in many sensory dimensions which have only been reported infrequently, but *colour* clearly dominates over other visual dimensions such as size, texture, shape, numerosity or location in concurrent synaesthetic experience (Baron-Cohen, Wyke and Binnie 1987; Cytowic and Wood 1982a; Karwoski, Odbert and Osgood 1942; Marks 1975; Riggs and Karwoski 1934). Why is colour the most common concurrent in synaesthesia? Colour is the only dimension of vision which is not shared by any other sense modality, so it may be the one sort of visual information processed by the brain which is not normally tethered to other senses. Other visual dimensions (such as texture) are linked to sensory dimensions in other sense modalities (tactile roughness) for processing specific kinds of multimodal information such as the surface roughness of objects (Grossenbacher 1993). The very lack of universal correspondence between colour and other modalities may make colour phenomena readily available for concurrent synaesthetic experience (by virtue of underdetermined intermodal neural connectivity).

A recently developed line of reasoning concludes that, other things being equal, more recently evolved cortical systems contribute more to conscious awareness than do older cortical systems (Grossenbacher 1995). Along this line, the evolutionary recency of cortical brain circuitry subserving colour processing explains why human consciousness is so often dominated by colour. Perhaps the same mechanism which confers greater salience on recently evolved cortical representations also leads to susceptibility for phenomenal appearance as a synaesthetic concurrent. Synaesthetic-like interaction between modalities may occur in both synaesthetes and non-synaesthetes, but might only crop up within the *conscious* experience of synaesthetes. When viewed in this way, it makes sense for synaesthetic concurrents to coincide with the most salient dimensions of sensory experience, such as colour.

Colour serves as an excellent mnemonic retrieval cue, and thus offers a natural cognitive resource which could get tapped by a clever system even when stimulus conditions preclude colour sensation. For example, under poor lighting conditions, perceived shape (known either through vision or touch) might automatically evoke colour imagery in order to facilitate memory retrieval for object recognition. In this manner, imagined colour cues could aid in the identification of many object classes, including edible foods such as fruit. This utility might enhance fitness for survival and thereby promote some forms of imagery through natural selection. It is not known whether the rate of occurrence of synaesthesia in the population is increasing or decreasing. It is possible that the neural underpinnings of synaesthesia may facilitate the identification of a large number of distinct objects, a benefit which could fuel increasing evolutionary selection for synaesthetic processing of sensory information. Novel colour-tone associations can be formed after single exposure to tones by a coloured-hearing synaesthete but not by a non-synaesthete (Rizzo and Eslinger 1989), potential evidence for the adaptive increase in memory ability presumed by this evolutionary account.

Perception requires the transduction of energy in the physical world by receptor cells which contribute to a complex system of neural signalling which mediates mental representation of the surrounding world. Perception thus supplies a model of reality which receives ongoing validation as each individual interacts with the world. How does the distinction between genuine perception and illusion get made in the case of synaesthesia? Are synaesthetic concurrents perceived *as real*? This is very important. Do concurrents contribute to the representation of reality, leading to a qualitatively distinct representation of the physical world compared to non-synaesthetes? Or are concurrents recognized as extrasensory non-perception and regarded as illusory? Does this vary across synaesthetes? Given differential access to verification by multimodal agreement, the very concepts of perception and reality may differ between synaesthetes and non-synaesthetes.

Many conscious percepts, at least exteroceptive ones, are mutually available for communication and comparison between people. Even many interoceptive sensations such as cold hands or warm belly are often amenable to consensus based on shared exposure to qualitatively similar stimulus conditions. But synaesthetically induced concurrents will not typically yield such agreement. This disagreement between others' perception and synthetically induced concurrent phenomena could mark part of the synaesthete's apparent sensory experience as false. Or such conflicts could instead convince the synaesthete that people simply differ in the way the world is perceived.

9.2.3 *Relations between inducer and concurrent*

In synaesthesia, an inducer provokes the usual percept as well as the synaesthetically induced concurrent phenomenon. That is, the concurrent appears in addition to, not instead of, the inducer. Are there ever occasions where only the concurrent is experienced, with complete lack of conscious awareness of the inducer? This is a difficult question to answer; if there were such cases, these experiences could get categorized as simple hallucinations if there were absolutely on awareness of the inducer. Perhaps reports of hallucination should be investigated with this question of modality-substitution in mind.

The fact that no temporal dimension (e.g. duration or rhythm) operates as either inducer or concurrent in synaesthesia tells us something about synaesthesia. The intersensory mapping is constrained by temporal regularities in sensory experience. Because inducers and concurrents both involve temporally bound percepts, we can ask whether they are experienced simultaneously. Generally speaking, inducers and concurrents do seem to be experienced more or less simultaneously (Devereux 1966; Paulesu et al. 1995). A psychophysically complete case description should specify temporal relations between inducer and concurrent with respect to apparent onset, offset and duration of each.

It is surprisingly easy to compare intensities across modalities (Luce 1990). Which seems more intense to the synaesthete, the inducer or the concurrent? Or are they equally matched? For example, as the intensity of the inducer changes, does the apparent intensity of the concurrent change accordingly? A carefully studied patient with a sub-cortical brain tumour which entailed experience of visual–auditory synaesthesia demonstrated this kind of induced intensity function (Vike, Jabbari and Maitland 1984). The synaesthetic experiences (which did not involve colour concurrents) stopped once this patient's tumour was removed. Some cases of constitutional synaesthesia may also involve concurrents whose intensity is proportional to that of the inducer (Cytowic 1989: 51; Marks 1975; Rizzo and Eslinger 1989).

Unlike the non-synaesthetic case, synaesthesia admits of only partial validation through multimodal agreement. In synaesthesia there may be strong agreement between sense modalities in timing, but the spatial aspects of inducer and concurrent can be very different (Baron-Cohen et al. 1993; Riggs and Karwoski 1934). Do the inducer and concurrent seem like two separate things or one unified composite to the synaesthete? Consider what it must be like for a coloured-hearing synaesthete for whom the apparent location of the concurrent colour is always in the left of the visual field. So as the head turns, the concurrent moves accordingly. This apparent movement must set concurrent colours apart from non-induced colour percepts which stay put in space whether the head moves or not. In this example, the induced photism stays with the person, a private sensation embedded in the bodily framework which constitutes the basis of physical self-perception. Presumably the apparent location of the inducer remains constant in environmental co-ordinates rather than moving with the head. This disparity between spatial frameworks of inducer and concurrent provides a ever-present clue that synaesthetically induced colour qualitatively differs from non-induced colour evoked by a visual object. Each synaesthete could develop one or more strategies for discerning whether a phenomenal impression is perceptually primary or has been synaesthetically induced.

There are many types of synaesthesia which can be distinguished according to the distribution of inducers and concurrents across sense modalities and sub-modalities. However, only certain pairings between inducers and concurrents tend to occur, leaving some conceivable types of synaesthesia without documented cases. It makes sense to distinguish between types of synaesthesia in this way because, for a given synaesthete, a concurrent dimension is not induced by more than one inducer dimension. The converse case has been observed: EW reported concurrent experience of both colours and shapes induced by perception of sounds (Cytowic 1989: 46). This case might be explained by the shared neural basis for processing colour and shape (Corbetta et al. 1990; Desimone and Schein 1987), but there are also cases in which multiple concurrents *in more than one sense modality* are induced by a unimodal stimulus (Cytowic 1993). According to the typology of synaesthesias determined by the sense modalities of inducers and concurrents (Simpson and McKellar 1955), these cases of multimodal concurrents entail multiple types of synaesthesia within a single individual.

For *any* synaesthete, the mapping from inducers to concurrents does not exhibit the complete regularity of a linear alignment between inducer and concurrent dimensions. Thus, three tones which are ordered from low to high pitch need not induce concurrent colours which follow the ordering of inducers. This apparent disorder, or non-linearity, could derive from biological imperfection in a pattern which otherwise exhibits some aspects of cross-modal regularity in ordering. But there is another possibility which casts the non-linear mapping in a more ideal light.

Cognitive experiments on different kinds of structure in redundant information have revealed that memory is best served when two sensory dimensions are combined in a highly non-linear pattern (Lockhead 1970). This result makes intuitive sense if we compare the ease with which subjects can identify stimuli which vary in both colour and tactile roughness when the stimuli are assembled using either (a) a pairwise linear rule so that similar colours are paired with similar levels of roughness, or (b) a sawtooth rule wherein a few successive colour values are paired with roughness values several levels apart, and this pattern is repeated but with the next colour value being paired with the lowest unpaired roughness value, these pairings forming a series of sawteeth if plotted (Garner 1974). When there are many stimuli which must be discriminated from each other in order to be accurately identified, it is not easy to tell the difference between two stimuli which differ only slightly in both colour and roughness, as for some stimuli generated by the linear pairing rule. However, under these same task conditions, stimuli generated by the sawtooth pairing rule are easy to tell apart as no two stimuli are highly similar in both colour and roughness. In terms of information theory, non-linear (sawtooth) pairing greatly increases information transmission relative to linear pairing. Thus the non-linear intermodal mapping between synaesthetic inducers and concurrents is ideally suited to aiding memory functions.

9.3 Possible Neurocognitive Mechanisms of Synaesthetic Experience

Two classes of neural circuitry which are potentially responsible for inducing synaesthetic experience can be termed 'crosstalk' and 'feedback'. This section examines both crosstalk and feedback in light of the perceptual-informational evidence presented above. While discussing the possible neural underpinnings of synaesthetic experience, perhaps we should also consider whether synaesthesia is mediated by neural circuits which exist in non-synaesthetes but are not readily observable in their psychological processes. Perhaps synaesthetes enjoy greater conscious awareness of cross-modal associations which non-synaesthetes may make only unconsciously. After all, there are synaesthetic-like aspects of normal perceptual and semantic processing (Marks 1982b; Melara 1989). Indeed, some aspects of information processing in non-synaesthetes closely resemble the very aspects of synaesthetic experience thought to distinguish synaesthetes from non-synaesthetes (Marks 1975). Perhaps synaesthetic and non-synaesthetic perception share much the same neuroanatomical foundation for interaction between sense modalities.

9.3.1 Crosstalk

The brains of some mammals contain direct connections between primary cortical receiving areas of each sense modality (Paperna and Malach 1991). But there is greater anatomical segregation between the senses within the cortex of primate brains, suggesting that the primary trend in our own evolution has been toward anatomical isolation between modalities (Pandya, Seltzer and Barbas 1988). In humans, the strict anatomical segregation between sense modalities so evident at the low level of receptor organs is largely maintained through several levels of the central nervous system, including numerous cortical areas which respond selectively to stimuli in a single sense modality (Haxby et al. 1991; Kawashima, O'Sullivan and Roland 1995). Beyond these unimodal primary and association areas, higher-level multimodal areas of cortex receive inputs from multiple senses and are important for meaningful thought (Amir, Harel and Malach 1993). The brain thus contains a hierarchy of sense modalities segregated at low and intermediate levels, combining into multimodal representations at higher levels. Synaesthetic experience seems to require some form of communication between neural representations in separate sensory pathways within this hierarchy. What pattern of anatomical connectivity (i.e. neural circuitry) could make synaesthetic experience possible?

Synaesthetic experience could result from crosstalk between separate sensory pathways. Figure 9.1 depicts the combined neural and phenomenal consequences of a sound stimulus heard by a coloured-hearing synaesthete. The stimulus evokes neural activity in the auditory pathway which leads to hearing the sound (auditory percept). But the upper part of the visual pathway is also activated by virtue of a crosstalk link which conveys neural signals from the auditory pathway. These crosstalk signals induce neuronal firing in the visual pathway which leads to the synaesthetic experience of a visual concurrent.

It is not known whether or where such direct cross-modal neural connections are to be found in humans (either synaesthetes or non-synaesthetes). The crosstalk hypothesis raises questions about the na-

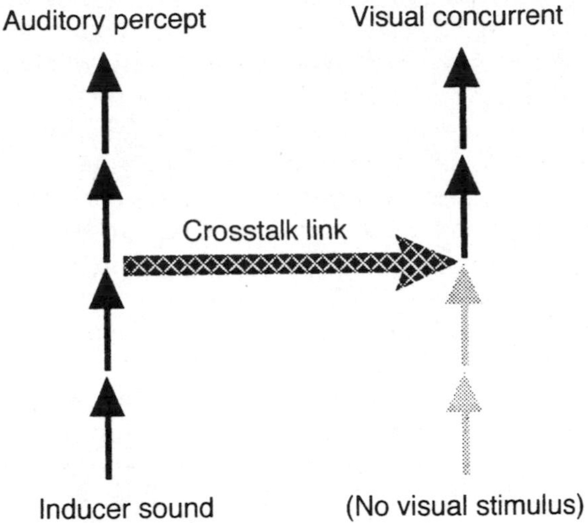

Figure 9.1 Crosstalk circuit

Note: Two parallel sensory pathways are depicted with ascending arrows. The auditory pathway on the left is fully activated (designated by darker arrows) because a sound is heard. The sound stimulus shown at the bottom is transduced into neural signals which lead to phenomenal experience of the sound (auditory percept). Somewhere along the ascending auditory pathway is the origin of a crosstalk link, depicted by a cross-hatched arrow, which sends signals to the visual pathway on the right of the figure. The upper part of the visual pathway becomes activated by these crosstalk signals, whereas the lower part of the visual pathway remains inactive (designated by lighter arrows).

ture of any neurobiological difference between synaesthetes and non-synaesthetes: are cross-modal neural connections numerically greater in synaesthetes than in non-synaesthetes? Or are comparable numbers of synaptic connections somehow used in a different way in synaesthetes as opposed to non-synaesthetes? There is no evidence yet available for deciding between these two alternative crosstalk mechanisms. Either way, assuming some form of crosstalk, the concurrent sensory pathway becomes activated via input from the inducer pathway without involvement of any additional neural system.

Where is the origin of the crosstalk link? We want to know, in particular, how high a level of sensory representation in the inducer neural pathway influences concurrent phenomenology. This origin can be inferred by the nature of the stimuli which induce synaesthetic experience. The synaesthetic experiences induced only by inherently meaningful stimuli such as words or music presumably involve higher-level crosstalk origins than those which can be induced by all kinds of sound.

We also want to know the lowest level of sensory representation in the concurrent pathway at which neural activity is synaesthetically induced. Where is the terminus of the crosstalk link? As with the origin, the terminus appears to vary among individual synaesthetes. For example, the apparent location of concurrent visual phenomena in the visual field is fixed (e.g. always appearing in the upper-left quadrant) for some synaesthetes and not fixed for others (Baron-Cohen et al. 1993; Riggs and Karwoski 1934). This observation suggests that the putative crosstalk link terminates at different neural levels of representation in different synaesthetes because neurons in low levels of the visual system distinguish between different locations in the visual field (e.g. some neurons represent only those stimuli appearing in the upper left) whereas neurons in high levels represent stimuli which appear in any part of the visual field (Rolls 1991).

Similar levels of sensory processing in different sense modalities can share anatomical proximity (e.g. in thalamic nuclei or in some areas of cortex). Such anatomical proximity makes cross-modal neural connection more likely to occur than cross-modal projections which must link widely disparate levels of two sensory pathways. So the closer inducer and concurrent levels of representation are to each other, the more likely synaesthetic experience really is mediated by crosstalk circuitry.

It may be important that the range of synaesthetic concurrents is limited to primitive features such as colour and shape, and does not include fully developed representations of familiar visual objects such as people or houses. Because the realistic complexity of natural objects is not induced in synaesthetic experience, the terminus of the crosstalk link must be lower in the concurrent pathway than the level at which entire objects are represented. Synaesthesias which demonstrate intensity parity between inducer and concurrent (Vike, Jabbari and Maitland 1984) support the idea of low-level crosstalk because it is the lower levels of sensory representation which most strongly reflect differences in stimulus intensity. However, many constitutional cases of synaesthesia do not seem to exhibit intensity parity, suggesting that at least the origin of the crosstalk link lies above these intensity-sensitive levels.

Repeated stimuli are typically experienced as gradually reducing in apparent intensity, a process known as 'adaptation'. For synaesthetes, as the inducer is presented multiple times in succession, how does this repetition affect the apparent intensity or vividness of the concurrent? Given a repeating inducer stimulus, equal decline in apparent intensity for the inducer and concurrent could most easily be accounted for by crosstalk. Such a finding would most strongly support a crosstalk account if there were very tight coupling between magnitude estimations of inducer and concurrent sampled over the course of inducer stimulus repetition.

Assuming that synaesthetic experience depends solely on crosstalk mechanisms, we might expect that for some synaesthetes there are occasions where only the concurrent phenomenon is experienced, without any conscious awareness of the inducer. Does such synaesthetic *replacement* ever occur? This would parallel the common experience of incomplete perception in which an individual notices only one stimulus among a set of two or more simultaneously displayed stimuli. Synaesthetic replacement phenomena have not been reported in the literature to date. Thus the universal observation that synaesthetic concurrents arise in addition to, not in replacement of, inducers could therefor be mustered for a (possibly weak) argument against crosstalk. To counter such an argument, suppose that the neural signals arising in the pathway which represents the inducer must be of some criterial strength in order to induce neural activity in the pathway which represents the concurrent (not an unreasonable proposition). Suppose further that this synaesthetic threshold of neural activation which represents a potential inducer is higher than the threshold for conscious awareness of the inducer. Given these suppositions of thresholds, neural activity in the inducer pathway sufficiently strong to induce a synaesthetic concurrent would always suffice for conscious awareness of the inducer. Without recourse to synaesthetic mechanisms other than crosstalk, this argument precludes the possibility of awareness of a synaesthetic concurrent without accompanying awareness of the inducer.

9.3.2 *Feedback*

An important lesson from modern neuroanatomy is that feedbackward connections pervade the brain's hierarchy of sensory pathways (Cynader et al. 1988). This means that the ascending neuronal projections which convey afferent (bottom-up) signals from one level of the sensory pathway to the next higher level are reciprocated by top-down signals going in the reverse direction. These reciprocal (feedbackward) connections are well positioned to convey various sorts of feedback to lower levels of sensory representation during the processing of sensory information. For example, feedback signals could play a crucial role in shaping neural activation when expectation precedes the beginning of actual sensory stimulation, as when you expect to see someone once you open the door to your home. Indeed, feedbackward connections probably contribute to a variety of cognitive functions including sensory attention, imagery and memory.

Feedbackward connections, presumably present in the sensory systems of every individual, synaesthete or not, provide for an alternative to the crosstalk account of synaesthesia. Figure 9.2 depicts a feedback circuit in which feedbackward connections within the visual pathway convey signals to lower-level visual areas. These feedback signals originated from higher-level multimodal brain areas activated by auditory inputs. In lower visual levels, neural proliferation of these feedback signals induces feedforward activation of the visual pathway. If synaesthesia is mediated by feedbackward connections, then it is reasonable to suspect that similar connections are present in non-synaesthetes.

Are feedbackward connections numerically greater in synaesthetes than in non-synaesthetes, or are comparable connections simply used

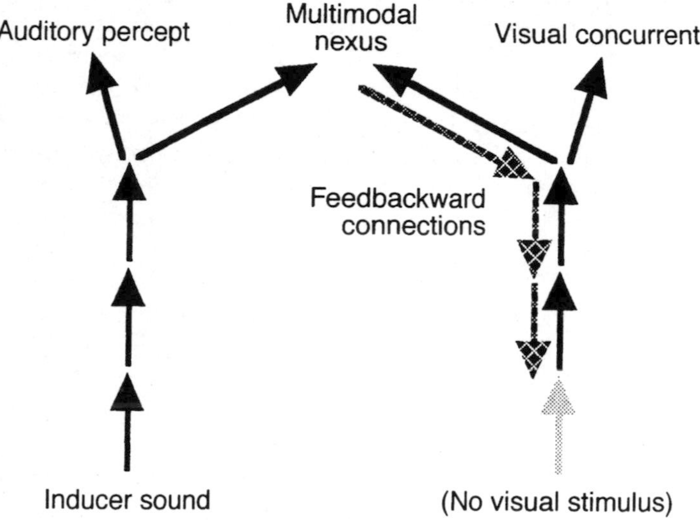

Figure 9.2 Feedback circuit

Note: Two parallel sensory pathways merge into a multimodal nexus which receives inputs from multiple sense modalities. The auditory pathway on the left is fully activated (designated by darker arrows) because a sound stimulus evokes neural signals which lead to phenomenal experience of the sound (auditory percept). Feedbackward projections, depicted by descending cross-hatched arrows, convey feedback signals along the reverse course taken by the ascending, afferent visual information stream. The upper part of the visual pathway becomes activated by feedback signals, whereas the lowest part of the visual pathway remains inactive (designated by a lighter arrow).

in a different way? In synaesthetes such connections may be prepotent, perhaps subject to less neural inhibition than in non-synaesthetes. There are several ways in which this prepotency could occur, and they all might differ from the neurobiology of non-synaesthetes only by a matter of degree. For example, it could be that the lowest-level brain area which processes the concurrent is hypersensitive, exhibiting enhanced responding to feedback signals which might be present in both synaesthetes and non-synaesthetes.

Feedback assumes that the inducer selectively activates neurons in a multimodal nexus, and the feedback signalling initiated in this multimodal brain area must be neurally conducted so as to reach some lower level of the concurrent pathway. What levels within the neural hierarchy of sensory representation send and receive the feedback signals? Presumably the information content of high-level representations is not accessible to low levels of the sensory hierarchy. So the lowest level at which the inducer *must* be represented in order to induce synaesthetic experience provides a lower limit to the origin of synaesthetic feedback. In terms of our ongoing example, how high in the auditory system is the most highly processed representation of sensory information which influences visual phenomenology? This critical level of inducer representation varies across individual synaesthetes, but can be as high as a level which differentiates between speech and non-speech sounds (Cytowic 1989: 37), or meaningful versus meaningless non-speech sounds (Marks 1975). Relatively few synaptic connections are required to link levels which are near to each other in the sensory hierarchy. So the higher the level of feedback origination, the more plausible is mediation by top-down feedbackward projections as opposed to putative crosstalk connections.

Explanation of synaesthesia in terms of feedback may be supported by the observation that voluntary imagery can induce a synaesthetic concurrent (Cytowic 1989: 41). The lower levels of representation in the inducer pathway need not be activated by mental imagery. For those synaesthetes who experience a synaesthetic concurrent while imagining an inducer, these bypassed levels are not viable candidates for originating a crosstalk link. So a crosstalk link could only originate in higher levels of the inducer pathway. Moreover, imagery may itself depend on feedback connections, given that feedforward connections cannot activate the pathway because no adequate stimulus is present during imagery. Co-activation of two sensory pathways by feedback signals presents a plausible mechanism for inducer-imagery spilling over into activity of the concurrent pathway.

The prevalence of words or music among synaesthetic inducers may also indicate a role for feedback in synaesthesia. Even *fractions* of words can induce synaesthetic experience: many synaesthetes experience concurrent phenomena which are induced by acoustic or orthographic *parts* of words (Rose 1909; Wheeler and Cutsforth 1922). Synaesthetic experience induced by meaningful stimuli may involve semantic association (Devereux, 1966; Marks 1982a). However, rather than seeking an explanation in terms of semantic association, a mental process for which the neural basis is not known, an alternative approach starts with the neural substrates of perceiving language and music, and asks how these cortical areas might communicate with brain areas involved in representing synaesthetic concurrents. This approach is especially motivated by synaesthetic experience induced by letters of the alphabet or phonemes, the sounds which comprise audible language (Baron-Cohen et al. 1993; Rose 1909; Wollen and Ruggiero 1983).

Humans may have recently evolved brain systems which are geared for perceiving symbolic information. For example, a cortical area selectively active in response to visual words has been discovered in left occipital cortex (Petersen et al. 1988). Cortical area V4, which is involved in processing colour (and shape), evolved relatively recently, appearing in only some primate species (Condo and Casagrande 1990; Krubitzer and Kaas 1990). The recent evolution of area V4 could help to explain why colour dominates among synaesthetically induced concurrent phenomena (as well as dominating visual experience). Recently evolved cortical systems might be more strongly connected to a large number of other cortical systems, either directly or via those systems involved in conscious awareness, compared to brain systems which evolved much earlier (Grossenbacher 1995).

It remains a puzzle why synaesthetic inducers and concurrents tend to separate themselves by clustering in language and natural object features respectively. That is, orthographic and phonemic features only induce synaesthetic experience and do not appear as concurrent phenomena. Conversely, colour is a common synaesthetic concurrent but not typically reported as an inducer. A feedback account of synaesthetic experience implies that representation of linguistic sensory information contributes to the initiation of feedback signalling more than does the representation of non-linguistic sensory information. Conversely, the neural representations of concrete object features may tend to receive more feedback signals than do the neural representations of linguistic stimuli. By pursuing an explanation of synaesthetic experience in terms of feedback, we have encountered an intriguing theoretical distinction which might apply equally well to neurocognitive systems among synaesthetes and non-synaesthetes alike.

9.3.3 Does synaesthetic experience depend on attention?

The fact that music is a common synaesthetic inducer suggests that it might be the *way* in which people listen to sounds that induces synaesthetic experience. Would concurrent phenomenal coloration arise if the listener were not consciously following the melody? This question can be phrased more generally: does synaesthetic experience depend on how attention is focused on the inducer stimulus? Actually, attention may be important to synaesthetic experience in more than one way: if there are many simultaneously available stimuli, must the inducer stimulus be selectively attended in order for synaesthetic experience to occur? Does the concurrent phenomenon draw attention towards or away from the inducer? Can a synaesthete attend to either the inducer or the concurrent without attending to the other?

In some cases synaesthetic experience occurs only intermittently, say only 20 per cent of the time rather than on all of the occasions in which a viable inducer stimulus is presented. Could it be that part of this variability is a function of attending, or a certain kind of attending? Perhaps the synaesthetic concurrent is experienced only when the inducer is carefully attended. This suggests that distraction from the inducer could reduce synaesthetic experience. Would an interference task such as threading a needle reduce synaesthetic experience induced by listening to a radio? The fact that synaesthetic experience can be intermittent provides a handle for asking quantitative empirical questions. Comparing those occasions when synaesthetic experience occurs with other, non-synaesthetic occasions, in which of them do the inducer stimuli appear more vivid, are identified with greater accuracy, or are remembered with greater accuracy? An experimental study could determine whether attention to the inducer does in fact boost (or diminish) synaesthetic experience.

It should be straightforward to compare the synaesthetic yield of potentially synaesthetic inducer stimulation (i.e. experience of synaesthetic concurrent or lack thereof) with accurate perception of the inducer. Suppose the experimental subject must discriminate between many possible inducer stimuli by identifying each stimulus (presented one at a time). On each occasion of inducer stimulation, the experimenter measures the synaesthete's concurrent experience and inducer perception. Synaesthetic experience could be assessed according to verbal report by the synaesthete, and perception of the inducer could be evaluated as correct or incorrect responding in the identification task. Analysis of the resulting data should reveal whether accurate discrimination of inducer and experience of the synaesthetic concurrent are correlated. Positive correlation (more synaesthetic experience associated with correct responses) would support the idea that synaesthetic experience depends on attention to the inducer. Negative correlation (more synaesthetic experience associated with incorrect responses) would indicate that the synaesthetic concurrent distracts the synaesthete from perceiving the inducer, and would weigh against the possibility of mediation by attention to the inducer.

One synaesthete reported: 'Concentration will tend to intensify the [concurrent] sensations, while distractions will minimize them' (Cytowic 1989: 41). This remark could be taken to support the idea that synaesthetic experience requires attention to the inducer. But an alternative interpretation places the concurrent at the centre of attention. Suppose that the experiment proposed above results in a negative correlation between inducer perception and synaesthetic experience. It could be that synaesthetic experience depends on attention focusing on the concurrent. For example, there could be some low level of synaesthetic concurrent activity induced in the sensory system, but the operation of selective attention might determine whether anything is made of this nascent activity. If indeed synaesthetic experience is boosted by attention to either the inducer or the concurrent, this raises the possibility that synaesthetic experience may be subject to the influence of the brain systems which mediate some forms of voluntary control.

9.4 Summary

This chapter has explored the perceptual structure of synaesthetic experience. A brief discussion of non-synaesthetic perception provided background for an informational analysis of synaesthetic experience. Aiming to describe the nature of synaesthetic experience in terms of sensory information, this analysis clarified some issues, but raised other questions which as yet go unanswered. Although incomplete, the resulting parametric description of synaesthetic experience did establish empirical constraints bearing on two ideas concerning the neurological basis of synaesthesia. Crosstalk concerns the perceptual consequences of potentially direct links between sensory channels. In contrast, feedback emphasizes the role of top-down influences arising in a high level of the brain's neural hierarchy. Crosstalk and feedback mechanisms may in fact each underlie different types of synaesthesia. Consideration of the psychological and neural mechanisms of crosstalk and feedback raised questions regarding possible roles of attention in synaesthetic experience.

There is still great empirical need to verify and extend the provisional catalogue of inducer stimulation, concurrent phenomena, and relations between synaesthetic inducers and concurrents provided in this chapter. If possible, sub-modalities (e.g. colour versus shape; warmth versus heavy) of inducers and concurrents should be specified, including their linguistic relevance. As has already been done in a small number of studies, it is important to test models of synaesthesia with perceptual experiments using synaesthetes as participants in quantitative assessment paradigms. In particular, the role of attention in synaesthesia should be explored with this approach.

References

Allison, T., Begleiter, A., McCarthy, G., Roessler, E., Nobre, A.C. and Spencer, D.D. 1993: Electrophysiological studies of color processing in human visual cortex. *Electroencephalography and Clinical Neurophysiology – Evoked Potentials*, 88(5), 343–55.

Amir, Y., Harel, M. and Malach, R. 1993: Cortical hierarchy reflected in the organization of intrinsic connections in Macaque monkey visual cortex. *Journal of Comparative Neurology*, 334, 19–46.

Baron-Cohen, S., Harrison, J., Goldstein, L.H. and Wyke, M. 1993: Coloured speech perception: is synaesthesia what happens when modularity breaks down? *Perception*, 22, 419–26.

Baron-Cohen, S., Wyke, M.A. and Binnie, C. 1987: Hearing words and seeing colours: an experimental investigation of a case of synaesthesia. *Perception*, 16, 761–7.

Colavita, F.B. 1974: Human sensory dominance. *Perception and Psychophysics*, 16, 409–12.

Condo, G.J. and Casagrande, V.A. 1990: Organization of cytochrome oxidase staining in the visual cortex of nocturnal primates (*Galago crassicaudatus* and *Galago senegalensis*). I: Adult patterns. *Journal of Comparative Neurology*, 293(4), 632–45.

Corbetta, M., Miezin, F.M., Dobmeyer, S., Shulman, G.L. and Petersen, S.E. 1990: Attentional modulation of neural processing of shape, color, and velocity in humans. *Science*, 248, 1556–9.

Cynader, M.S., Andersen, R.A., Bruce, C.J., Humphrey, D.R., Mountcastle, V.B., Niki, H., Palm, G., Rizzolatti, G., Strick, P., Suga, N., von Seelen, W. and Zeki, S. 1988: General principles of cortical operation. In P. Rakic and W. Singer (eds), *Neurobiology of Neocortex*, New York: John Wiley, 353–71.

Cytowic, R.E. 1989: *Synaesthesia: a union of the senses*. New York: Springer-Verlag.

Cytowic, R.E. 1993: *The Man Who Tasted Shapes*. London: Abacus.

Cytowic, R.E. and Wood, F. B. 1982a: Synaesthesia. I: A review of major theories and their brain basis. *Brain and Cognition*, 1(1), 23–35.

Cytowic, R.E. and Wood, F.B. 1982b: Synaesthesia. II: Psychophysical relations in the synaesthesia of geometrically shaped taste and colored hearing. *Brain and Cognition*, 1(1), 36–49.

Desimone, R. and Schein, S.J. 1987: Visual properties of neurons in area V4 of the macaque: sensitivity to stimulus form. *Journal of Neurophysiology*, 57(3), 835–68.

Devereux, G. 1966: An unusual audio-motor synaesthesia in an adolescent: significance of this phenomenon in psychoanalytic therapy. *Psychiatric Quarterly*, 40(3), 459–71.

Farah, M.J. 1988: Is visual imagery really visual? Overlooked evidence from neuropsychology. *Psychology Review*, 95, 307–17.

Farah, M.J. 1989: Mechanisms of imagery-perception interaction. *Journal of Experimental Psychology: Human Perception and Performance*, 15(2), 203–11.

Garner, W.R. 1974: *The Processing of Information and Structure*. Hillsdale, N.J.: Lawrence Erlbaum.

Glicksohn, J., Salinger, O. and Roychman, A. 1992: An exploratory study of syncretic experience: eidetics, synaesthesia and absorption. *Perception*, 21, 637–42.

Godefroy, O., Cabaret, M. and Rousseaux, M. 1994: Vigilance and effects of fatigability, practice and motivation on simple reaction time tests in patients with lesion of the frontal lobe. *Neuropsychologia*, 32(8), 983–90.

Greenwood, P.M., Parasuraman, R. and Haxby, J.V. 1993: Changes in visuospatial attention over the adult lifespan. *Neuropsychologia*, 31(5), 471–85.

Grossenbacher, P.G. 1993: Interaction between touch and vision: correspondence between frequency dimensions. [Abstract]. *Dissertation Abstracts International*, 54(1), 526B.

Grossenbacher, P.G. 1995: Consciousness and evolution in neocortex. In P.A. Mellars and K.R. Gibson (eds), *Modelling the Early Human Mind*, Cambridge: McDonald Institute for Archaeological Research.

Haxby, J.V., Grady, C.L., Ungerleider, L.G. and Horwitz, B. 1991: Mapping the functional neuroanatomy of the intact human brain with brain work imaging. *Neuropsychologia*, 29(6), 539–55.

Hollister, L.E. 1968: *Chemical psychoses, LSD and related drugs*. Springfield, Ill.: Charles C. Thomas.

Karwoski, T.F., Odbert, H.S. and Osgood, C.E. 1942: Studies in synaesthetic thinking. II: The role of form in visual responses to music. *Journal of General Psychology*, 26, 199–222.

Kawashima, R., O'Sullivan, B.T. and Roland, P.E. 1995: Positron-emission tomography studies of cross-modality inhibition in selective attentional tasks: closing the 'mind's eye'. *Proceedings of the National Academy of Sciences of the United States of America*, 92(13), 5969–72.

Kennedy, C., Sakurada, O., Shinohara, M. and Miyaoka, M. 1982: Local cerebral glucose utilization in the newborn macaque monkey. *Annals of Neurology*, 12(4), 333–40.

Krubitzer, L.A. and Kaas, J.H. 1990: Cortical connections of MT in four species of primates: areal, modular, and retinotopic patterns. *Visual Neuroscience*, 5(2), 165–204.

Lockhead, G.R. 1970: Identification and the form of multidimensional discrimination space. *Journal of Experimental Psychology*, 85, 1–10.

Luce, R.D. 1990: 'On the possible psychological laws' revisited: remarks on cross-modal matching. *Psychological Review*, 97(1), 66–77.

Marks, L.E. 1975: On colored-hearing synaesthesia: cross-modal translations of sensory dimensions. *Psychological Bulletin*, 82(3), 303–31.

Marks, L.E. 1982a: Bright sneezes and dark coughs, loud sunlight and soft moonlight. *Journal of Experimental Psychology: Human Perception and Performance*, 8, 177–93.

Marks, L.E. 1982b: Synaesthetic perception and poetic metaphor. *Journal of Experimental Psychology: Human Perception and Performance*, 8(1), 15–23.

Melara, R.D. 1989: Similarity relations among synaesthetic stimuli and their attributes. *Journal of Experimental Psychology: Human Perception and Performance*, 15(2), 212–31.

Nickerson, R.S. 1970: The effect of preceding and following auditory stimuli on response times to visual stimuli. *Acta Psychologica*, 33, 5–20.

Pandya, D.N., Seltzer, B. and Barbas, H. 1988: Input–output organization of the primate cerebral cortex. In *Comparative Primate Biology*, vol. 4: *Neurosciences*, New York: Alan R. Liss, 39–80.

Paperna, T. and Malach, R. 1991: Patterns of sensory intermodality relationships in the cerebral cortex of the rat. *Journal of Comparative neurology*, 308, 432–56.

Paulesu, E., Harrison, J., Baron-Cohen, S., Watson, J.D., Goldstein, L., Heather, J., Frackowiak, R.S. and Frith, C.D. 1995: The physiology of coloured hearing: a PET activation study of colour–word synaesthesia. *Brain*, 118(Pt 3), 661–76.

Perret, D.I., Harries, M.H., Mistlin, A.J. and Chitty, A.J. 1990: Recognition of objects and actions: frameworks for neuronal computation and perceptual experience. In D.M. Guthrie (ed.), *Higher Order Sensory Processing*, vol. 8, New York: Manchester University Press, 155–73.

Petersen, S.E., Fox, P.T., Posner, M.I., Mintun, M. and Raichle, M.E. 1988: Positron emission tomographic studies of the cortical anatomy of single-word processing. *Nature*, 331(18 February), 585–9.

Posner, M.I. 1980: Orienting of attention. *Quarterly Journal of Experimental Psychology*, 32, 3–25.

Posner, M.I. and Rothbart, M.K. 1991: Attentional mechanisms and conscious experience. In D. Milner and M. Rugg (eds), *The Neuropsychology of Consciousness*, New York: Academic Press, 91–111.

Posner, M.I., Grossenbacher, P.G. and Comption, P.E. 1994: Visual attention. In M. Farah and G. Ratcliff (eds), *The Neuropsychology of High-level Vision: collected tutorial essays*, Hillsdale, N.J.: Lawrence Erlbaum, 217–39.

Posner, M.I., Nissen, M.J. and Klein, R.M. 1976: Visual dominance: an information-processing account of its origins and significance. *Psychological Review*, 83(2), 157–71.

Posner, M.I., Sandson, J., Dhawan, M. and Shulman, G.L. 1989: Is word recognition automatic? A cognitive-anatomical approach. *Journal of Cognitive Neuroscience*, 1, 50–60.

Riggs, L.A. and Karwoski, T. 1934: Synaesthesia. *British Journal of Psychology*, 25, 29–41.

Rizzo, M. and Eslinger, P.J. 1989: Colored hearing synaesthesia: an investigation of neural factors. *Neurology*, 39(6), 781–4.

Rolls, E.T. 1991: Neural organization of higher visual functions. *Current Opinion in Neurobiology*, 1(2), 274–8.

Rose, K.B. 1909: Some statistics on synaesthesia. *America Journal of Psychology*, 20, 446.

Simpson, L. and McKellar, P. 1955: Types of synaesthesia. *Journal of Mental Science*, 101, 141–7.

Ungerleider, L.G. and Haxby, J.V. 1994: 'What' and 'where' in the human brain. *Current Opinion in Neurobiology*, 4(2), 157–65.

Vike, J., Jabbari, B. and Maitland, C.G. 1984: Auditory–visual synaesthesia: report of a case with intact visual pathways. *Archives of Neurology*, 41(6), 680–1.

Wheeler, R.H. and Cutsforth, T.D. 1922: Synaesthesia and meaning. *American Journal of Psychology*, 33, 361–84.

Wollen, K.A. and Ruggiero, F.T. 1983. Colored-letter synaesthesia. *Journal of Mental Imagery*, 7(2), 83–6.

10

Possible Implications of Synaesthesia for the Hard Question of Consciousness

Jeffrey A. Gray, Steven C.R. Williams, Julia Nunn and Simon Baron-Cohen

10.1 Introduction: the Hard Question of Consciousness

A central unresolved problem in cognitive neuroscience is posed by the relation of, on the one hand, 'conscious experience' and, on the other, 'brain event'. The first of these terms refers to the subjective experiences that make up what Jackendoff (1987: 3–4) calls 'primary awareness', including above all the perceived world with all its various qualities, but also bodily sensations, proprioception, mental images, dreams, internal speech, hallucinations, and so on. As to 'brain events', this is used here as a portmanteau term to cover neural functioning, the information processing carried out by such neural functioning, and the behaviour that these control.

Until relatively recently, the relation between brain events and conscious experience was not addressed at all within the scientific community, being left for philosophical enquiry and usually dismissed as a pseudo-problem arising from conceptual or linguistic confusion. While it is now, in contrast, widely accepted that the relation of conscious experience to brain events is a legitimate target for scientific research (Gray 1992; Marsh 1993), it is still far from clear how to approach the problem. No specific hypothesis appears yet to have been proposed which, if correct, would meet Nagel's (in Marsh 1993: 4) test of providing a 'transparent' account of how brain events generate conscious experience – that is, one that goes beyond mere 'brute' correlation and shows just how these two apparently incommensurable sets of phenomena are causally related one to the other. Indeed, it is not yet possible to choose on empirical grounds to which among whole classes of theory such hypotheses might belong. Should we, for example, seek explanations of the occurrence of conscious experiences in terms of neural events alone, information processing (syntax, semantics, etc.) alone, these two jointly (Gray 1971, 1996a), or at some deeper level of the physics of brain events (Penrose 1989)? (This list is by no means exhaustive.)

Most current accounts of cognitive neuroscience, if they include conscious experience at all, beg these questions. In general they provide statements to the effect that (a) certain neural circuits (for example, in the cerebral cortex) carry out (b) certain kinds of information processing (for example, the analysis of movement in the visual field) and result in (c) certain kinds of behaviour (for example, eye or limb movement), all this accompanied – or not – by (d) certain kinds of conscious experience (for example, the visual perception of movement) (Gray 1996a). In principle, and sometimes even in practice, it is known how to construct detailed accounts of the links between steps (a)–(c) in this type of chain; but, if one goes on to ask for details of how (a)–(c) are linked to (d) (the Hard Question about consciousness), no principled answer can as yet be given.

Worse still, there is as yet no empirically grounded way of answering, for any such account, the following more general questions. Suppose we tried to change the neural circuitry specified in step (a) – moved it, say, from cortical circuits to circuits in the limbic system – but kept the information processing the same: would this be possible; and, if so, would it change the nature of conscious experience? Suppose, instead, we kept the circuits the same, but tried to give them other kinds of information processing to carry out: again, would this be possible; and, if so, would it change the nature of conscious experience? Quite different types of answer to these questions are assumed to be correct in different types of general approach to the problem of consciousness: functionalists assume that conscious experience is tied to information processing; proponents of the mind–brain identity approach assume that it is tied to neural function; and still others assume that it is tied to both (for examples, see Blakemore and Greenfield 1987; Marsh 1993; and commentaries on Gray 1996a as summarized in Gray 1996b).

Each of these assumptions is equally lacking in empirical justification; nor, apparently, have attempts yet been made to gather relevant experimental evidence. It will perhaps be possible to do so, however, by studying brain function in synaesthesia.

10.2 Synaesthesia

Synaesthesia is discussed in all chapters in this volume, so only the key points are summarized here. It is a condition in which the individual experiences a sensation in one sensory modality triggered involuntarily and automatically by a sensation in a different sensory modality (Motluk 1994). It appears to be consistent across the individual's whole life-time, and is present from as early in childhood as the individual can recall. It can occur between any two sensory modalities, though in practice some combinations are more common than others. The most common form appears to be seeing colours when hearing sounds. Typically, in 'coloured hearing', the person sees a different colour when hearing a different sound, but in a highly consistent fashion. For example, when hearing speech, each word heard triggers a different colour, and over time the same word always triggers the same colour.

One possibility is that coloured speech perception represents coloured visual imagery of the orthography of words. Indeed, synaesthetes frequently report that words with the same initial sound but different initial letters (e.g. 'fish' and 'photo') trigger different colours, while words with a different initial sound but the same initial letter (e.g. 'psychology' and 'photo') trigger the same colour (Baron-Cohen et al. 1993). This indicates that letters rather than sounds determine the colours. However, if synaesthetes showing this effect are asked the question, 'Are the colours of words always determined by an inital or dominant letter?', many of them answer 'No'. Some state that the colour is triggered by phonemic features of the word (so that 'sex' and 'psychology' have the same colour) whilst in other cases there is no connection between the word and its colour at all (for example, 'Jane' and 'July', despite sharing both the initial sound and letter, trigger different colours). Presumably, since word processing occurs at several levels, colours can be triggered at any of them (Baron-Cohen 1995).

One hundred years ago, synaesthesia was a topic of considerable scientific interest (Binet 1893; Galton 1883; Myers 1911, 1914). By the 1940s, the topic had virtually vanished from science, for two reasons: introspection had become an unrespectable method of data collection in experimental psychology; and there appeared to be no objective way of validating that synaesthesia was actually occurring, over and above the self-report data from the subject him- or herself. This scepticism as to whether synaesthesia was real or not is understandable, though it is worth noting that many psychiatric phenomena (hallucinations, delusions, and so on) rely purely on data obtained via self-report.

Baron-Cohen et al. (1987) reported on a single case (EP) of a woman with synaesthesia, with the aim of overcoming the problem posed by the potential unreliability of self-report data. When EP was given a long word list and was asked to describe the colours triggered by each word in the list, she gave very detailed descriptions (for example, the word 'Maria' triggered a dark purple colour, with a shiny texture, and with speckled spinach-green at the edges). When retested on the same

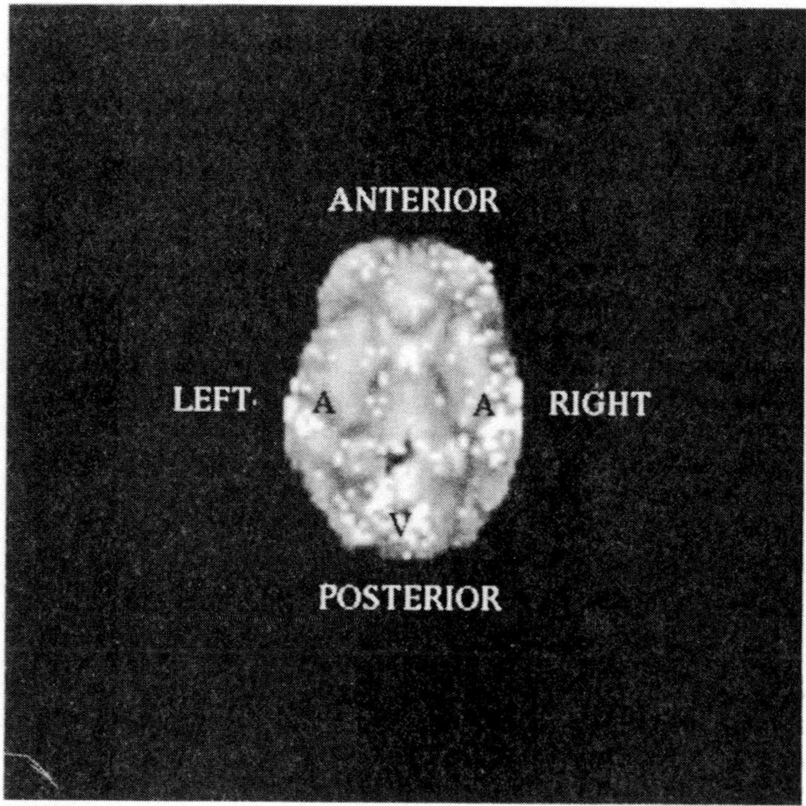

Figure 10.1 Functional MR image from a single case with synaesthesia (coloured-speech perception)

Note: The data show a t-test map at 97.5 per cent confidence (white pixels) of all imaged pixels responding in synchrony with the external stimulus. These data are superimposed on to one of the original echoplanar images acquired in the near-axial plane. This case shows clear activation of both auditory (A) and visual (V) cortices even though, during the condition, our subject was simply hearing words.

word list one year later, without any prior warning, she was 100 per cent consistent in the colours she described for each word. In contrast, a normal control subject, matched for intelligence and memory, who was asked to associate colours with words in the same word list, and who had the advantage that she was warned that she would be retested after two weeks (and so could attempt to use mnemonics), was only 17 per cent consistent. Since a memory strategy could not plausibly account for such performance, it was concluded that synaesthesia was a genuine phenomenon. This finding was replicated on a larger group of synaesthetes in a later study (Baron-Cohen et al. 1993).

Establishing that synaesthesia is highly consistent within an individual is one way of testing its genuineness. A second way has been to use functional neuroimaging to investigate if there is a neural basis to the condition. Paulesu et al. (1995), using positron emission tomography (PET), compared six synaesthetic women with six matched controls. When hearing words, the group of synaesthetes showed abnormal activation in some areas of visual cortex (for example, the left lingual gyrus, a putative portion of human area V2) relative to controls. This finding has received support in our recent pilot study of a single synaesthete using functional magnetic resonance imaging (fMRI). This showed clear activation of the visual cortex when the subject listened to words, in contrast to a normal control (see figure 10.1). This is clearly an abnormal finding, and suggests that visual imagery indeed occurs when synaesthetes hear words.

These results suggest the possibility that there is abnormal neuronal connectivity between auditory and visual cortical areas, and so a neurological basis for synaesthesia. Further evidence in support of this possibility comes from studies showing that synaesthesia can be induced in normal individuals by hallucinogenic drugs such as lysergic acid (LSD) and mescaline (see Motluk 1994). It should be stressed, however, that the subjects studied in the above experiments have synaesthesia 'naturally' – they are not taking any form of drug.

10.3 The Relevance of Synaesthesia to the Study of Consciousness

Because both synaesthesia and the hard question of consciousness have both received so little scientific attention, it is necessary to bring out why their conjunction might be of scientific importance. There are three main reasons to highlight:

1 Fodor's (1983) view, that the sensory systems are *modular*, has received widespread discussion within neuroscience. Synaesthesia, in being a mixing of the senses, may be a natural experiment demonstrating the consequences of 'a breakdown in modularity' (Baron-Cohen et al. 1993). This view of synaesthesia suggests that in the normal individual there must be a mechanism, possibly under genetic control, which leads to the modularization of the senses, and which thus prevents most of us from having synaesthesia. The study of this condition may therefore throw light on the organization of the normal brain, as well as the nature of the synaesthetic brain.

2 One possibility is that synaesthesia results from a disruption in the normal process of selective neuronal cell death during infancy. In the normally developing brain in many species, many more neuronal connections are made than are finally retained (see, for example, Dehay et al. 1984), redundant or maladaptive connections being 'pruned' during infancy. In synaesthesia, the suggestion is that these may persist. This has led some (for example, Maurer 1993) to argue that perhaps synaesthesia has its origins in infancy. The study of synaesthesia may therefore throw light on mechanisms of neural development (see Baron-Cohen 1995).

3 Most pertinent to the major line of argument pursued here, there are two different hypotheses as to how synaesthesia occurs in the brain. One is that there are permanent neural connections between modalities which are not normally present (see, for example, Baron-Cohen et al. 1993), perhaps due to the processes indicated in 2. The other is that synaesthesia is simply the result of learned associations between stimuli (reflecting the vagaries of individual life events). The choice between these two hypotheses is a specific instance of the general issues concerning consciousness outlined in the Introduction. If a synaesthete has an experience of colour upon hearing a word, is this due to a particular type of information processing (the formation of an association between the word and the colour) or to a particular type of neuronal event (activity in specific neurons in a specific part of the visual system)? If it were possible to choose between the two types of hypothesis in the case of synaesthesia, this might have important implications for the construction of a general theory of consciousness. It might, of course, be impossible to make this choice, because the experiments are too coarse. More interestingly, the choice might be impossible because conscious experiences depend upon *both* appropriate information processing *and* appropriate neuronal events, these being

in some as-yet-unknown way indissolubly linked. However, it is only by the attempt to dissociate information processing and neuronal events that one is likely to uncover such a tight linkage.

In order to differentiate between these two hypotheses we have recently commenced a study, using fMRI (see figure 10.1), to measure regional cerebral blood flow (rCBF). Here we describe the design of our study rather than its results, since this work is still in progress. We measure rCBF:

1 in synaesthetes exposed to verbal stimuli which spontaneously evoke experiences of colour;
2 in normal controls exposed to the same verbal stimuli during and after associative learning in which they are paired with visual stimuli comparable to those described as part of the synaesthetes' experience;
3 in normal controls exposed to the same verbal stimuli but with no prior associative learning task;
4 in synaesthetes given associative learning tasks involving stimuli to which they do not have a spontaneous associative response; and
5 in normal controls given the same tasks as for 4.

If the special features of the synaesthetic experience are due to hard wiring between normally separate, modality-specific regions, we would expect to see activation patterns (including, in particular, activation of visual colour cortex by words) in condition 1 that differ from those seen in the remaining four conditions. In contrast, if the synaesthetic experience reflects prior associative learning, the results in conditions 1, 2, 4 and 5 should all resemble each other, but differ from those in condition 3. Finally, if synaesthetes differ from normals in the nature of their associative learning, their results in conditions 1 and 4 should differ from those seen in the controls in conditions 2, 3 and 5.

An outcome to these experiments consistent with the 'hard wiring' hypothesis (in italic above) would have the most far-reaching implications for a general theory of consciousness. If synaesthetes have colour experiences when they hear words because unusual patterns of neuronal connectivity lead to activity in particular brain circuits, without there being any need for a particular life history of associative learning, this would imply that *the particular features that characterize specific conscious experiences depend upon neuronal events, not upon information processing*. If correct, this inference would further imply that much current effort to explain consciousness by appeal simply to informational transactions that could go on in non-neuronal systems, such as computers (see, for example, Johnson-Laird 1987), is fundamentally misdirected.

Acknowledgements

We are grateful to the McDonnell-Pew Program in Cognitive Neuroscience, which is supporting our current research using fMRI to study synaesthesia. We also thank Chris Andrew and John Harrison for their technical assistance in the development of our MR-compatible paradigms.

References

Baron-Cohen, S. 1995: Is there a phase of synaesthesia in normal development? *Psyche* (special issue on Synaesthesia), in press.

Baron-Cohen, S., Wyke, M. and Binnie, C. 1987: Hearing words and seeing colours: an experimental investigation of a case of synaesthesia. *Perception*, 16, 761–7.

Baron-Cohen, S., Harrison, J., Goldstein, L. and Wyke, M. 1993: Coloured speech perception: is synaesthesia what happens when modularity breaks down? *Perception*, 22, 419–26.

Binet, A. 1893: L'application de la psychometrie à l'étude de l'audition colorée. *Recherches philosophiques*, 36, 334–6.

Blakemore, C. and Greenfield, S. (eds) 1987: *Mindwaves*. Oxford: Blackwell.

Dehay, C., Bullier, J. and Kennedy, H. 1984: Transient projections from the fronto-parietal and temporal cortex to areas 17, 18, and 19 in the kitten. *Experimental Brain Research*, 57, 208–12.

Fodor, J. 1983: *The Modularity of Mind*. Cambridge, Mass.: MIT/Bradford Books.

Galton, F. 1883: *Enquiries into the Human Faculty*. London: Denton.

Gray, J.A. 1971: The mind–brain identity theory as a scientific hypothesis. *Philosophical Quarterly*, 21, 247–52.

Gray, J.A. 1992: Consciousness on the scientific agenda. *Nature*, 358, 277.

Gray, J.A. 1996a: The contents of consciousness: a neuropsychological conjecture. *Behavioral and Brain Sciences*, in press.

Gray, J.A. 1996b: Consciousness and its (dis)contents. *Behavioral and Brain Sciences*, in press.

Jackendoff, R. 1987: *Consciousness and the Computational Mind*. Cambridge, Mass.: MIT Press.

Johnson-Laird, P. 1987: How could consciousness arise from the computations of the brain? In C. Blakemore and S. Greenfield (eds), *Mindwaves*, Oxford: Blackwell, 247–57.

Marsh, J. (ed.) 1993: *Experimental and Theoretical Studies of Consciousness*, Ciba Foundation Symposium 174. Chichester, Sussex: John Wiley.

Maurer, D. 1993: Neonatal synaesthesia: implications for the processing of speech and faces. In B. de Boysson-Bardies, S. de Schonen, P. Jusczyk, P. McNeilage and J. Morton (eds), *Developmental Neurocognition: speech and face processing in the first year of life*. Dordrecht: Kluwer.

Motluk, A. 1994: The sweet smell of purple. *New Scientist*, 13 August, 33–7.

Myers, C. 1911: A case of synaesthesia. *British Journal of Psychology*, 4, 228–38.

Myers, C. 1914: Two cases of synaesthesia. *British Journal of Psychology*, 7, 112–17.

Paulesu, E., Harrison, J., Baron-Cohen, S., Watson, J.D.G., Goldstein, L., Heather, J., Frakowiac, R.S.J. and Frith, C.D. 1995: The physiology of coloured hearing: a PET activation study of colour-word synaesthesia. *Brain*, 118, 661–76.

Penrose, R. 1989: *The Emperor's New Mind*. Oxford: Oxford University Press.

11

Synaesthesia: Is a Genetic Analysis Feasible?

Mark E.S. Bailey and Keith J. Johnson

11.1 Introduction

The biological study of synaesthesia is in its first bloom, but a fundamental understanding of the neural processes that lead to this unusual faculty has been made feasible by recent advances in technological and theoretical approaches to a number of mental phenomena. These methods have most often been applied to overt diseases, such as schizophrenia, manic depression and Alzheimer's disease, but synaesthesia has some unique features which will combine to make a genetic approach to its study fruitful, if challenging. A genetic study of synaesthesia is unlikely to encounter the ethical problems associated with the study of diseases of the brain, such as Huntington's disease, since synaesthetes tend to be very positive about their possession of the trait. It carries no apparent stigma, has no obvious implications for health or longevity and is enjoyed throughout life, so that there are none of the potential problems associated with early diagnosis of 'delayed onset' diseases.

These characteristics of synaesthesia make it very attractive to geneticists keen to unravel the cellular and biochemical mechanisms underlying the trait. In this chapter, we have addressed what is known about the familial transmission of synaesthesia, the modes of inheritance that could explain these patterns of transmission, what implications there are for finding one or more 'synaesthesia genes', and a summary of the technology that now exists to make this feasible. To clarify the arguments and specialized jargon this entails for non-biologists we have started with a brief overview of some of the important concepts in human genetics. Finally, we have made educated guesses regarding the kinds of genes that might be involved in determining synaesthesia, based on current knowledge of the functional anatomy and neurophysiology of synaesthetes' brains.

11.2 A Basic Guide to Human Genetics

For synaesthesia to have a genetic basis, there must be an identifiable point or set of points within the genome that differ(s) between individuals that have and those that do not have the trait. A brief guide to some of the concepts and terms needed to understand the principles involved in finding these differences can be found in Box 11.1. A few

Box 11.1 A basic guide to human genetics

Glossary

Genome	Inherited information stored as a DNA double helix in all human cells, comprising 3,300 million base pairs (A, C, G and T), organized into 46 chromosomes (22 homologous pairs of autosomes; X and Y sex chromosomes, which are partially homologous). Bases pair on opposite strands of the helix according to the rule A + T, C + G.
Gene	Functional unit of genome, specified by sequence of DNA that can be translated into functional protein. Number of genes = 50–100,000. Organized into exons (coding) and introns (non-coding), interspersed with much longer regions of non-coding DNA.
Allele	Sequence variants found at any position (locus) in the genome. Also, the variants carried by an individual at any position on homologous chromosomes.
Marker	Any means of identification of variants at a locus, discovered by 'genotyping'.
Polymorphism	The presence of variants at any locus at significant frequency in a population.
Homozygote	Possessing the same allele at a polymorphic locus on both homologous chromosomes.
Heterozygote	Possessing different alleles at a polymorphic locus on the two homologues.

Meiosis	Type of cell division employed in the reproductive phase to generate gametes. Involves a halving of the genomic constitution, i.e. each gamete contains one of each pair of homologous chromosomes, and, hence, one of the two alleles at every polymorphic locus.
Recombination	Crossing-over of homologous chromosomes at meiosis. This process 'shuffles' the existing combination of alleles at every locus on a chromosome. It is measured in terms of the number of offspring per hundred that show a recombination in the genetic interval between two loci. 1 centiMorgan (cM) indicates an approximated rate of recombination of 1/100.
Restriction site	Specific DNA sequence that can be cut by one of a range of 'restriction enzymes'.
RFLP	Restriction fragment length polymorphism; occurs when alleles at a polymorphic locus differ with respect to the presence or absence of a restriction site. Detected by cutting an individual's DNA, separating out the fragments on the basis of size, and using a specific labelled DNA 'probe' for the locus of interest. The alleles (two maximum) are identified ('genotyped') by their size difference.
STR	Short tandem repeat ('microsatellite'). Tracts of repeated DNA sequence units, such as the dinucleotide $(CA)_n$, where n varies between individuals. Often highly polymorphic, most individuals being heterozygous (e.g. if one's two homologous chromosome 5s carry alleles with, for example, $n = 15$ and $n = 18$ at a particular $(CA)_n$ repeat locus).
PCR	Polymerase chain reaction. Using a thermostable DNA polymerase enzyme to create new strands of DNA using a specific DNA primer annealed to a DNA template, PCR can amplify, through many rounds of temperature cycling, a target DNA sequence up to a million-fold or more. Often used to amplify DNA segments around STR markers to enable alleles to be identified ('genotyping', *see* 'Allele' above).

Genetic parameters

Mode of inheritance	An observed pattern of inheritance of a trait that is explained by a theoretical genetic model.
Autosomal/ X-linked	A trait or disease gene is located on one of the autosomes (chr. 1–22)/X-chromosome, respectively.
Dominant	An allele is dominant if its associated phenotype is apparent when the allele is carried in only one copy by an individual.
Recessive	Two copies of an allele are required for visualization of the associated phenotype. Alternatively, no normal copy must be present (i.e. in males, for X-linked genes; see table 11.1a).
Mendelian transmission	The phenotypic ratios in offspring match those predicted by Mendel for autosomal dominant and recessive, and X-linked dominant and recessive inheritance respectively (see table 11.1).
Penetrance	The probability that an individual, having inherited a trait allele, will display the phenotypic effect of that allele. Reduced penetrance can show up as 'skipped' generations within a pedigree segregating a trait or as a lower than predicted proportion of affected offspring, given a particular mode of inheritance.
Variable expressivity	The symptoms or characteristics of an inherited trait may vary between individuals, within and between pedigrees, even though they have inherited the same trait allele. Often due to 'genetic background' effects (i.e. alleles at other loci influence expression of the trait).
Monogenic vs. polygenic	Traits may be substantially determined at a single locus (monogenic), for example Duchenne muscular dystrophy; or they may be brought about by combinations of specific alleles at several loci simultaneously (polygenic), for example fingertip ridge count. Most traits in the latter category are also influenced to greater or lesser degree by non-genetic, environmental influences (multifactorial traits).

points on genetics are particularly relevant to the discussion below. Each human chromosome exists as a pair of homologues, and the order of genes and markers on each homologue is identical. This enables the interpretation of data generated from recombinations between polymorphic markers. As the only exception to this, the Y chromosome contains only a tiny fraction of the genes carried on the X chromosome, which means that only one copy of most X-linked genes exists in males (whose karyotype, or complement of chromosomes, is 46, XY), unlike females (46, XX). The genetic distance between two polymorphic markers is estimated from the rate of recombination between them. During recombination, a pair of homologous chromosomes swap material at identical positions, thus bringing together new combinations of variants at polymorphic sites and ensuring that each sex cell, or gamete, is unique. The shuffling of the genome by recombination can be followed (that is, the grand-parental origin of the chromosome carrying a particular variant at any chromosomal position can be traced) in the offspring of any mating, provided that a parent is heterozygous at the polymorphic marker of interest. This ability can be put to use in mapping genes by the method of 'linkage analysis', as discussed in sub-section 11.6.1.

There are two major types of variation that can be used as genetic markers in this way: restriction fragment length polymorphisms (RFLPs) and polymorphic short tandem repeat (STR) markers. Both types include a large number of almost identical DNA features spread across the genome. The 'trick', however, is to identify the unique DNA sequence flanking the variable bases at the locus of interest and to use it to detect the presence or absence of the restriction site in the case of RFLPs, or to measure by polymerase chain reaction (PCR) (Saiki et al. 1988) the variation in number of repeat units at that site, in the case of STRs.

Polymorphisms are, by definition, relatively common and so are unlikely to be directly involved in a causative role in less common traits and diseases. When they do affect the function of a gene, they will more often be found to underlie a portion of the variance in a common polygenic or multifactorial trait. Here, the contribution of alleles at polymorphic markers is to be understood in terms of increased 'risk' of developing a trait. An example might be late-onset Alzheimer's disease, in which possession of a particular variant of a gene known as apolipoprotein E (in this case, the apoE4 allele) is associated with increased risk of developing the disease (Corder et al. 1993). In the case of rarer traits, most polymorphisms will act merely as markers of the positions of nearby genes because they have no effect on the expression or function of the genes. Common polymorphisms are, however, a necessary ingredient in the mapping of those genes and traits.

Variations in human DNA sequence are not only due to polymorphisms. Rarer variants originate as mutations and are much more likely to be observed as the direct cause of genetic traits and diseases. Such diseases are more often Mendelian, single gene disorders, than they are multifactorial in character. Mutations are usually impossible to detect using the same techniques as for polymorphic markers because they result in a change in a restriction site or disrupt and STR only occasionally. This then requires that mutations be identified by direct sequencing of the DNA within the disrupted gene in affected individuals and this can only take place after identification of the appropriate gene.

The second genetic principle of importance here is 'mode of inheritance'. Single gene, Mendelian, disorders may demonstrate a dominant or recessive mode of inheritance, as described in Box 11.1 and illustrated in Table 11.1. The implications of mode of inheritance for gene searches and interpretation of family data in synaesthesia are discussed below, but first an examination of the evidence for synaesthesia being a familial, and thus possibly genetic trait, is warranted.

11.3 Does Synaesthesia Run in Families?

Harrison and Baron-Cohen refer, in the Introduction to this book, to the fact that several early workers on synaesthesia viewed the trait as a largely heritable condition. These included Galton, whose classic paper on the mind has been reproduced in chapter 4 and, more recently, Cytowic (1989a). Extremely few studies, however, have attempted to gauge the population prevalence of synaesthesia or even to report a focused study of the family history of those presenting with the condition. Calkins (1895) reported the results of a three-year study at Wellesley College. The prevalence increased from 6 per cent to more than 23 per cent over the course of this study. A separate study by Rose (1909) came up with a figure of 9 per cent of those questioned having experienced involuntary colour–word associations. These figures are surprisingly high for a trait that is not well known in the general population. A similar study referred to by Calkins yielded a figure of around 2 per cent prevalence amongst pupils at another college. This figure is more similar to those observed in some mental disorders, such as schizophrenia, which may be regarded as unusual but not rare.

More recent estimates suggest a substantially lower prevalence of the trait. Cytowic (1993) refers to a figure of 1/100,000 for all synaesthesias. Motluk (1994) reported an estimated prevalence of 1/25,000. A recent survey conducted by advertisements in the local Cambridge, UK, media produced a minimum prevalence of coloured-hearing synaesthesia of 1/2,100 (Baron-Cohen et al. submitted). This could be an underestimate of the prevalence, since self-referrals often represent less than 100 per cent of available subjects.

A brief survey of the scientific literature on synaesthesia generates the impression that most studies have been concerned with the characteristics of the trait itself in those who manifested it, and not so much with the reasons for its appearance in that person. However, it is clear that a distinction must be drawn between those who presented with idiopathic synaesthesia and those whose symptoms were acquired, as has been discussed in more detail in chapter 1. There have been several reports of isolated cases of apparently idiopathic synaesthesia, most without giving details of family history, or reporting its exclusion (Coriat 1913; Rizzo and Eslinger 1989; Starr 1893). Amongst the published studies that do include these data are those of Baron-Cohen et al. (1987 and 1993), in which about a quarter of those interviewed claimed to have affected family members. Cytowic has also reported the existence of synaesthetic individuals with strong family histories (Cytowic 1989a) including at least one family with affected members in three or possibly four generations (Cytowic 1989b). Almost a third of the respondents to the Cambridge survey mentioned above reported that they had affected relatives.

Baron-Cohen and colleagues have also analysed six families (manuscript submitted) ascertained from their previous survey (Baron-Cohen et al. 1993) through reports from index cases of additional affected family members. All six have multiple affected relatives in more than one generation (multiplex) but were selected at random with respect to family structure. About a third of the individuals have had the test of genuineness applied, the rest being ascertained by interview of the proband in each family.

11.4 What Modes of Inheritance are Compatible with Observed Family Structures?

Mode of inheritance (MOI) of a genetic trait is an important parameter that is required to be known, or at least estimated, for some forms of analysis to be statistically valid. It is useful, therefore, to examine what can be concluded about possible MOIs in synaesthesia. The difference between dominant and recessive trait or disease alleles has been covered in Box 1. Other facets of MOI must also be considered. Table 11.1

Table 11.1 Patterns of transmission of traits under Mendelian inheritance

(a) X-linked traits

Parental genotype and affected status		*Genotype and affected status of offspring, by sex*								
		Dominant traits				*Recessive traits*				
		Son		*Daughter*		*Son*		*Daughter*		
Father	*Mother*	*Affected* ■	*Unaffected* □	*Affected* ●	*Unaffected* ○	*Affected* ■	*Unaffected* □	*Affected* ●	*Carrier* ◐	*Unaffected* ○
TY ■	TT ●	TY 100%	–	TT 100%	–	TY 100%	–	TT 100%	–	–
TY ■	TN ● (or ◐)	TY 50%	NY 50%	TT 50% TN 50%	–	TY 50%	NY 50%	TT 50%	TN 50%	–
TY ■	NN ○	–	NY 100%	TN 100%	–	–	NY 100%	–	TN 100%	–
NY □	TT ●	TY 100%	–	TN 100%	–	TY 100%	–	–	TN 100%	–
NY □	TN ● (or ◐)	TY 50%	NY 50%	TN 50%	NN 50%	TY 50%	NY 50%	–	TN 50%	NN 50%

Table 11.1 Continued

(b) Autosomal

Parental genotype and affected status				*Genotype and affected status of offspring*									
				Dominant traits				*Recessive traits*					
Father		*Mother*		*Affected* ■, ●		*Unaffected* □, ○		*Affected* ■, ●		*Carrier* ⊡, ⊙		*Unaffected* □, ○	
TT	■	TT	●	TT	100%	–		TT	100%	–		–	
TT	■	TN	● (or ⊙)	TT, TN	100%	–		TT	50%	TN	50%	–	
TT	■	NN	○	TN	100%	–		–		TN	100%	–	
TN	■ (or ⊡)	TT	●	TT, TN	100%	–		TT	50%	TN	50%	–	
TN	■ (or ⊡)	TN	● (or ⊙)	TT, TN	75%	NN	25%	TT	25%	TN	50%	NN	25%
TN	■ (or ⊡)	NN	○	TN	50%	NN	50%	–		TN	50%	NN	50%
NN	□	TT	●	TN	100%	–		–		TN	100%	–	
NN	□	TN	● (or ⊙)	TN	50%	NN	50%	–		TN	50%	NN	50%

1 Letters represent alleles at a Mendelian locus: T = trait allele, N = normal allele, Y indicates absence of second allele in hemizygous males for X-linked genes.
2 Percentages relate to the proportion of affected and carrier/unaffected offspring within each category, dominant and recessive (by sex for X-linked traits).
3 Dashes within table indicate phenotypic categories for which no possible genotype exists.
4 Symbols beside parents depict affected status of parent: ■, ● = affected, male or female; ⊡, ⊙ = carrier male or female; □, ○ = unaffected male or female.
5 Symbols in parentheses are status in the case of recessive traits.

summarizes the transmission characteristics of all combinations of genotypes of a single gene trait under Mendelian inheritance.

A few points should be stressed. The inheritance of genes carried on the X- and Y-chromosomes is different to that of autosomal genes. For example, in X-linked recessive traits, affected males, if fertile, will pass on the trait allele to all their female offspring (who will thus be carriers), but to none of their male offspring, since fathers contribute their single X chromosome to all their daughters and their Y chromosome to all their sons. In the dominant case, affected males will transmit a trait to all their daughters, all of whom should be affected, but, again, to none of their sons. Maternal transmission of recessive X-linked traits usually proceeds from unaffected, heterozygous 'carrier' mothers (with one trait and one normal allele on their two X chromosomes) to affected and unaffected sons in the ratio 1:1. Similarly, 50 per cent of daughters of a carrier mother should inherit the trait allele and become carriers also. In the rare instances where a carrier female marries an affected male, half the female offspring will be carriers and the other half will be affected. X-linked dominant trait genes can be passed from females to yield 50 per cent affected offspring of both sexes, with no unaffected carriers.

Autosomal disease genes are more straightforward. Dominant alleles present in one parent (of either sex) will be transmitted to 50 per cent of sons and daughters; all who receive one copy of this allele will be affected. Autosomal recessive alleles will produce, on average, 25 per cent affected offspring of both sexes if both parents are unaffected heterozygotes. If one parent is affected and the second parent is a carrier, then 50 per cent of their offspring will be affected, while the other 50 per cent will be carriers. It is important to realize that the proportions of affected offspring detailed above are the predicted statistical averages over many families and it should also be remembered that, in reality, these figures predict the risk of developing affected status for each and every offspring on conception. Mode-of-inheritance estimation becomes much more complicated when these Mendelian rules are not obeyed.

A few alternative MOIs are worthy of mention. Occasionally, dominant alleles are described as having incomplete penetrance or variable expressivity (see Box 1). In the latter, affected status may be difficult to ascertain because a spectrum of severity and symptoms may be observed, no individual conforming precisely to a simple definition of the trait. (cf. for example, myotonic dystrophy; Harper 1989). The proportion of affected offspring will vary from predictions if the function of a gene undergoes modification by alleles present at another locus (a modifier locus). Similarly, in polygenic traits, the proportion of affected relatives falls off much more sharply with decreasing genetic relationship than for dominant Mendelian traits.

Quantitative 'threshold' models have been postulated in a number of cases of polygenic inheritance of qualitative (presence or absence) traits and diseases. The only quantitative aspect to synaesthesia is the cut-off point adopted in the test of genuineness. This should be employed with caution in assessing whether an individual contributing genetic information to the analysis of a pedigree should be classed as affected or not. The inheritance of synaesthesia as a contiguous gene syndrome as a result of chromosomal deletion is unlikely, assuming a lack of other symptoms that characteristically segregate with the trait.

Having summarized the major possible modes of inheritance to look for in synaesthesia, we would like to be able to pull together the available information on MOI in this trait. Data relating to transmission patterns are, however, very scarce in synaesthesia. The six families studied by Baron-Cohen et al. and referred to above form the only set of data at present amenable to analysis, since all the affected families were ascertained by the same method and evaluated by a single team of psychologists applying a consistent set of diagnostic tests. In this study, individuals with >75 per cent consistency were assumed to have the trait, and all those answering negatively in the interviews or by reporting from other family members were assumed not to carry the trait.

Table 11.2 summarizes the available transmission data from these six families. The female:male affected ratio of 7.7:1 is of considerable note, as discussed below. In no family are both parents affected, and there is no indication that the trait is being transmitted bilineally (from both halves of a family). The two affected males who transmit the trait do so to all their offspring, all of whom are female. There is thus no opportunity to determine whether synaesthesia can be excluded as an X-linked trait by its transmission from fathers to male offspring. Inheritance through the maternal line shows a markedly higher rate of transmission to affected daughters than to affected sons. Although the numbers involved are small, this bias is statistically significant ($P < 0.002$, Fisher's Exact Test). If the paternal transmissions are included in this analysis (a further 5/5 affected female offspring) it becomes clear that the trait may show what is called sex-limited expression (equivalent to reduced penetrance of the risk allele in one sex), in which offspring of one sex are much more likely to develop the trait, given that they have inherited the risk allele.

The simplest model that could explain these data would be autosomal dominant transmission. Cytowic (1989a) has argued that the familial cases he has observed can be passed down the paternal or

Table 11.2 Transmission data for synaesthesia families

No. of families		= 6	
Total no. of individuals		= 51	
No. of affected individuals		= 26	
Sex ratio of affected individuals	23♀:3♂	= 7.7:1	
Total no. of offspring of affected individuals		= 32 (23♀ and 9♂)	
Sex ratio " " " " females		= 18♀:9♂	
males		= 5♀:0♂	
Transmissions from affected parents to offspring, by sex (affected/total)	♀ → ♀	14/18	77.7%[a]
	♀ → ♂	1/9	11.1%[b]
	♂ → ♀	5/5	100%
	♂ → ♂	0/0	–
Proportion of affected offspring of affected mother/ unaffected father		15/24	62.5%

[a] This proportion changed to 10/14 = 71.4% when transmission rates to multiple female offspring only was considered.

[b] $P < 0.002$ (Fisher's Exact Test) for comparison with proportion affected in female-to-female transmission.

maternal line to affected offspring of either sex, with no skipped generations, in keeping with this MOI. An X-linked dominant MOI would, however, be even more appropriate, given the data from the Cambridge families (see table 11.1), because of the high rate of transmission from affected males to affected daughters (5/5 meioses), although again the numbers are small. In support of this, the proportion of affected offspring from maternal transmissions is a little over the 50 per cent expected under this MOI.

The high ratio of female to male affecteds does not fit well with simple dominant transmission, however. The sex ratio of affected individuals in the general population is also markedly biased towards females. Amongst a self-selected cohort of synaesthetes gathered by Harrison and Baron-Cohen, less than 5 per cent of respondents were male (Baron-Cohen et al. 1993), and most of the respondents reporting affected relatives specified that these were female. Other recent studies have reported female-biased ratios of 2.5:1 (Cytowic 1989a) and 4:1 or 6:1 (Baron-Cohen et al. 1987 and 1993). It should be noted that, other things being equal, an X-linked dominant allele may be more common in females than males purely because of the transmission characteristics of this MOI. Affected heterozygous females will transmit the trait allele to half their offspring of both sexes, but males transmit to all female offspring and to no male offspring, leading to instant bias in the sex ratio of 3:1 in favour of females.

An interesting alternative that would be more in keeping with a female-biased sex ratio of >3:1 would be X-linked dominant inheritance with lethality in hemizygous males. The difference between 'dominant' and 'recessive' alleles in this scenario requires clarification; the lethality aspect would be recessive, acting only in males, where no normal allele is present. In contrast, the synaesthesia (the aspect of the trait we are defining the MOI for) would act in dominant fashion, even in the presence of a normal allele. This MOI is discussed further in section 11.5, but if it is the true MOI, one would predict that the overall sex ratio of offspring of affected mothers would be heavily biased towards females, since 50 per cent of the male foetuses should die *in utero*. The figures for the six families described here are 18 female:9 male offspring (see table 11.2), which matches this prediction. A further prediction under this model would be an increase in the proportion of miscarriages amongst women with synaesthesia.

Autosomal recessive (AR) inheritance cannot be excluded in this small sample, but given the observed family structures, the chance of an affected homozygote having married an unaffected heterozygote (leading to a predicted 50 per cent affected offspring of both sexes, which is not observed here) is low. X-linked recessive inheritance is also extremely unlikely, given the high proportion of female–female transmissions, on the grounds that females should only be affected if they have inherited two copies of the risk allele, one from an affected father and one from a carrier mother. A possible exception to this rule is discussed in the following section.

Each of the studies referred to in this section is liable to various forms of ascertainment bias and this must be taken into account in the interpretation of both the transmission and the prevalence and sex ratio data. Two possible sources of bias are particularly noteworthy. First, most of the subjects gathered from studies reported to date have been to some extent self-referred. This may bias ascertainment towards the more outgoing people with the trait and may under-represent sectors of the affected population in unknown ways. In these cases unsolicited ascertainment may provide a more representative sample of the population. Secondly, in studies of multiply affected families, one must guard against the possibility of the erroneous inclusion of unaffected family members and the exclusion of affected members by misreporting through ignorance. In this case, the extensive use of the test of genuineness would provide the most reliable data at the expense of some of the power of the analysis (if relatives cannot be tested).

Other potential biases may also be of importance. Penetrance of a dominant gene cannot be accurately estimated from these six families, since families in which the affected proband reported *no* affected first-degree relatives are not represented. The status of synaesthesia as a welcome and unusual faculty likely to promote an individual's self-worth (at least after that individual has become apprised of the condition in others), rather than as an abnormality associated with social stigma, is likely to reduce the impact of these biases.

In summary, the likely MOI of synaesthesia in its genetic forms based on earlier studies is unclear. The new study described by Baron-Cohen et al. (submitted) yields some interesting data, but the number of transmissions is insufficient for statistical rigour. In spite of these limitations, two possible MOIs have emerged, namely autosomal dominant and X-linked dominant, with partially sex-limited expression and possibly a high risk of lethality in males in the latter case. These hypotheses cannot be distinguished without knowing whether women with synaesthesia suffer an increased spontaneous miscarriage rate. Further studies should be aimed at gathering larger samples, possibly including the collection and testing of more individuals in each family with multiple affected relatives, and certainly through the use of random sampling methods. The incidence of apparently sporadic cases without parental transmission should also be ascertained in order to estimate the rate of new mutations resulting in trait alleles. Absence of family history does not necessarily preclude a genetic basis to a trait, since apparently sporadic occurrences of a trait are a feature of recessive and complex, polygenic modes of inheritance.

More data on the prevalence in males, transmission rates and sex ratios in paternal transmissions, and the proportion of affecteds amongst siblings of affected males and their offspring will all be useful. It will also be important that all unaffected family members have been ascertained by direct interview rather than by reports from other family members, since some genetic analysis strategies are particularly sensitive to misspecification of affected status.

11.5 Genetic Mechanisms that Could Account for the Possible Modes of Inheritance of Synaesthesia

It may be of some benefit to speculate on the likely genetic mechanisms that could account for the patterns of inheritance described above. One possible, and perhaps the most likely, MOI is X-linked dominant. Examples of diseases thought to show this kind of inheritance (reviewed in Wettke-Schäfer and Kantner 1983) are Rett syndrome (see below), X-linked hypophosphatemia, otherwise known as vitamin D-resistant rickets (Read et al. 1986), Aicardi syndrome (Donnenfeld et al. 1989) and incontinentia pigmenti/focal dermal hypoplasia (Wettke-Schäfer and Kantner 1983).

As we have seen, the very high ratio of females:males with the trait (at least as far as coloured-hearing synaesthesia is concerned) argues against this simple explanation. A modified form of X-linked dominant inheritance has been postulated in a handful of diseases with some of the same transmission characteristics as synaesthesia, including some of those listed above. One of the more interesting of these is Rett syndrome (Rett 1977). This disease is characterized by developmental stagnation, followed by loss of higher brain function and other neurological symptoms, but is not always progressive thereafter. The frequency of the disorder has been estimated at 1/15,000 in parts of Sweden (Hagberg et al. 1985). The interesting feature of the genetics of this disease is that it appears exclusively in girls.

There have been several explanations proposed for this heavily female-biased pattern of inheritance. The first relates to X-linked dominant inheritance with lethality in males, which proposes that possession of a single copy of the gene variant is lethal in hemizygous male foetuses before birth, so that no affected boys are born. Heterozygous female foetuses carrying one normal X chromosome and one with the variant gene would be less severely affected but would develop the disease. The implication is that somehow the presence of one normal copy in females prevents the full, lethal effect of the disease-causing variant, as seen in males, from being expressed.

The explanation for this effect may involve the phenomenon of X-chromosome inactivation ('Lyonization'). Since males only carry one X chromosome, the genes on that chromosome have to function efficiently in single 'dosage' in male cells. Evolution has provided a mechanism for counteracting the undesirable effects of the possession by females of two X chromosomes, through inactivation of the expression of genes from one X chromosome in each of their cells. This means that the genes on only one of a female's two X chromosomes are expressed, producing proteins with normal cellular functions, in any given cell. The important feature of this process is the random nature of the choice, from cell to cell, of which of the two X chromosomes is inactivated. This means that in a woman who is heterozygous for a disease-causing variant of an X-linked gene, approximately 50 per cent of the cells in each of her tissues should express the normal copy and the rest will express the variant ('X-inactivation mosaicism'), giving rise to a phenotype only in the latter cells.

If the disease-causing variant acts by killing the cells in which it is expressed, the normal cells can often take over their function, or their reduced numbers will still suffice for the normal function of the organ or tissue. This is particularly relevant when the gene of interest is expressed in neurons, since there is considerable redundancy in the human brain; a moderate decrease in the number of normally functioning cells in those regions of the brain in which a deleterious gene product is expressed may have little or no observable phenotypic effect at the level of whole-brain function. In the case of Rett syndrome, one could postulate that the variant gene product is lethal to, or compromises the potential for cell division of, all the cells in which it is expressed, thereby preventing antenatal development of the brain in males, with females suffering the severe but non-lethal effects of a reduced number of cells in the relevant brain regions.

A feature of some diseases which operate in this fashion is that most cases are apparently sporadic. In this case, the mothers are not affected, either because they carry new mutations only in a sub-set of eggs ('gonadal mosaicism') or because they tend to inactivate the X chromosome carrying the mutation preferentially (skewed X-inactivation, a common feature of X-linked dominant traits). Alternatively, the affected offspring may have inherited two copies of the maternal X chromosome carrying the disease ('maternal isodisomy'); in this case, skewed X-inactivation in the mother is necessary to explain her lack of symptoms. None of these hypotheses is obviously indicated in synaesthesia, since a high proportion of affected females have affected mothers. Furthermore, there is some dispute over whether any of these phenomena can explain Rett syndrome (Webb et al. 1993) or even whether the Rett locus is on the X chromosome at all (Migeon et al. 1995).

A second possible explanation for the phenomenon of apparent X-linked dominant inheritance with only female affecteds involves the concept of 'metabolic interference'. Johnson (1980) proposed a model in which a deleterious interaction occurs between the normal and variant products of a gene. For X-linked loci the idea is that a hemizygous male carrier of one copy or a homozygous female carrier of two copies of the variant gene produces only variant gene products in expressing cells, just as a normal homozygote or male hemizygote would produce only normal gene product. The products are predicted to function efficiently in their interactions with like products, so that the affected penotype would not be observed in either case. A phenotype will be apparent when the cells of a heterozygous female carrier express both normal and variant products. For this effect to appear dominant, the variant product would have to endow itself or the normal product with a new, deleterious function not observed in the presence of variant product only. Wilkie (1994) has discussed the different ways in which alleles can exert dominant phenotypic effects. Multi-subunit proteins with complex regulatory systems are particularly likely candidates for disruption by this means.

A third possibility relates to the behaviour of the mutation in certain members of a special class of dominant diseases, those caused by expanding trinucleotide repeats. In such diseases, for example Huntington's disease, fragile X syndrome and myotonic dystrophy, the pathology is associated with the inheritance of an expanded tract of tandem copies of a simple sequence repeat at a particular location within the affected genes. The pathological effects of the expansion are triggered when the repeat length exceeds a threshold, typically about 40–50 repeat units. It has become apparent that complicated transmission characteristics of the repeat expansion underlie previously inexplicable phenomena such as reduced penetrance (Shelbourne et al. 1992; Wieringa 1994). Additionally, in fragile X syndrome, expansions in the range 50–200 repeats constitute a 'premutation', unstably transmitted by females, but with no overt symptoms (Fu et al. 1991). Several of the expanding trinucleotide diseases display unusual biases in the transmission of the expansion, with parent-of-origin effects interacting with biased sex-of-offspring effects (Ashizawa et al. 1994; Lavedan et al. 1993; Trottier, Biancalana and Mandel 1994). The relative lack of affected males in synaesthesia could be explained if repeat number was relatively stable on transmission through females, but always expanded after transmission through the male line. Sons of unaffected mothers carrying a premutation would not themselves be affected, but would tend to pass on expanded repeats to all their daughters and to none of their sons, if the gene was X-linked. An analogous mechanism has been proposed for X-linked incontinentia pigmenti (Traupe and Vehring 1994).

Genetic heterogeneity could in principle explain the presence of affected males in the six families discussed above. It is not possible to say whether the same mutation is responsible for all the familial cases of synaesthesia. Different mutations that are not functionally identical may exist in the same gene (allelic heterogeneity) or in completely different genes (locus heterogeneity). Many human diseases display these characteristics, for example allelic heterogeneity in cystic fibrosis and locus heterogeneity in familial Alzheimer's disease. The latter provides a case in point, since mutations in two unlinked but closely related genes, the presenilins, have recently been shown to cause broadly similar but subtly different forms of early onset Alzheimer's in different families (Levy-Lahad et al. 1995; Rogaev et al. 1995; Sherrington et al. 1995). A similar phenomenon occurring in synaesthesia might explain the presence of affected males in a situation where most mutations are lethal *in utero*. One could speculate that mutations leading to novel or modified interactions between the gene product and other proteins could vary in their biological effects; for example, one mutation might lead to the death (by activation of apoptosis pathways perhaps) of all cells containing the product, while another might leave enough cells alive to be compatible with normal but altered brain function, as in the heterozygous females.

Other genetic mechanisms that could explain the observed transmission data are more complicated and will not be discussed in depth. A number of possible explanations exist for the presence of affected males in X-linked dominant conditions with lethality in males. One involves 'half-chromatid mutations', which leaves affected males with one functional copy of the gene in half the cells deriving from the cell in which the mutation took place (Gartler and Francke 1975). Alternatively, affected males could have a partial Klinefelter syndrome karyotype (47, XXY), with an extra, normal copy of the gene on the second X-chromosome, but without the sterility usually associated with this syndrome, possibly as a result of mosaicism.

The apparent dominant nature of the trait allele could also be explained by (a) skewed patterns of X-inactivation in cells of heterozygous females, in which more cells have inactivated the normal chromosome than the trait allele-bearing one; or (b) by maternal isodisomy, as discussed above. Naumova et al. (1995) have reported that skewed X-inactivation patterns may result in an unusual distortion of the expected random segregation of the active and inactive X chromosome to males. There is some evidence that the tendency to undergo X-inactivation skewing may be inherited as a Mendelian trait in some cases (Hoffman and Pegoraro 1995), and concurrence of such a gene with a gene for synaesthesia could conceivably occur. A very few traits have been postulated to be autosomal dominant with female sex-limited expression, but these will not be discussed further. The pattern of inheritance, with no obvious reduction in proportion of affected offspring as one descends a pedigree, is not, however, consistent with a simple polygenic model for this trait.

11.6 Strategies for Detecting and Locating Genes for Synaesthesia

Further studies on the prevalence and transmission characteristics of synaesthesia will be necessary before a full-scale gene search can be instigated. Segregation analysis may prove to be an indispensable tool in this effort, being used to test a series of transmission models, and resulting in an estimate of the most likely mode of inheritance. It can be used to assess the true prevalence of a trait, whether there is significant familial clustering, and the risk to different degrees of relative of affected probands. Being sensitive to ascertainment bias, however, this powerful tool must be used with caution (Lander and Schork 1994). The planning of truly random surveys of a population with minimal admixture (mixing of populations) is crucial.

Once a suspected MOI is established for synaesthesia, the next problem will be to define affected status in such a way that the power to detect trait genes is maintained while keeping the size of the family resource within manageable limits. A useful parameter in this respect is λs, roughly defined as the increased risk to siblings (or other relatives) over the population risk (prevalence) of being affected. Risch (1990) has delineated the constraints on power to detect trait genes that are determined by sample size for this type of study. Detecting and narrowing down the localization in the genome of both simple and complex trait loci is largely achieved by three main types of analysis: linkage (meiotic recombination estimates); allele sharing (within families, the trait will be inherited with particular alleles at closely linked loci); and association (as for allele sharing, but the sharing applies between as well as within families). A typical set of strategies, largely determined by the population prevalence and distribution and mode of inheritance, is summarized below. Two alternative scenarios are discussed.

11.6.1 Autosomal inheritance

Strategies for autosomal dominant and recessive trait mapping begin similarly. Assuming that no cytogenetic or other physical clues as to the location of the trait gene are available (for example, affected probands with chromosomal translocations), the optimal strategy would be to screen the entire autosomal genome with polymorphic markers (a 'genome scan') in the hope of detecting significant evidence for linkage to one or more markers. Linkage analyses yield results in terms of 'lod scores'. An odds ratio of about 2,000:1 in favour of linkage to any one marker (a lod score of 3.3) corresponds to a genome-wide significance level of 5 per cent. This figure has been proposed as the minimum required to demonstrate significant linkage in a genome scan (Lander and Kruglyak 1995). The screen is performed by choosing representative markers spanning each autosome, genotyping families at those markers and running linkage analyses.

Choice of families is crucial to the success of such a screen. Ambiguous individuals may be left out of the analysis because of its sensitivity to misclassification of affected status (Hodge and Greenberg 1992). Paternity of each individual should be examined (confidentially) during the course of the screen. Genotyping is now usually performed by PCR using fluorescent probes incorporated into the PCR product. This technology enables many markers to be analysed simultaneously by polyacrylamide gel electrophoresis. A typical genome scan would include more than 200 individuals from 50 or more medium-sized families, genotyped at 300 or more polymorphic markers. Reed et al. (1994) have established a screening set of 254 highly informative markers at an average spacing in the genome of 13cM. The choice of markers is important, since large gaps may mean that linkage is missed. Marker sets for screening will undoubtedly evolve as chromosomal regions that are particularly gene-rich become the focus for genotyping effort (Antonarakis 1994).

New analytical tools are being developed (O'Connell and Weeks 1995) to eliminate the bottleneck in gene searches – the requirement for vast computer resources and speed when traditional methods of linkage analysis are used (Cottingham et al. 1993; Lathrop et al. 1984). Linkage analysis does, however, suffer from some limitations when applied to traits with complex inheritance. Recently, simpler methods for assessing the extent of gene-sharing amongst affected members of pedigrees, which are applicable to genome scans and do not require any assumptions about MOI, have been employed (Kruglyak and Lander 1995; Weeks and Lange 1992), also with revised guidelines for the interpretation of positive results (Lander and Kruglyak 1995).

If the trait MOI is recessive, other scanning options are available, such as homozygosity mapping (Lander and Botstein 1987). This technique is only possible when there is some guarantee that the two copies of the trait allele segregating in affected individuals are identical by descent, due to consanguinity (inbreeding), so may not be appropriate to a relatively common trait in the general population.

At the end of the genome scan one would hope to have one or more regions thought to contain trait genes. This can be confirmed by replication in independently ascertained families. Promising candidate regions can be narrowed down to less than 1cM by saturation with informative markers. These would be chosen from the very high resolution linkage maps now available (Dib et al. 1996). With luck, linkage disequilibrium may be demonstrated between the trait and some markers. This implies that the marker and trait loci lie so close together that recombinations between them have not dissipated the association between the originally mutated trait gene and the surrounding region.

Association/disequilibrium analysis has been used in several recent studies to refine the position of a disease gene to within 100kbp (for example, see Hastbäcka et al. 1994). At this point, physical techniques can be used to identify possible candidate genes in the region. Clones containing expressed sequences are selected by their position and pattern of expression and analysed to reveal whether they show similarity to other proteins with known functions. Likely candidates are then screened for mutations which segregate exclusively with affected status in the families and which are absent in the general population. Thus a gene 'for' synaesthesia may be identified.

11.6.2 X-linked inheritance

The X-chromosome presents special challenges with respect to gene searches. The basic scan strategy is similar to that for the autosomes, with linkage analysis parameters set for dominant or recessive MOI as appropriate. The difficulties appear when the structure of the X chromosome, its functional attributes and their consequences for patterns of inheritance are considered. Inheritance patterns will be affected, except in very rare cases, if the trait locus lies within the pseudosautosomal region (the region which pairs with the Y chromosome at meiosis), as has been found with several disease genes. Genes have also been found which lie in a region that escapes X-inactivation, or show skewed X-inactivation ratios, either of which could alter expected phenotypes in heterozygous females. Complications can also relate to altered chromosome constitutions. Isodisomy for the affected parental chromosomes in females and partial Klinefelter's syndrome (XXY sex chromosomes) in males can both be involved, as discussed earlier. Both of these possibilities should be evaluated as part of the analysis of the genotyping data for X-linked markers.

11.7 Candidate Processes Lead to Candidate Genes

As discussed in chapter 14 in this volume, by Kennedy, Dehay, Batardiere and Barone, and in chapter 8, by Frith and Paulesu, evidence for a specific neurological basis for coloured-hearing synaesthesia is accumulating. An important feature of the results of the PET study conducted by Paulesu et al. (1995) was that some of the brain areas demonstrating altered blood flow (and hence neuronal activity) during synaesthetic experiences lie at the anatomical junction between areas involved in visual and language processing. There is still much controversy about the source of synaesthetic percepts, those in favour of a model of altered connectivity between associative processing areas (Victor 1989, for example) standing in opposition to those who prefer a hypothesis of unusually strong cross-modal association during higher level, synthetic processing (Rizzo and Eslinger 1989, for example). The latter may or may not be subject to genetically programmed variation, being strongly influenced through learning and experience, but the former undoubtedly has that aptitude. However, a model of altered connectivity would provide molecular geneticists with the easier basis on which to predict possible candidate neural processes, and hence candidate genes, for coloured-hearing synaesthesia.

Altered connectivity may develop in two ways, essentially. First, it may result from the maintenance of early synaptic connections between neurons in different prospective cortical domains. Support for this in synaesthesia is scant, but there is evidence for transient connections between auditory and visual areas in newborn primates (Kennedy, Bullier and Dehay 1989). This might result from an excess of growth factors in the target area for one set of neurons, or from the failure of a group of neurons to undergo apoptosis (programmed cell death) during cortical maturation. Candidates in these two scenarios would include secreted neuronal growth factors, neurotransmitters and their receptors, or enzymes involved in the transduction of signals from these systems.

Secondly, novel neuronal connections may be made mistakenly during development. Good candidates in this scenario would be extracellular matrix molecules involved in axon guidance and survival, ectopically expressed target ligands and, possibly, proteins involved in neuronal migration. Several human genetic disorders have been shown to have aberrant migration of neurons, including those in which specific subsets of neurons are involved. A good example of this is Kallman syndrome, which is caused by mutations in the *KALIG-1* (or *ADMLX*) gene (Hardelin et al. 1992). The primary symptoms, a disrupted sense of smell and altered secondary sexual characteristics, can be traced back to the failure of a specific group of immature neurons to migrate properly from the olfactory placode to their final positions in the olfactory bulb and hypothalamus. Interestingly, the protein product of this gene bears some resemblance to the neuronal cell adhesion molecule, NCAM-L1, which is mutated in, amongst other diseases, X-linked hydrocephalus (Rosenthal et al. 1992). The roles played by growth factors, axonal guidance cues and cell adhesion molecules in the proper development of the human brain are highlighted by these and other neuronal migration disorders.

11.8 Conclusion

This brief exploration of the possible underlying features of synaesthesia has uncovered in the order of several hundred possible candidate genes for the trait, which may seem to be unhelpful. As identification and characterization of the region-specific expression of all brain genes approaches completion, however, it will become increasingly possible to select candidate genes that map to chromosomal regions detected by genetic analysis of a trait. The construction of a combined gene and physical map, necessary for this to work, is well underway (Berry et al. 1995), as is the integration with polymorphic marker maps (Hudson et al. 1995). The burden of analysis will shortly shift away from gene cloning and identification as such, towards the art of gathering appropriate families. The recent prevalence and transmission data for synaesthesia give cause for an optimistic outlook.

References

Antonarakis, S.E. 1994: Genome linkage scanning: systematic or intelligent. *Nature Genetics*, 8, 211–12.

Ashizawa, T., Dunne, P.W., Ward, M.S., Seltzer, W.K. and Richards, C.S. 1994: Effects of the sex of myotonic dystrophy patients on the unstable triplet repeat in their affected offspring. *Neurology*, 44, 120–2.

Baron-Cohen, S., Wyke, M.A. and Binnie, C. 1987: Hearing words and seeing colours: an experimental investigation of a case of synaesthesia. *Perception*, 16, 761–7.

Baron-Cohen, S., Harrison, J., Goldstein, L.H. and Wyke, M. 1993: Coloured speech perception: is synaesthesia what happens when modularity breaks down? *Perception*, 22, 419–26.

Baron-Cohen, S., Burt, L., Smith-Laittan, F., Harrison, J. and Bolton, P. submitted: Synaesthesia: Prevalence and familiality.

Berry, R., Stevens, T.J., Walter, N.A.R., Wilcox, A.S., Rubano, T., Hopkins, J.A., Weber, J., Goold, R., Bento Soares, M. and Sikela, J.M. 1995: Gene-based sequence-tagged-sites (STSs) as the basis for a human gene map. *Nature Genetics*, 10, 415–23.

Calkins, M.W. 1895: Synaesthesia. *American Journal of Psychology*, 7, 90–107.

Corder, E.H., Saunders, A.M., Strittmatter, W.J., Schmechel, D.E., Gaskell, P.C., Small, G.W., Roses, A.D., Haines, J.L. and Perikak-Vance, M.A. 1993: Gene dose of apolipoprotein E type 4 allele and the risk of Alzheimer's disease in late onset families. *Science*, 261, 921–3.

Coriat, I.H. 1913: A case of synesthesia. *Journal of Abnormal Psychology*, 8, 38–43.

Cottingham, R.W., Idury, R.M. and Schaffer, A.A. 1993: Faster sequential genetic-linkage computations. *American Journal of Human Genetics*, 53, 252–63.

Cytowic, R.E. 1989a: *Synesthesia: a union of the senses*. New York: Springer-Verlag.

Cytowic, R.E. 1989b: Synesthesia and mapping of subjective sensory dimensions. *Neurology*, 39, 849–50.

Cytowic, R.E. 1993: *The Man Who Tasted Shapes*. New York: Putnam.

Dib, C., Fauré, S., Fizames, C., Samson, D., Drouot, N., Vignal, A., Millasseau, P., Marc, S., Hazan, J., Seboun, E., Lathrop, M., Gyapay, G., Morissette, J. and Weissenbach, J. 1996: A comprehensive genetic map of the human genome based on 5,264 microsatellites. *Nature*, 380, 152–4.

Donnenfeld, A.E., Packer, R.J., Zackai, E.H., Chee, C.M., Sellinger, B. and Emanuel, B.S. 1989: Clinical, cytogenetic, and pedigree findings in 18 cases of Aicardi syndrome. *American Journal of Medical Genetics*, 32, 461–7.

Fu, Y.-H., Kuhl, D.P.A., Pizzuti, A., Pieretti, M., Sutcliffe, J.S., Richards, S., Verkerk, A.J.M.H., Holden, J.J.A., Fenwick, R.G. Jr, Warren, S.T., Oostra, B.A., Nelson, D.L. and Caskey, C.T. 1991: Variation of the CGG repeat at the fragile X site results in genetic instability: resolution of the Sherman paradox. *Cell*, 67, 1047–58.

Gartler, S.M. and Francke, U. 1975: Half chromatid mutations: transmission in humans? *American Journal of Human Genetics*, 27, 218–23.

Hagberg, B., Aicardi, J., Dias, K. and Ramos, O. 1985: A progressive syndrome of autism, dementia, ataxia, and loss of purposeful hand use in girls: Rett's syndrome: report of 35 cases. *Annals of Neurology*, 14, 471–9.

Hardelin, J.-P., Levilliers, J., del Castillo, I., Cohen-Salmon, M., Legouis, R., Blanchard, S., Compain, S., Bouloux, P. et al. 1992: X chromosome-linked Kallman syndrome: stop mutations validate the candidate gene. *Proceedings of the National Academy of Sciences of the USA*, 89, 8190–4.

Harper, P. 1989: *Myotonic Dystrophy*, 2nd edn. Philadelphia: Saunders.

Hastbäcka, J., de la Chapelle, A., Mahtani, M.M., Clines, G., Reeve-Daly, M.P., Daly, M., Hamilton, B.A., Kusumi, K. et al. 1994: The diastrophic dysplasia gene encodes a novel sulfate transporter: positional cloning by fine-structure linkage disequilibrium mapping. *Cell*, 78, 1073–87.

Hodge, S.E. and Greenberg, D.A. 1992: Sensitivity of lod scores to changes in diagnostic status. *American Journal of Human Genetics*, 50, 1053–66.

Hoffman, E.P. and Pegoraro, E. 1995: Skewed X-inactivation can be inherited as a Mendelian trait in humans. *American Journal of Human Genetics*, 57, A49.

Hudson. T.J., Stein, L.D., Gerety, S.S., Ma, J.L., Castle, A.B., Silva, J., Slonim, D.K., Baptista, R. et al. 1995: An STS-based map of the human genome. *Science*, 270, 1945–54.

Johnson, W.G. 1980: Metabolic interference and the + − heterozygote: a hypothetical form of simple inheritance which is neither dominant nor recessive. *American Journal of Human Genetics*, 32, 374–86.

Kennedy, H., Bullier, J. and Dehay, C. 1989: Transient projection from the superior temporal sulcus to area 17 in the newborn macaque monkey. *Proceedings of the National Academy of Sciences of the USA*, 86, 8093–7.

Kruglyak, L. and Lander, E.S. 1995: Complete multipoint sib-pair analysis of qualitative and quantitative traits. *American Journal of Human Genetics*, 57, 439–54.

Lander, E.S. and Botstein, D. 1987: Homozygosity mapping: a way to map human recessive traits with the DNA of inbred children. *Science*, 236, 1567–70.

Lander, E. and Kruglyak, L. 1995: Genetic dissection of complex traits: guidelines for interpreting and reporting linkage results. *Nature Genetics*, 11, 241–7.

Lander, E.S. and Schork, N.J. 1994: Genetic dissection of complex traits. *Science*, 265, 2037–48.

Lavedan, C., Hofmann-Radvanyi, H., Shelbourne, P., Rabes, J.-P., Duros, C., Savoy, D., Dehaupas, I., Luce, S., Johnson, K. and Junien, C. 1993: Myotonic dystrophy: size- and sex-dependent dynamics of CTG meiotic instability, and somatic mosaicism. *American Journal of Human Genetics*, 52, 875–83.

Lathrop, G.M., Lalouel, J.M., Julier, C. and Ott, J. 1984: Strategies for multilocus linkage analysis in humans. *Proceedings of the National Academy of Sciences of the USA*, 81, 3443–6.

Levy-Lahad, E., Wijsman, E.M., Nemens, E., Anderson, L., Goddard, A.B., Weber, J.L., Bird, T.D. and Schellenberg, G.D. 1995: A familial Alzheimer's disease locus on chromosome 1. *Science*, 269, 970–3.

Migeon, B.R., Dunn, M.A., Thomas, G., Schmeckpeper, B.J. and Naidu, S. 1995: Studies of X-inactivation and isodisomy in twins provide further evidence that the X-chromosome is not involved in Rett-syndrome. *American Journal of Human Genetics*, 56, 647–53.

Motluk, A. 1994: The sweet smell of purple. *New Scientist*, 143, 33–7.

Naumova, A.K., Olien, L., Bird, L.M., Slamka, C., Fonseca, M., Verner, A.E., Wang, M., Leppert, M., Morgan, K. and Sapienza, C. 1995. Transmission-ratio distortion of X-chromosomes among male offspring of females with skewed X-inactivation. *Developmental Genetics*, 17, 198–205.

O'Connell, J.R. and Weeks, D.E. 1995: The VITESSE algorithm for rapid exact multilocus linkage analysis via genotype set-recoding and fuzzy inheritance. *Nature Genetics*, 11, 402–8.

Paulesu, E., Harrison, J., Baron-Cohen, S., Watson, J.D.G., Goldstein, L., Heather, J., Frackowiak, R.S.J. and Frith, C.D. 1995: The physiology of coloured hearing. *Brain*, 118, 661–76.

Read, A.P., Thakker, R.V., Davies, K.E., Mountford, R.C., Brenton, D.P., Davies, M., Glorieux, F., Harris, R. et al. 1986: Mapping of human X-linked hypophosphatemic rickets by multilocus linkage analysis. *Human Genetics*, 73, 267–70.

Reed, P.W., Davies, J.L., Copeman, J.B., Bennett, S.T., Palmer, S.M., Pritchard, L.E., Gough, S.C.L., Kawaguchi, Y. et al. 1994: Chromosome-specific microsatellite sets for fluorescence-based, semiautomated genome mapping. *Nature Genetics*, 7, 390–5.

Rett, A. 1977: Cerebral atrophy associated with hyperammonaemia. In P.J. Vinken and G.W. Bruyn (eds), *Handbook of Clinical Neurology*, vol. 29, Amsterdam: North-Holland, 305–29.

Risch, N. 1990: Linkage strategies for genetically complex traits. I: Multilocus models. *American Journal of Human Cenetics*, 46, 222–8.

Rizzo, M. and Eslinger, P.J. 1989: Colored hearing synesthesia: an investigation of neural factors. *Neurology*, 39, 781–4.

Rogaev, E.I., Sherrington, R., Rogaeva, E.A., Levesque, G., Ikeda, M., Liang, Y., Chi, H., Lin, C. et al. 1995: Familial Alzheimer's disease in kindreds with missense mutations in a gene on chromosome 1 related to the Alzheimer's disease type 3 gene. *Nature*, 376, 775–8.

Rose, K.B. 1909: Some statistics on synaesthesia. *American Journal of Psychology*, 20, 447.

Rosenthal, A., Joulet, M. and Kenwrick, S. 1992: Aberrant splicing of neural cell adhesion molecule L1 mRNA in a family with X-linked hydrocephalus. *Nature Genetics*, 2, 107–12.

Saiki, R.K., Gelfand, D.H., Stoffel, S., Scharf, S.J., Higuchi, R., Horn, G.T., Mullis, K.B. and Erlich, H.A. 1988: Primer-directed enzymatic amplification of DNA with a thermostable DNA-polymerase. *Science*, 239, 487–91.

Shelbourne, P., Winqvist, R., Kunert, E., Davies, J., Leisti, J., Thiele, H., Bachmann, H., Buxton, J., Williamson, R. and Johnson, K. 1992: Unstable DNA may be responsible for the incomplete penetrance of the myotonic dystrophy phenotype. *Human Molecular Genetics*, 1, 467–73.

Sherrington, R., Rogaev, E.I., Liang, Y., Rogaeva, E.A., Levesque, G., Ikeda, M., Chi, H., Lin, C. et al. 1995: Cloning of a gene bearing mis-sense mutations in early-onset familial Alzheimer's disease. *Nature*, 375, 754–60.

Starr, F. 1893: Note on colour-hearing. *American Journal of Psychology*, 5, 416–18.

Traupe, H. and Vehring, K.-H. 1994: Unstable pre-mutation may explain mosaic disease expression of incontinentia pigmenti in males. *American Journal of Medical Genetics*, 49, 397–8.

Trottier, Y., Biancalana, V. and Mandel, J.-L. 1994: Instability of CAG repeats in Huntington's disease: relation to parental transmission and age of onset. *Journal of Medical Genetics*, 31, 377–82.

Victor, J.D. 1989: Coloured hearing synesthesia. *Neurology*, 39, 1409–10.

Webb, T., Watkiss, E. and Woods, C.G. 1993: Neither uniparental disomy nor skewed X-inactivation explains Rett-syndrome. *Clinical Genetics*, 44, 236–40.

Weeks, D.E. and Lange, K. 1992: A multilocus extension of the affected-pedigree-member method of linkage analysis. *American Journal of Human Genetics*, 50, 859–68.

Wettke-Schäfer, R. and Kantner, G. 1983: X-linked dominant inherited diseases with lethality in hemizygous males. *Human Genetics*, 64, 1–23.

Wieringa, B. 1994: Myotonic dystrophy reviewed: back to the future? *Human Molecular Genetics*, 3, 1–7.

Wilkie, A.O.M. 1994: The molecular basis of genetic dominance. *Journal of Medical Genetics*, 31, 89–98.

Part IV
Developmental Perspectives

12

Synaesthesia: Implications for Modularity of Mind

Gabriel M.A. Segal

12.1 Introduction

I shall argue that synaesthesia provides further evidence for the existence of cognitive modules, in Fodor's (1983) sense of the term. The argument is not entirely conclusive, but it has some plausibility and raises some interesting issues along the way.

A module, in Fodor's sense, is a classical computer in the mind/brain. As such, it is the kind of thing standardly posited to explain cognitive capacities by classical cognitive science. But Fodor modules are characterized by a list of further features:

1 dedicated neural architecture;
2 mandatory operation;
3 informational encapsulation;
4 inaccessibility to central processes;
5 rapid speed;
6 shallow outputs;
7 domain specificity;
8 characteristic pattern of breakdown;
9 fixed pattern of development.

One of Fodor's aims is to delineate a psychological natural kind; a type of cognitive mechanism that is a real and important component of cognition, and an interesting topic of enquiry for psychology. I think it is fair to say that Fodor made an impressive start at characterizing a psychological natural kind, but that his work should be seen as the beginning of a larger enterprise which would involve, among other things, clarifying which are the most important features of modules and which are incidental; how the features interrelate; which areas of cognition are explicable by modules and which are not, and so on. Fodor formed valuable initial hypotheses about these matters, but further work needs to be done to get a full picture.

I shall be particularly concerned with the developmental aspect of modularity. Modules have characteristic patterns of development. The natural explanation of this feature, which Fodor would certainly accept, is that the pattern is genetically determined. Modules grow in the mind/brain according to a genetically specified pattern. What this means is that for each module, M, some property, P, of the subject's genetic code is (a) *ceteris paribus*, a necessary condition of development of M: unless something absolutely extraordinary occurs, an embryo lacking P will not grow into a being with M; and (b) a sufficient condition for the development of M, in normal circumstances. That is to say, there exist environmental and endogenous conditions that are in fact the normal ones for humans, and, in those conditions, P suffices for growth of M.

The key point here is not affected by the details of how genetic programming interacts with the environment to determine the pattern and endpoint of growth. Rather, it is that whatever account applies to the growth of physical characteristics also applies to modules. The growth of mental organs is the same kind of phenomenon as the growth of physical ones.

Most humans grow two arms, one heart, two eyes and so on. This is what is normally coded in the genes. But, of course, some humans do not: they may lack arms, they may grow an extra eye or nipple, they may grow webbing between their toes, they may grow fewer than the normal number of fingers. Often such abnormalities are due to some abnormal characteristic of the genetic code. So, if a theory predicts that the development of mental organs is like that of physical ones, it will predict the occasional abnormality. Sometimes a genetic abnormality will lead to a lack of some or all of a mental organ. Sometimes it may lead to selective impairment – or improvement. And sometimes it will lead to the growth of an extra module or sub-module.

The reader will perhaps have predicted my argument. Synaesthetes have an abnormal genetic property that leads to the growth of an extra module – roughly analogous to the growth of an extra finger or pupil. This lends support to Fodor's general conception of modularity in two ways. First, the conception would predict the existence of some genetic abnormalities that yield abnormalities in the growth of modules in ways that parallel such phenomena in the physical realm. Secondly, if synaesthetes have an extra module, then it is one more instance of the psychological natural kind the existence of which Fodor argued for.

12.2 The Colour–Grapheme Synaesthetic Mechanism as a Computer

Since a module is a special kind of computer, the first point to investigate is whether it is plausible to suppose that the synaesthetic mechanism is a computational one. I shall focus on the special case of synaesthesia that Baron-Cohen et al. (1993) call CG (colour–grapheme) synaesthesia. This appears to be the most common form of synaesthesia: nine out of nine subjects tested by Baron-Cohen et al. and five out five tested by Paulesu et al. (1995) were found to have CG synaesthesia, rather than some other form. In CG synaesthesia, subjects experience colours when they hear spoken words, and the mapping from words to colours is typically determined by the first letter of the word as it is spelt. Sometimes the mapping isn't perfect, the colour of some words not being determined by their first letters. And often CG synaesthetes also experience colours on hearing non-verbal sounds. But I shall ignore these complications, except where they are clearly relevant to my argument, and for the most part consider only the CG mapping property of the synaesthetic mechanism.

A computer is a representation processor. It is a mechanism that takes representations as inputs and produces representations as outputs. A representation is a physical configuration of some kind that has both syntactic and semantic properties. Utterances and inscriptions of English sentences are examples of representations in the relevant sense. The physical configuration might be vibrations in the air (utterances) or chalk dust on a blackboard, or pencil lead on paper. These configurations have syntactic properties: that is to say, they have an identity as symbols that can be specified independently of what they mean. Thus 'fish swim' is a particular sentence, composed of a particular common noun (the word 'fish') and a particular verb (the word 'swim'). And the very same sentence, syntactically specified, can be realized by vastly different physical configurations: vibrations in the air, collections of chalk dust, and so on. And these configurations also have semantic properties: 'fish' means fish and 'swim' means swim and 'fish swim' means that fish swim.

A computer maps representations on to representations. Thus, given the physical realization of a certain representation, physical, causal processes ensue that culminate in the production of another physical configuration that is also a representation. If the computer is a pocket calculator, and you type in ⟨'4' ^ '−' ^ '2' ^ '='⟩, causal processes occur that will culminate in the production of a '2'. Further, the input–output relation is a function that is determined by the representations' syntactic properties. So, given an input of syntactic type T1, there is a specific output of syntactic type T2 that the machine will produce.

Computers compute functions. The function is fixed by the semantic properties of the representations. The input representations represent elements in the domain of the function, and the output representations represent elements in its range. For example, an adding machine computes a function from pairs of numbers to their sums. The pairs of numbers are represented by the numerals that are the input representations, and their sums are represented by the numerals that are the output representations. Thus if you type in the numerals, 2 and 3 the machine will produce 5. The inputs represent the numbers 2 and 3, and the output represents the number 5.[1]

There are, in fact, three functions involved in computation. There is a 'syntactic function' from input representations to output representations; there is a 'semantic function' from what the input representations represent to what the output representations represent; and, finally, there is an 'interpretation function' that connects the two and maps the representations on to their semantic interpretations.

When one posits a module to explain some aspect of a being's cognition, it must be possible to characterize that aspect of cognition in terms of a semantic function. For example, the early visual system can be seen as computing a function from pairs of light patterns (on the retinas) to the shapes, locations, orientations, and so on of three-dimensional objects in objective space (see Marr 1982). Various modules are also involved in language acquisition and use, for example, effecting the mapping from speech sounds to meaning that is required for understanding a heard utterance (for extensive discussion, see Larson and Segal 1995).

It is often useful to think of computers as having tasks or goals. An adding machine has the goal of adding; the visual system has the goal of extracting information about the physical structure of the world from retinal images; a chess-playing machine has the goal of winning games of chess. The goal of a computer will usually be closely related to the function it computes. But it need not be identical to it. For example, it is useful to view the visual system as having the goal of extracting veridical information about the world. And it is reasonably successful: the function it computes usually produces true outputs, veridical representations of the external world. But the visual system need not be, and is not, perfect. Sometimes it computes false representations, and we get visual illusions.

There are at least three different attitudes we might take to the idea that computers, particularly those that are also cognitive systems, have goals. At one extreme is the view that it is essential to computers, at least those that are cognitive systems, that they actually have goals which derive from an actual designer; either a sentient one or natural selection (Lycan 1987; Millikan 1984; Papineau 1993). Thus the visual system has the goal of constructing veridical representations because this is what nature designed it to do. In the middle is the view that computers have goals, but these are directly determined by their intrinsic properties. Roughly, the idea is that if one can make sense of the activity of a system by ascribing it a goal, then that by itself validates the ascription. Thus the visual system really has the goal of constructing veridical representations. But it has this goal because this is what it usually does, and not because this is what Mother Nature designed it to do. One adopts what Daniel Dennett calls the 'design stance', but does not literally require any actual designer (Cummins 1989). At the other extreme is the fully reductive view that all talk of goals and design is a mere *façon de parler*. Adopting heuristic assumptions about design might sometimes be a useful guide to research, but amounts to no more than that. On this view, the visual system computes the function it does, and that is all there is to it. When the system is confronted with, for example, a Muller–Lyer illusion, it computes a representation that is false of the external world. But it is not, in any literal sense, making a mistake or failing to do what it should be doing. It is just doing what it does. Beyond the truth or falsity of the representations, there is no normativity involved.

I shall adopt the third, fully reductive view. One reason for doing this follows from the parallel between physical and cognitive development. If we want to understand how the how various tendons and ligaments hold the knee joint together, or how the kidneys regulate fluids in the body, evolutionary considerations are beside the point. As Chomsky (1995) points out, if it was discovered that our ancestors had been constructed in a laboratory 30,000 years ago, so that natural selection played no role in the evolution of the kidney, this would not lead to any revisions of the technical sections of physiology books concerned with its actual functioning. As Chomsky also says, the same point applies to cognitive systems. The visual system, for example, does what it does, computes what it computes, however it got there.

Of course, evolutionary speculations can be a useful aid to research into the actual workings of a system; and they can be interesting in themselves. But cognitive systems are what they are and do what they do independently of their origins, just as the actual workings of the knee joint or kidneys are as they are, whatever their historical origins.

Ultimately, whether a cognitive system is a computer is a factual question about its intrinsic and current features. If it is a physical system that effects a syntactically determined mapping from representations to representations, and in virtue of doing this computes some kind of semantic function from what the input representations represent to what the output representations represent, then it is a computer. It need not have any actual designer, nor any actual goal. And if it is a computer that has most or all of the characteristics of a Fodor module, then it is a Fodor module – irrespective of whether it was designed by Mother Nature to solve a problem.

If the CG synaesthetic mechanism (hereafter CGM) is a module, it must be a computer in the sense just explained. My first claim is that this is, indeed, so. Here is what I take to be a reasonable but not conclusive argument for the claim. Consider, first, the fact that the CGM maps sounds of words to colours via the words' orthography. Thus when a subject hears someone say, for example, 'phonology', the mechanism produces the particular colour experience that, in this subject, is always associated with 'p' words. There is very good reason to suppose that both the language-precessing and visual mechanisms are themselves computers. And on a standard picture of language processing, the spellings of words are recorded in representations in the lexicon, a particular component of the larger language mechanisms. Further, there is a computational system that maps representations of sounds on to these representations of spellings. This system is the one that allows you to do such things as take dictation. So there is already a mechanism in place to effect the first part of the mapping performed by the CGM – a computer that takes representations of speech sounds to representations of spellings of words. The natural hypothesis, then, is that at least part of the CGM is that very computational mechanism.

The second part of the mapping effected by the CGM is from spellings to colours. We have already supposed that the spellings are internally represented by representations in a computational system involved in language use. So the inputs to the second part of the CGM are representations. What about the outputs? This case is a little harder to make out. But it is reasonably plausible that the colour experiences produced by the visual system are themselves, at least in part, representations. Some philosophers have argued that all colour experiences are purely representational, that sensations of seeing blue or red are really just representations of colours (see, for example, Dretske 1995; Lycan 1987; Tye 1992; Tye 1995). But even if one does not take this extreme view, it is surely fair to suppose that there is at least a representational element in colour experience – that is to say, such experiences may in part be, as it were, 'raw feels'; may have some interesting, introspectible properties that are not representational, but they may also be representations, representing particular colours. Moreover, a number of subjects (six out of seven examined by Baron-Cohen et al. 1993) report that what they experience is the shape of the word in colour: they either see the word as it is spelt, or they see a specific shape uniquely associated with the word. These experiences certainly appear to be representational: what is represented is a certain specific-coloured shape. This fact also suggests an additional computational complexity in the CGM: it draws on information about the spelling of a word in order to construct a corresponding shape. (Think about what would be involved in programming a computer to produce representations of coloured word-shapes given representations of acoustic signals.)

It does, then, seem reasonable to suppose that the CGM is a computer: it maps representations of sounds on to representations of spelling, and it maps these on to representations of coloured shapes.[2]

12.3 The CGM as a Fodor Module

The available evidence does indeed suggest that the CGM has most of the characteristic features of a Fodor module.

12.3.1 *Dedicated neural architecture*

Paulesu et al. (1995) used positron emission topography (PET) to study the neurophysiological correlates of synaesthesia in seven subjects of CG synaesthesia. In comparison with a control group, these subjects 'showed greater activation in a series of multimodal areas including the posterior inferior temporal cortex and the parieto-occipital junctions'. Paulesu et al. take their results to suggest 'that colour word synaesthesia may result from engagement of brain areas associated with language and visual feature integration and that colour word synaesthesia is generated by a unique functional connectivity between these language and vision associated areas'.

Thus the evidence does suggest that the CGM is realized in dedicated neural architecture.

12.3.2 *Mandatory operation*

A cognitive system's operations are mandatory if the subject cannot stop it functioning once it has received a characteristic input. For example, if a normal, open-eyed subject is confronted by a red cube, he or she will be unable to prevent the visual system from forming a representation of a red cube.

All synaesthetes report that they have no control over synaesthetic experiences: on receiving the relevant auditory input, the colour experience occurs willy-nilly. Thus CGM operations are wholly mandatory.

12.3.3 *Informational encapsulation*

A cognitive system is informationally encapsulated if it does not have access to some of the information in the subject's mind. The clearest illustrations of informational encapsulation involve information that is potentially relevant to what the system is doing, but somehow does not affect its functioning. This also may be illustrated by the visual system: visual illusions persist even when the subject knows that they are illusions. Consider, for example, the Muller–Lyer illusion:

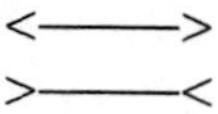

Even if the subject knows that the lines are of the same length, this information does not prevent the visual system representing them as being of different lengths. This shows that potentially relevant information about the perceived world which the subject possesses may fail to affect the workings of the visual system.

It is difficult to see how to conceive of an exact analogy of a visual illusion in the case of the CGM, since the latter does not construct representations that are true or false of an independent reality. Or if it does, then they are always false: representing coloured words or colour patches that do not exist in the external world.

The underlying problem is that is hard to see what would count as 'potentially relevant' information to the CGM. The notion of relevance is clearest when we adopt the design stance, and view the computer as having a goal. Information is potentially relevant if it could be relevant to the pursuit of the goal. It is because we view the visual system as aiming at the construction of veridical representations of the external world that we view information about the length of lines in the Muller–Lyer illusion as potentially relevant to the system's functioning. If we thought of the system as doing something else, we might not count the information as potentially relevant. Since there is no obvious goal we could view the CGM as directed towards, there is no obvious way of saying what information is potentially relevant. Consequently, we cannot easily use the notion of 'potential relevance' to help decide if the CGM is informationally encapsulated.

However, the idea of informational encapsulation does not actually require 'potential relevance'. The real point is that only information from a limited range of sources is accessible to the system. What visual illusions show is that only information from retinal images and information within the system itself is accessible to early vision. Information in central processes is not. And the CGM does appears to be informationally encapsulated in that sense. It appears as though no information available to the subject has any effect on the workings of the CGM: the mapping is fixed by the mechanism's internal properties, and is not responsive to any beliefs or desires on the subject's part.

12.3.4 *Inaccessibility to central processes*

A cognitive system is inaccessible to central processes if some of the information deployed within the system is unavailable to the subject.

The CGM appears to have this feature as well. Subjects may be aware that the association is between graphemes and colours. But they do not appear to be aware of how the system effects the mapping. They do not report awareness of the processes involved in accessing a lexical representation of a word, locating its first letter, constructing the appropriate coloured shape, and so on.

12.3.5 *Rapid speed*

I am not aware of any experimental data on the speed of operation of the CGM. However, it does appear to be rapid.

12.3.6 *Shallow outputs*

An output is shallow if it is phenomenological; that is, if it represents the way world appears and does not represent theoretically inferred, hidden features of the world. The CGM certainly produces shallow outputs in this sense.

12.3.7 *Domain specificity*

Modules are domain-specific in the sense that they are only good for one thing: they aren't general, or multipurpose problem solvers. Fodor emphasizes that domain specificity is not the 'boring' property that all input systems (perceptual and linguistic systems) have, in that each does its own thing: if the visual system maps patterns on retinal images to representations of shape and so on, then *ipso facto*, its domain is restricted to retinal images. Rather, domain specificity requires that the internal workings of the system are specific to a narrow domain; that is, the types of computation involved are specialized, and do not apply in other domains. For example, there is good evidence that language processors used in speech perception deploy information about universal grammar. This information is highly eccentric, and the processes involved in applying it to speech sounds are presumably eccentric as well.

It is not clear to me to what extent the CGM is domain-specific. If most cases of CGM were pure, in the sense that colour experiences were only produced when subjects heard what they could identify as speech, this would be evidence of domain-specificity. This is because, as just mentioned, speech analysers are themselves domain-specific. So if the first component of the CGM, mapping sounds to lexical representations, were comprised of speech analysers, then the CGM would inherit the latters' domain-specificity. But, unfortunately, most CG synaesthetes also report colour experiences on hearing non-words. This suggests that at least part of the synaesthetic mechanism may not be very domain-specific. It may be that it effects a somewhat arbitrary mapping, using computational methods of a non-specialized kind.

It seems, then, that there is a domain-specific component of the CGM, one which deploys specifically linguistic information to specifically linguistic inputs, and one or more further components that may or may not be domain-specific. Further conclusions await further research.

12.3.8 Characteristic pattern of breakdowns

I know of no evidence bearing on this issue. Presumably the CGM is composed of sub-modules, or sub-processors; so there might be cases of selective impairment due to lesions in specific areas. For example, if a subject were to suffer an aphasia which interfered with the ability to spell words, say, with certain types of orthographic irregularity, this might result in corresponding interference to the CGM. However, no test cases for this hypothesis appear to have come to light, as far as I know.

12.3.9 Fixed pattern of development

This is a crucial aspect of modularity, since it points to a specific genetic component. There are good reasons to believe that development of a CGM is genetically determined. First, all subjects report having had synaesthesia for as long as they can remember. This suggests the CGM has a genetic basis, rather than being acquired through some special environmental influence. Secondly, it appears to run in families. All seven of the subjects examined by Baron-Cohen et al. (1993) reported that other family members had synaesthesia. Thirdly, it appears to be very largely confined to females.

Since little is known about the development of synaesthesia, little is known about how characteristic the pattern of development is. However, it is clear that CG synaesthesia cannot precede literacy. If, as most researchers believe, synaesthesia of some other form (say colour–phoneme synaesthesia) is present at birth, it looks as though there is a reasonably characteristic developmental pattern. Initially there is a mechanism that effects some sort of sound–colour mapping and, on acquisition of literacy, they specifically CG mechanism develops. Here again, more substantial conclusions await further research.

12.4 Discussion

It appears that, overall, there is a good case to be made that CG synaesthesia is to be accounted for, at least in part, by presence of an extra module that computes a function from speech sounds to coloured word-shapes. The GC mechanism definitely has most of the Fodor features, and the evidence suggests that it may have the others, at least to some degree, as well.

This conclusion is slightly at odds with the view of Baron-Cohen et al. (1993), endorsed by Paulesu et al. (1994), that synaesthesia is a case of the breakdown of modularity. Certainly in synaesthesia there is, in some sense, a breakdown of the normal development of modularized cognitive systems: in normal adult humans there is no system that causes the specific synaesthetic action of auditory or linguistic modules on visual modules.

It is also possible that synaesthetic mechanisms are the result of an uncompleted process of modularization in the ontogenesis of an individual's cognitive make-up. Maurer (1993) suggests that neonates are normally highly synaesthetic: that sensory inputs in one modality generally cause experiences in others. For example, sounds cause auditory, visual and tactile sensations. During maturation, sensory processing becomes modularized, special-purpose sensory systems developing. If this hypothesis is correct, then adult synaesthesia might be the result of an incomplete process of modularization.

But even if this is so, it does not seem that the failure of the modularization process to arrive at its normal conclusion is a cognitive architecture that is less modular than normal. For synaesthetes do not lack visual or auditory modules: the existence of an additional connection between auditory and visual systems does not make the latter any the less modular. All the criteria for modularity still apply to them. Nor is GC synaesthesia a case of leaking buckets, as if the language-processing modules had not been fully formed and had leaked information into some neighbouring area. Rather, some mechanism draws on information about the orthography associated with an acoustic signal and then actually builds up a representation of a coloured shape. The cognitive architecture of synaesthesia is not less modular than normal but, at least in a sense, more so.[3]

Notes

1 This paragraph makes an idealization, for the sake of simplicity. Some computers do not compute functions in exactly the sense I just explained, but I shall ignore that for the purposes of this chapter.

2 Obviously, my argument that the CGM is a computer hinges on the view that it is not a necessary condition of something's being a computer, or being a genuine cognitive system, that it have a designer. However, most philosophers who view design as essential to cognition do so only because they view it as essential to representationality. Interestingly, my argument does not necessarily conflict with this view. I argued that the representations mediated by the CGM already feature in linguistic and visual systems. Thus their representationality could derive from the evolution of these latter systems.

3 Thanks to Simon Baron-Cohen, Michael Martin and David Papineau for helpful comments and criticisms on earlier drafts of this paper.

References

Baron-Cohen, S., Harrison, J., Goldstein, L. and Wyke, M. 1993: Coloured speech perception: is synaesthesia what happens when modularity breaks down? *Perception*, 22, 419–26.

Chomsky, N. 1995: Language and nature. *Mind* 104, 413, 1–61.

Cummins, R. 1989: *Meaning and Mental Representation*. Cambridge, Mass.: MIT Press.

Dretske, F. 1995: *Naturalizing the Mind*. Cambridge, Mass.: MIT Press.

Fodor, J. 1983: *The Modularity of Mind*. Cambridge, Mass.: MIT Press.

Larson, R. and Segal, G. 1995: *Knowledge of Meaning: an introduction to semantic theory*. Cambridge, Mass.: MIT Press.

Lycan, W.G. 1987: *Consciousness*. Cambridge, Mass.: MIT Press.

Marr, D. 1982: *Vision*. San Francisco, Cal. W.H. Freeman.

Maurer, D. 1993: Neonatal synaesthesia: implications for the processing of speech and faces. In B. de Boysson-Bardies, S. de Schonen, P. Jusczyk, P. McNeilage and J. Morton (eds), *Developmental Neurocognition: speech and face processing in the first year of life*, Dordrecht: Kluwer.

Millikan, R. 1984: *Language, Thought and Other Biological Categories: new foundations for realism*. Cambridge, Mass.: MIT Press.

Papineau, D. 1993: *Philosophical Naturalism*. Oxford: Blackwell.

Paulesu, E., Harrison, J., Baron-Cohen, S., Watson, J.D.G., Goldstein, L.H., Heather, J., Frackowiak, R.S.J. and Frith, C.D. 1995: The physiology of coloured-hearing: a PET activation study of colour–word synaesthesia. *Brain*, 118, 661–76.

Tye, M. 1992: Visual qualia and visual content. In T. Crane (ed.), *The Contents of Experience*, Cambridge: Cambridge University Press.

Tye, M. 1995: *Ten Problems of Consciousness: a representational theory of the phenomenal mind*. Cambridge, Mass.: MIT Press.

13

*Neonatal Synaesthesia: Implications for the Processing of Speech and Faces**

Daphne Maurer

13.1 Introduction

The focus of this chapter is the integration of vision and hearing with each other and with the other senses. Based on a re-analysis of the published literature and some new data of my own, I will hypothesize that the young infant confuses the input from different senses. Early cross-modal transfer is based on that confusion rather than the recognition of objects in more than one modality. I will then discuss the implications for studies of babies' reactions to faces and to speech during early infancy.

13.2 Background to the Hypothesis

13.2.1 Development of cross-modal transfer

Many of the data on the development of cross-modal transfer fit Piaget's description of the baby's gradually learning to interrelate separate schemas toward the end of the first year of life (Piaget 1952). For example, according to Piaget, the baby develops separate schemas for listening, for looking, and for sucking, which the functional principle of organization causes subsequently to become interrelated. Although automatic reciprocal assimilations can form early in development,

*Reprinted from B. de Boysson-Bardies et al. (eds) *Developmental Neurocognition: speech and face processing in the first year of life*, Dordrecht: Kluwer, 109–24.

connections involving the understanding of an object's identity are not apparent until Stage 4 of sensorimotor development, typically in the second half of the first year of life.

The data from many studies fit Piaget's description (reviewed in Rose and Ruff 1987). For example, Rose, Gottfried and Bridger (1978, 1981b) found that full-term, middle-class 12-month-olds looked longer at a novel object than at an object they had just explored for 30 seconds by mouth. In contrast, lower-class or preterm 12-month-olds showed no such preference. Neither did full-term, middle-class 6-month-olds even when the object remained in the mouth during the visual test and even when the oral familiarization time was increased to 60 seconds. (In every case, babies looked longer at the novel object following a comparable period of *visual* exposure to the other object.) Taken together, these results suggest that cross-modal transfer is an ability just emerging toward the end of the first year of life. That conclusion is also supported by evidence that 6- to 12- month-olds are likely to demonstrate cross-modal transfer only after long and active exploration of the object in the first modality, longer and more active exploration than is required for intra-modal recognition (e.g. Hernandez-Reif 1992; Rose, Gottfried and Bridger 1981a).

13.2.2 Cross-modal effects in the first month of life

Cross-modal transfer At the same time, there are cross-modal effects in the first month of life. The best-known example is the study by Meltzoff and Borton (1979) with smooth and nubby pacifiers. One-month-olds sucked on a pacifier for 90 seconds, then were shown large versions of the two pacifiers side-by-side for 20 seconds. Both in the original study and in a replication, most babies (72 and 67 per cent) looked longer at the pacifier shaped like the one they had just sucked on. Walker-Andrews and Gibson (1986) reported similar results for one-month-olds who had sucked on a rigid or a soft pacifier, except in this case babies looked longer at the pacifier they had *not* just sucked on.

Further evidence of cross-modal matching comes from a study by Lewkowicz and Turkewitz (1980) on auditory and visual intensity. One-month-olds were familiarized for 20 trials with a patch of white light of 39 cd/m^2, then presented with bursts of white noise at seven levels of intensity between 68 and 80 dB, interspersed with the familiar patch of light. Instead of the normal monotonic increase in cardiac response with increased auditory intensity, infants' heart rate changed least when they heard the 74 dB white noise and changed increasingly for sounds either more or *less* intense. Interestingly, adults chose 74 dB as the best cross-modal match to 39 cd/m^2, the intensity of light to which the babies had been habituated. In other words, exposure to light influenced one-month-olds' reaction to sound, and the pattern of reaction suggested the matching of intensity between vision and hearing: least response to the 'familiar' intensity. To verify this interpretation, Lewkowicz and Turkewitz familiarized another group of babies with a more intense light (138 cd/m^2). As expected, this time the least change in heart rate occurred at a higher intensity of sound. Adults' heart rate in response to each intensity of sound was not influenced by prior exposure to light. Together, the results suggest that, unlike adults, one-month-olds do not register the modality through which a stimulus is presented and respond to changes in the intensity of stimulation impinging anywhere on the nervous system.

Cross-modal effects in primary sensory cortex There are also reports of cross-modal effects in the cortical responses of young babies. For example, Wolff and his colleagues (1974) reported that in newborns, unlike adults, the amplitude of the somatosensory potential evoked by electrical stimulation of the wrist increases when white noise is also played. During early infancy – and only during early infancy – Neville (in Boysson-Bardies et al. 1993) recorded evoked responses to spoken language not just over the temporal cortex, where one would expect to find them, but over the occipital cortex as well. There are similar reports of widespread cortical responses to visual stimuli during the first two months of life (e.g. Hoffmann 1978). Results such as these suggest that primary sensory cortex is not so specialized in the young infant as in the adult.

Optimal level of stimulation Young infants also appear to seek out an optimal level of stimulation, summed across all sensory modalities. In a quiet lab, they prefer middling stimulation. They look longer at a light flashing at 6–8 Hz than at a light flashing faster or slower (Karmel et al. 1977). They look longer at a mid-grey square than at a black or a white square (Hershenson, Kessen and Munsinger 1967). They look longest at a figure with a middling number of elements (Miranda and Fantz 1971; Hershenson, Munsinger and Kessen 1965), extend their fingers most toward a sound of middling intensity (Turkewitz et al. 1971), and suck most for a sucrose solution of middling concentration (Crook 1978).

But only in a quiet lab. If the babies have just heard a lot of noise – or been stimulated by an intense stimulus in any other sensory modality – the preference shifts to a lower value (reviewed in Turkewitz, Gardner and Lewkowicz 1984). For example, Lewkowicz and Turkewitz (1981) found that, as expected, newborns look longer at a middling grey square than at a lighter or darker square – unless they have just been stimulated by a burst of white noise. In that case, they look longest at the darkest square. Results like these suggest that the newborn seeks an optimal level of stimulation summed across all the senses (a very low level at first, although with development it increases: Schneirla 1959).

If the baby receives too much stimulation, he or she will go to sleep. This happens when the baby is exposed to intense stimulation through one modality – say intense light or sound – but also if the baby is exposed to moderate stimulation simultaneously through several modalities – say moderate light plus moderate sound. This pattern is apparent in a compilation of studies on infants' sleep (Maurer and Maurer 1988: 69–70) and in several studies by Brackbill (1970, 1971, 1973, 1975). For example, Brackbill (1971) observed newborns exposed to two different levels of sound, light and temperature, and who were either swaddled or not. The sources of stimulation were interchangeable in their effect. What mattered was how many modalities were stimulated at the higher level: the more modalities stimulated, the more likely the babies were to be asleep.

13.3 Neonatal Synaesthesia

In sum, during the first month of life, there is evidence of cross-modal matching, of 'inappropriate' responses in primary sensory cortex, and of cross-modal summation in the determination of preferences and of sleep. Yet at the same time there is evidence of the emergence of cross-modal transfer much later during infancy. All of this evidence makes sense if one postulates that the newborn's senses are not well differentiated but are instead intermingled in a synaesthetic confusion. If this is true, then for the newborn, energy from the different senses, including the proprioceptive sense of his or her own movement, is largely if not wholly undifferentiated: the newborn perceives changes over space and time in the quantity of energy, not the sense through which it arose.

Two principles appear to govern the baby's behaviour: (a) keep the sum of energy entering all sensory channels within an optimal range and (b) when the sum is at an appropriate level, attend to the familiar patterning of the energy *regardless of the modality of origin* until a schema is well-formed, then search out a novel pattern of energy. During early infancy the optimal range of stimulation is so low that the sum is rarely at a level appropriate for the second principle to operate. Furthermore, only with development do the sensory systems become differentiated enough that adult patterns of cross-modal transfer can develop.

The first principle is apparent from experimental evidence of the type summarized above. The second principle is well-established within the visual modality (e.g. Hunter, Ames and Koopman 1983; Rose et al. 1982; Wagner and Sakovits 1986): after short exposure to a visual stimulus, babies look longer at it than at a novel object, but after longer exposure – presumably after a schema is well-formed – babies look longer at a novel object. My second principle is similar, only it applies to patterns of energy regardless of the modality through which they arise.

13.3.1 Anatomical evidence

Two anatomical mechanisms could cause neonatal synaesthesia. First is that babies, like other mammals, are born with transient connections between many neural structures (reviewed in Bourgeois, in Greenough and Alcantara, in Scheibel, in Garey, and in Kennedy and Dehay, all in Boysson-Bardies et al. 1993). For example, the neonatal hamster has transient connections between the retina and the main somatosensory and auditory nuclei of the thalamus (Frost 1984; reviewed in Frost 1990). The kitten has transient connections between visual, auditory, somatosensory and motor cortices (Dehay, Bullier and Kennedy 1984; Dehay, Kennedy and Bullier 1988). Although these specific connections have not been found in the monkey, the monkey's brain does contain many transient connections at birth and subsequently undergoes considerable rewiring (Kennedy, Bullier and Dehay 1989; Meissierel et al. 1991; see also Kennedy and Dehay, and Gross and Rodman, both in Boysson-Bardies et al. 1993). Such transient connections could explain why, in babies, primary sensory cortex responds to stimuli from the 'wrong' modality. They could well support synaesthetic interactions in the newborn and, for that matter, in the young of other species (e.g. Spear et al. 1988).

Alternatively, or additionally, the newborn's apparent synaesthesia could be the manifestation of connections within the midbrain which later become inhibited by the cortex. This possibility is suggested by Cytowic's (1988) study of a gustatory synaesthete for whom tastants and odorants induced tactile perceptions. Spearmint evoked the feeling of smooth, cold, glass columns; strawberry evoked round spheres. Cortical depressants – ethanol and amyl nitrate – increased the synaesthetic experiences so that spearmint evoked the perception of being in among the columns, touching and feeling their surfaces on the hands, back, cheeks and arms. Cortical stimulants – nicotine, amphetamines and caffeine – diminished the synaesthesia: the columns seemed more distant, slipping out of the hands. This pattern suggests that the cortex can inhibit synaesthesia. That suggestion was confirmed by a study of how blood flowed through the synaesthete's brain. At the same time that spearmint evoked synaesthesia, the level of blood flow in the parietal cortex and parts of the frontal and temporal cortex dropped to nearly the level observed in strokes. Note that this man showed no other evidence of cortical abnormality and has a full-scale IQ of 129.

Cytowic's data indicate that cross-modal intrusions can occur when the cortex is not functioning fully. Because the cortex is not functioning fully during early infancy (reviewed in Johnson and in Atkinson, both in Boysson-Bardies et al. 1993), the young infant might be synaesthetic. With development, any such synaesthesia will decrease both because the cortex functions better and because transient connections have been pruned. As a result, the sensory systems will become more differentiated and so will the baby's perceptions. The baby will become better aware of whether he or she is seeing an object, tasting it or feeling it. Then he or she is set to develop 'real' cross-modal matching and transfer.

13.3.2 Predictions

Meltzoff and Borton's (1979) results should be replicable but ephemeral, most likely to be demonstrated when the overall level of stimulation is low. From the perspective presented here, Meltzoff and Borton did not discover cross-modal transfer between the feel and the sight of a nubby or a smooth pacifier. Instead they documented one-month-olds' confusion between oral and visual stimulation. The babies sensed smoothness or nubbiness – continuity or discontinuity of energy – through the mouth *and* through the eyes. Since most one-month-olds do not form complete schemas for shapes in 90 seconds, babies attended to the familiar pattern of energy, unaware that it was now coming from a new modality.

As predicted, two- to four-week-olds failed to demonstrate cross-modal transfer from the mouth to the eyes in two studies (Pecheux, Lepecq and Salzurolo 1988; Brown and Gottfried 1986) in which the overall level of stimulation was higher than in the original study by Meltzoff and Borton (1979). In the study by Pecheux et al. (1988),[1] the babies were slightly younger (and hence likely to have a lower range of optimal stimulation), the pacifiers were larger and more malleable, the visual stimuli were larger, and the experimenter attracted the baby's attention to the screen before the visual test. In the study by Brown and Gottfried (1986), each baby was tested with four different pair of shapes arranged into two oral–visual problems and two manual–visual problems. Differences in overall level of stimulation may also explain why Born, Spelke and Prather (1982) found that newborns looked toward the visual pattern which matched the sound they were hearing for only one of the three visual/auditory combinations they tested.

As the cortex matures, the early apparent cross-modal transfer should decrease, to be followed by the development of a more analytic cross-modal transfer. Although some aspects of synaesthesia probably never disappear (see, for example, Marks 1975; Zellner and Kautz 1990), the older infant, like the adult, differentiates between hearing, seeing and feeling an object, and must learn to interconnect these different experiences of the same object. Indeed, in two of the few studies to test babies with the same paradigm at different ages, young babies appeared to show cross-modal transfer, yet on the same task, four- to six-month-olds did not. Thus, after Streri (1987; Streri and Pecheux 1986) repeatedly gave babies a shape to hold until they became habituated tactually, two-month-olds looked longer at a novel shape, appearing to show cross-modal transfer, yet four- to five-month-olds did not. Similarly, Pickens, Nawrocki and Soutullo (1992) reported that five- to six-month-olds looked equally often toward a face reading a passage that they were hearing and a face reading a different passage, yet younger (three- to four-month-olds) and older (seven- to eight-month-olds) babies looked at the matching face. These odd developmental patterns make sense if the baby changes from apparent cross-modal transfer based on synaesthetic confusion to cross-modal transfer based on connections between differentiated sensory modalities.

Cross-modal transfer with nubby and smooth pacifiers at one and three months of age To test whether cross-modal transfer also disappears for the smooth and nubby pacifiers introduced by Meltzoff and Borton (1979), we have repeated their study at one and three months of age. As in the original study, babies sucked on a smooth or nubby pacifier for 90 seconds (n = two groups of 16 at each age), then were presented with large orange versions of the two pacifiers against a black background for 20 seconds from the time of the first look. Unlike Meltzoff and Borton, we included a second 20-second test trial with the positions of the pacifiers reversed left-to-right and, as a baseline, we included a third group of 16 babies at each age who sat in the apparatus without sucking during the 90 seconds before the visual test. At neither age was there evidence of cross-modal transfer. The three-month-olds in the baseline group looked significantly longer at the nubby pacifier than at the smooth pacifier, a preference which was reduced following 90 seconds of sucking on *either* a smooth or nubby pacifier (see figure 13.1). In other words, extra stimulation with either form reduced their preference for discontinuous energy. In contrast to the three-month-olds and to the results of Meltzoff and Borton (1979), the visual preferences of one-month-olds were not altered by sucking on either pacifier (Stager 1992).

There is no ready explanation of our failure to replicate the results of Meltzoff and Borton (1979) with one-month-olds. One possibility is our addition of the second test trial and the baseline group, but even restricting the analyses to the two used in the original article, the results are significant only for one of the two analyses, and then in the

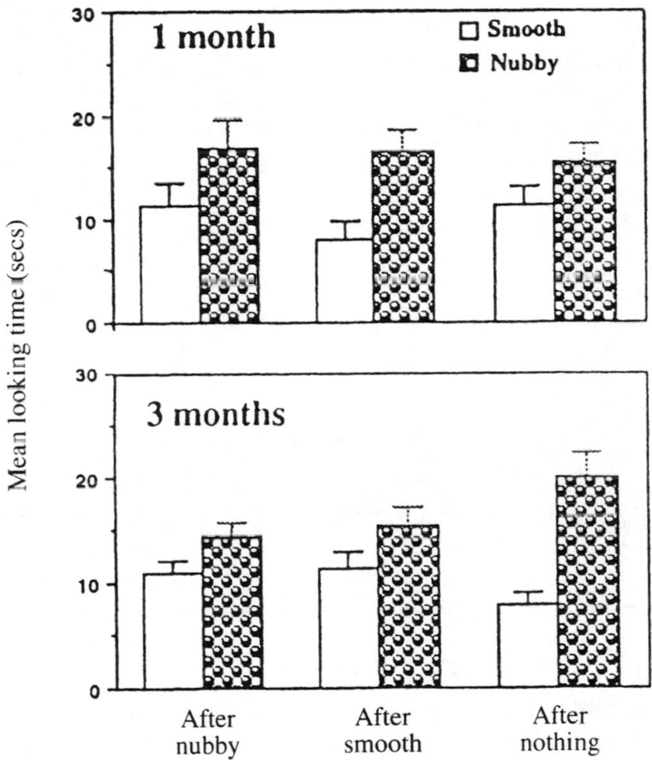

Figure 13.1 Mean looking time (+1 S.E.) summed across the two test trials for one-month-old babies (top) and three-month-old babies (bottom) presented with smooth (white bars) and nubby (spotted bars) pacifiers following 90 seconds of sucking on a nubby pacifier (left bars), of sucking on a smooth pacifier (middle bars), or of no oral stimulation (baseline group; right bars)

opposite direction: a significant number of babies looked at the *novel* shape, not the familiar shape as Meltzoff and Borton found in both their original study and its replication.[2] A more likely explanation is that we changed some aspect of the procedure which would be unimportant to an adult but which changes the task profoundly for the synaesthetic infant. In retrospect we are aware of three changes: a slide projector added some white noise to the room; the babies wore green or blue capes to prevent them from putting their hands in their mouths; and the experimenter did not rotate the baby 180° and centre his or her head just before the visual test, as Meltzoff and Borton had done. Whatever the explanation, the results, like previous research (Brown and Gottfried 1986; Pecheux, Lepecq and Salzarulo 1988; Lewkowicz et al. 1984), indicate that cross-modal transfer during early infancy is ephemeral and may be overridden by the baby's seeking an optimal level of stimulation across all modalities.

Shifting visual preferences If babies seek out patterns of energy regardless of modality, then cross-modal transfer during early infancy should not be specific. The baby should show transfer from sucking on a smooth or nubby pacifier to looking at a variety of visual stimuli which capture smoothness or nubbiness, or continuity or discontinuity of energy. There should be similar transfer from hearing continuous or fluttering tones. Such general transfer should decrease with age, as the senses become better differentiated and as cross-modal transfer develops based on the identification of objects and their properties.

To test whether early cross-modal transfer reflects cross-modal matching or cross-modal confusion, we created pairs of stimuli matched in total contour and in area which differed in the continuity of their contours (see figure 13.2). We also included photographs of orange smooth and nubby pacifiers. The experiments are not complete, but the baseline results indicate the influence of synesthesia.

We tested one-month-olds after they had sat in the dark for 90 seconds (the period during which the babies in the experimental groups will suck on nubby or smooth pacifiers or listen to continuous or fluttering tones). We then presented each pair of stimuli until the baby had looked for ten seconds on each of two trials, with the position of the two stimuli reversed left-to-right between trials.

One group of 24 one-month-olds we tested with four pair of stimuli. They looked significantly longer at the nubby pacifier and a split circle than at the smooth pacifier and an intact circle (see figure 13.2, top panel). For the other two pairs, they showed no preference. In contrast, when another group of 32 one-month-olds saw these same four pairs of stimuli intermixed with three other comparable pairs, they looked

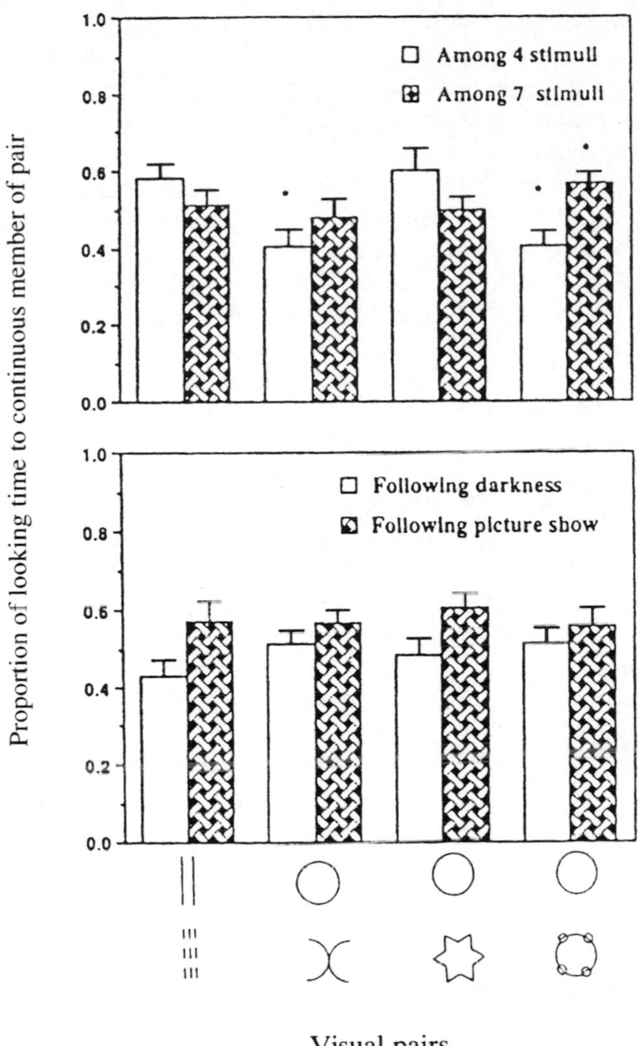

Figure 13.2 Visual preferences of one-month-old babies for three pairs of stimuli differing only in continuity versus discontinuity of energy and for photographs of nubby and smooth pacifiers

Note: Figure shows the proportion of looking time directed to the continuous member of each pair. Top graph contrasts results when these four pairs were presented alone (white bars) with results when these four pairs were intermixed with three other pairs (hatched bars). Asterisks indicate significant preferences by one-sample t-test against a chance value of 0.50. The bottom graph contrasts results when the test followed 90 seconds of darkness (white bars) or a 90-second picture-show (hatched bars). An ANOVA indicated that infants looked longer at the continuous member of each pair following the picture-show.

significantly longer at the smooth pacifier than at the nubby and looked equally long at the split and intact circles. Note that the babies exposed to only four pairs of stimuli had received less visual stimulation overall and looked longer at the more variable discontinuous member of two of the pairs.

To verify the interpretation that babies' preferences are easily modified by overall level of stimulation, we repeated the test with the four pairs of stimuli following either (a) 90 seconds of darkness (n = 24) or (b) 90 seconds of a slide show formed by seven pictures of natural objects, each presented for ten seconds with a three-second interstimulus interval (n = 24). An ANOVA showed a main effect of condition: babies looked longer at the continuous members of the pair after the picture show – after receiving more stimulation (see figure 13.2, bottom panel).

The results imply that one-month-olds' looking preferences are modified by overall level of stimulation, not only when stimuli differ in the amount of visual energy (e.g. Lewkowicz 1991; Turkewitz et al. 1984), but even when they differ only in the patterning of that energy. They imply that all previous reports on visual preferences in young infants are questionable. Negative results might be the result of an experimental situation which was too busy for the babies and positive results might not replicate if the testing conditions were more or *less* stimulating. They also imply that when babies show visual preferences following exposure to a stimulus in another modality, those preferences may reflect cross-modal transfer but they may equally well reflect a shift in visual preferences caused by an alteration of the general level of stimulation. It will be very difficult to distinguish these possibilities.

13.4 Implications for the Processing of Speech and Faces

Synaesthesia has profound implications for understanding how babies process speech and faces. How a young infant reacts in an experiment will depend on the overall level of stimulation and its pattern. Those variables will affect whether or not we see preferences and the form of those preferences. That prediction is supported by a re-examination of the literature on facedness. Studies of babies during the first two months of life have produced conflicting results. Some experimenters report that babies look at, or follow, a realistically drawn face longer than a face in which the features are distorted, but most experimenters report no differential reaction (reviewed in Johnson and Morton 1991; Maurer 1985). Table 13.1 summarizes the studies for one-month-olds.

Table 13.1 Tests of one-month-olds' sensitivity to facedness

Study	Positive result?	Number of: Stimuli	Presentations[a]	Other stimulation
Thomas (1973)	Yes	3	24	?
Johnson et al. (1991: exp. 3)	Yes	4	6–8	Infant moved away Between: small red light
Dannemiller and Stephens (1988)	No	4	5–8	Between: flashing bar
Johnson et al. (1992: exp. 1)	No	4	6–8	Between: small red flashing light
Sherrod (1979)	No	5	2–20	?
Fantz (1966)	No	6	'Presented repeatedly'	?
Johnson et al. (1992: exp. 2)	No	6	6	Between: 'attractor' Half of stimuli had internal movement
Maurer and Barrera (1981)	No	7	10–14	White noise Slide on screen at start
Wilcox (1969)	No	7	16–49	?
Fantz and Nevis (1967)	No	36	42	Between: rocked, talked to, pacified, aroused Could be distributed over repeated visits

[a] Range indicates minimum and maximum number of visual presentations through the test for sensitivity to facedness, with the variation caused by different orders of presentation. A pair of stimuli presented during on trial was counted as two visual presentations.

It shows that positive results were obtained only in two studies, one of which presented the fewest stimuli and the other of which is tied for next-to-fewest.

Greenberg and Blue (1977) presented similar results for checkerboards: two- and four-month-olds' looking times were related systematically to the number of checks in the stimulus when they were tested with three or four different checkerboards, but not when they were tested with five different checkerboards. Like table 13.1, Greenberg and Blue's results suggest that the extra stimulation from seeing more stimuli interferes with the baby's processing of the patterning of that energy.

Table 13.1 also shows that the studies of one-month-olds' response to facedness differed on a number of other variables which provided additional stimulation: the number of times each stimulus was presented, whether another stimulus was presented at the beginning of the procedure and/or between trials, the complexity of the 'irrelevant' stimulus, whether white noise was played, whether the baby was rocked between trials, etc. Given this extra stimulation, it is impossible to order the studies by their overall level of stimulation to the baby: experimenters have not always provided the necessary information and we do not know the importance of each type of stimulation to the baby. Nevertheless, this table suggests one reason why the literature on young infants' preferences seems so inconsistent: experimenters have been insensitive to the many ways in which they have complicated the testing situation for their young subjects.

13.5 Comparison to Other Theories

In sum, a variety of evidence supports the hypothesis that young infants confuse their senses in a synaesthetic mixture: cross-modal matching is present but ephemeral, especially if the overall level of stimulation is high; primary cortical areas respond to information from the 'wrong' senses; the senses sum in determining whether the baby is at the optimal level of stimulation, which in turn influences sleep and visual preferences for stimuli varying in their energy level; visual preferences even for stimuli matched in energy level can be shifted by accompanying visual stimulation; and cross-modal transfer decreases with age, to re-emerge later in the first year of life. Other theoretical positions can account for some of these phenomena but not all. Take, for example, the view that the baby is influenced solely by intensity as summed across the senses and from internal sources (e.g. Karmel, Gardner and Magnano 1991; Lewkowicz 1991; Turkewitz et al. 1984). This view can easily account for changes in visual preferences for stimuli differing in energy level, and it could encompass the cortical responses, but it does not explain shifts in visual preferences for stimuli matched in energy and it cannot account for early cross-modal matching. Gibson's (1969) positing of early amodal perception of shape, duration, size and rhythm can explain early cross-modal matching but is hard to reconcile with the ephemeral nature of the matching and with its diminution during development. And Piaget's

(1952) view, with which I began this paper, does not cover any of the early cross-modal effects.

All of the data are consistent with the hypothesis that the young infant confuses input from different senses, that is, is synaesthetic. By this account, the newborn baby forms schemas independent of modality. He or she responds to changes in energy over space or over time ignoring the modality of input. Depending on how easily the change is recognized, the baby may attend selectively to the old pattern or to a novel pattern, but will do so regardless of whether the pattern is in the same or a novel modality. At the same time, the baby seeks an optimal level of stimulation summed across all the senses. As a consequence, cross-modal matching is eqhemeral and visual preferences are easily shifted. With development, the senses become better differentiated and the early cross-modal confusion diminishes, so apparent matching becomes more difficult to observe. The unspecialized cortical responses are the physiological manifestation of the early synesthesia.

13.6 Extensions

My account can be extended to encompass other phenomena. At the same time that other evidence suggests that babies are in transition between synaesthesia and the formation of 'real' cross-modal connections (see section 13.3.2), infants seem not to expect to be able to feel a visible object: five- to six-month-olds show neither distress nor surprise when they reach for it and find only empty space (Field 1977; Gordon and Yonas 1976).

Moreover, from this perspective, early imitation (Meltzoff, in Boysson-Bardies et al. 1993) is merely the babies' lack of differentiation between changing patterns of visual and proprioceptive stimulation (Maurer and Maurer 1988). As would be expected, the imitation rarely matches the model exactly and extends to grossly similar patterns of energy (Jacobson 1979), the baby may imitate with the wrong part of the body (Gardner and Gardner 1970), and imitation becomes more difficult to elicit during middle infancy (Abravanel and Sigafoos 1984; Fontaine 1984; Heimann, Nelson and Schaller 1989). Together, the evidence implies that phenomena demonstrated during early infancy may bear only a superficial resemblance to similar phenomena later in life. It also implies that our understanding of how babies process speech and faces – or, indeed, how they process anything at all – will not progress until we consider all of the stimuli in our experimental situations which might be relevant to our infant subjects.

Acknowledgements

This chapter extends ideas developed with Charles Maurer and first described in *The World of the Newborn*. I thank Terri Lewis and Christine Stager for their comments on an earlier draft of this chapter. This work was supported by grant OGP0009797 from the National Science and Engineering Council of Canada.

Notes

1 Pecheux et al. (1988) concluded that they did find evidence of cross-modal transfer despite there being no evidence for it in the group overall. When they divided the group *post hoc* into those whose mouthing of the pacifier had decreased during the 90 seconds – suggesting that it had been well processed – and those whose mouthing had not changed, they found evidence of cross-modal transfer only in the group whose mouthing had not changed. However, that is the group in which there was no evidence that babies had done sufficient processing to have anything to transfer and even in this group the result was significant only at the .055 level by a one-tailed test.

2 When we ignored the data from the second test trial and the baseline group, to make the analyses identical to those of Meltzoff and Borton, we found that 22 out of 32 babies looked longer at the *novel* shape ($p < 0.05$ by a binomial test), but there was no significant bias in their looking time on either the first test trial or both test trials ($ps > 0.10$ by t-tests). Similarly, Lewkowicz et al. (1984) found that newborns looked longer at the novel smooth object after sucking on a nubby pacifier but there was no effect on their visual preferences of sucking on a smooth pacifier. Moreover, sucking on the smooth or nubby pacifier in some cases also altered the babies' looking preferences for 4×4 and 64×64 checkerboards: this may indicate some sort of systematic effect but it does not indicate cross-modal transfer.

References

Abravanel, E. and Sigafoos, A.D. 1984: Exploring the presence of imitation during early infancy. *Child Development*, 55, 381–92.

Born, W., Spelke, E. and Prather, P. 1982: Detection of auditory–visual relationships by newborn infants. Presented at the International Conference on Infant Studies, Austin, Texas.

Boysson-Bardies, B. de, Schonen, S. de, Jusczyk, P., McNeilage, P. and Morton, J. (eds) 1993: *Developmental Neurocognition: speech and face processing in the first year of life*. Dordrecht: Kluwer.

Brackbill, Y. 1970: Acoustic variation and arousal level in infants. *Psychophysiology*, 6, 517–25.

Brackbill, Y. 1971: Cumulative effects of continuous stimulation on arousal level in infants. *Child Development*, 42, 17–26.

Brackbill, Y. 1973: Continuous stimulation and arousal level: stability of the effect over time. *Child Development*, 44, 43–6.

Brackbill, Y. 1975: Continuous stimulation and arousal level in infancy: effects of stimulus intensity and stress. *Child Development*, 46, 364–9.

Brown, K.W. and Gottfried, A.W. 1986: Cross-modal transfer of shape in early infancy: is there reliable evidence? In L.P. Lipsitt and R. Rovee-Collier (eds), *Advances in Infancy Research*, vol. 4. Norwood, N.J.: Ablex, 163–70.

Crook, C. 1978: Taste perception in the newborn infant. *Infant Behavior and Development*, 1, 52–9.

Cytowic, R.E. 1988: *Synesthesia: a union of the senses*. New York: Springer Verlag.

Dehay, C., Bullier, J. and Kennedy, H. 1984: Transient projections from the fronto-parietal and temporal cortex to areas 17, 18, and 19 in the kitten. *Experimental Brain Research*, 57, 208–12.

Dehay, C., Kennedy, H. and Bullier, J. 1988: Characterization of transient cortical projections from auditory, somatosensory, and motor cortices to visual area 17, 18, and 19 in the kitten. *Journal of Comparative Neurology*, 272, 68–9.

Field, J. 1977: Coordination of vision and prehension in young infants. *Child Development*, 48, 97–103.

Fontaine, R. 1984: Imitative skills between birth and six months. *Infant Behavior and Development*, 7, 323–3.

Frost, D.O. 1984: Axonal growth and target selection during development: retinal projections to the ventrobasal complex and other 'nonvisual' structures in neonatal Syrian hamsters. *Journal of Comparative Neurology*, 230, 576–92.

Frost, D.O. 1990: Sensory processing by novel, experimentally induced cross-modal circuits. *Annals of the New York Academy of Sciences*, 608, 92–112.

Gardner, J. and Gardner, H. 1970: A note on selective imitation by a six-week-old human infant. *Child Development*, 41, 1209–13.

Gibson, E.J. 1969: *Principles of Perceptual Learning and Development*. New York: Appleton-Century Croft.

Gordon, F.R. and Yonas, A. 1976: Sensitivity to binocular depth information in infants. *Journal of Experimental Child Psychology*, 22, 413–22.

Greenberg, D.J. and Blue, S.Z. 1977: The visual preference technique in infancy: effect of number of stimuli presented upon experimental outcome. *Child Development*, 48, 131–7.

Heimann, M., Nelson, K.E. and Schaller, J. 1989: Neonatal imitation of tongue protrusion and mouth opening: methodological aspects and evidence of early individual differences. *Scandinavian Journal of Psychology*, 30, 90–101.

Hernandez-Reif, M.A. 1992: Visual tactile matching: perception of shape as a function of efficient haptic exploration and study time. Presented at the International Conference on Infant Studies, Miami, Florida.

Hershenson, M., Kessen, W. and Munsinger, H. 1967: Ocular orientation in the human newborn infant: close look at some positive and negative results'. In W. Wathen-Dunn (ed.), *Models for the Perception of Speech and Visual Form*. Cambridge, Mass.: MIT Press, 282–90.

Hershenson, M., Munsinger, H. and Kessen, W. 1965: Preference for shapes of intermediate variability in the human newborn. *Science*, 147, 630–1.

Hoffmann, R. 1978: Developmental changes in human visual-evoked potentials to patterned stimuli recorded at different scalp locations. *Child Development*, 49, 110–18.

Hunter, M.A., Ames, E.W. and Koopman, R. 1983: Effects of stimulus complexity and familiarization time on infant preferences for novel and familiar stimuli. *Developmental Psychology*, 19, 338–52.

Jacobson, S.W. 1979: Matching behavior in the young infant. *Child Development*, 50, 425–30.

Johnson, M.H. and Morton, J. 1991: *Biology and Cognitive development: the case of face recognition*. Oxford: Blackwell.

Karmel, B.Z., Gardner, J.M. and Magnano, C.L. 1991: Attention and arousal in early infancy. In M.J. Weiss and P.R. Zelazo (eds), *Newborn Attention*: Norwood, N.J. Ablex, 339–76.

Karmel, B.Z., Lester, M., McCarvill, S., Brown, P. and Hofmann, M. 1977: Correlation of infants' brain and behavior response to temporal changes in visual stimulation. *Psychophysiology*, 14, 134–42.

Kennedy, H., Bullier, J. and Dehay, C. 1989: Transient projection from the superior temporal sulcus to area 17 in the newborn macaque monkey. *Proceedings of the National Academy of Sciences*, 86, 8093–7.

Lewkowicz, D.J. 1991: Development of intersensory functions in human infancy: auditory/visual interactions. In M.J. Weiss and P.R. Zelazo (eds), *Newborn Attention*. Norwood, N.J.: Ablex, 308–38.

Lewkowicz, D.J., Gardner, J.M., Turkewitz, G. and Lawson, K.R. 1984: Oral prestimulation and visual preferences in neonates: non-specific effects without cross-modal transfer of shape. Unpublished manuscript.

Lewkowicz, D.J. and Turkewitz, G. 1980: Cross-modal equivalence in early infancy: auditory–visual intensity matching. *Developmental Psychology*, 16, 597–607.

Lewkowicz, D.J. and Turkewitz, G. 1981: Intersensory interaction in newborns: modification of visual preferences following exposure to sound. *Child Development*, 52, 827–32.

Marks, L.E. 1975: On colored-hearing synesthesia: cross-modal translations of sensory dimensions. *Psychological Bulletin*, 82, 303–31.

Maurer, D. 1985: Infants' perception of facedness. In T. Field and N. Fox (eds), *Social Perception in Infants*. New York: Ablex, 73–100.

Maurer, D. and Maurer, C. 1988: *The World of the Newborn*. New York: Basic Books.

Meissirel, C., Dehay, C., Berland, M. and Kennedy, H. 1991: Segregation of callosal and association pathways during development in the visual cortex of the primate. *Journal of Neuroscience*, 11, 3297–316.

Meltzoff, A.N. and Borton, R.W. 1979: Intermodal matching by human neonates. *Nature*, 282, 403–4.

Miranda, S. and Fantz, R. 1971: Distribution of visual attention by newborn infants among patterns varying in size and number of details. *Proceedings of the 79th Annual Convention of the American Psychological Association*, 6, 181–2.

Pecheux, M.-G., Lepecq, J.-C. and Salzarulo, P. 1988: Oral activity and exploration in 1–2-month-old infants. *British Journal of Developmental Psychology*, 6, 245–56.

Piaget, J. 1952: *The Origins of Intelligence in Children*. New York: International University Press.

Pickens, J.N., Nawrocki, T. and Soutullo, D. 1992: Auditory–visual integration in preterm infants. Presented at the International Conference on Infant Studies, Miami, Florida.

Rose, S.A. and Ruff, H.A. 1987: Cross-modal abilities in human infants. In J.D. Osofsky (ed.), *Handbook of Infant Development*. New York: John Wiley, 318–62.

Rose, S.A., Gottfried, A.W. and Bridger, W.H. 1978: Effects of visual, haptic, and manipulatory experiences on infants' visual recognition memory of objects. *Developmental Psychology*, 14, 305–12.

Rose, S.A., Gottfried, A.W. and Bridger, W.H. 1981a: Cross-modal transfer and information processing by the sense of touch in infancy. *Developmental Psychology*, 17, 90–8.

Rose, S.A., Gottfried, A.W. and Bridger, W.H. 1981b: Cross-modal transfer in 6-month-old infants. *Developmental Psychology*, 17, 661–9.

Rose, S.A., Gottfried, A.W., Carminar-Melloy, P.M. and Bridger, W.H. 1982: Familiarity and novelty preferences in infant recognition memory: implications for information processing. *Developmental Psychology*, 5, 704–13.

Schneirla, T. 1959: An evolutionary and developmental theory of biphasic processes underlying approach and withdrawal. In M.R. Jones (ed.), *Nebraska Symposium on Motivation*, vol. 7. Lincoln: University of Nebraska Press, 1–42.

Spear, N.E., Kraemer, P.J., Molina, J.C. and Smoller, D.E. 1988: Developmental change in learning and memory: infantile disposition for 'unitization'. In J. Delacour and J.C.S. Levy (eds), *Systems with Learning and Memory Abilities: proceedings of the workshop held in Paris, June 15–17, 1987* Amsterdam: North-Holland, 27–52.

Stager, C.L. 1992: Tactual–visual transfer in one-month-old human infants. Unpublished undergraduate thesis, McMaster University.

Streri, A. 1987: Tactile discrimination of shape and intermodal transfer in 2- to 3-month-old infants. *British Journal of Developmental Psychology*, 5, 213–20.

Streri, A. and Pecheux, M.-G. 1986: Vision-to-touch and touch-to-vision transfer of form in 5-month-old infants. *British Journal of Developmental Psychology*, 4, 161–7.

Turkewitz, G., Gardner, J. and Lewkowicz, D.J. 1984: Sensory/perceptual functioning during early infancy: the implications of a quantitative basis for responding. In G. Greenberg and E. Tobach (eds), *Behavioral Evolution and Integrative Levels*. Hillsdale, N.J.: Lawrence Erlbaum, 167–95.

Turkewitz, G., Moreau, T., Birch, H. and Davis, L. 1971: Relationships among responses in the human newborn: the non-association and non-equivalence among different indicators of responsiveness. *Psychophysiology*, 7, 233–47.

Wagner, S.H. and Sakovits, L.J. 1986: A process analysis of infant visual and cross-modal recognition memory: implications for an amodal code. In L.P. Lipsitt and R. Rovee-Collier (eds), *Advances in Infancy Research*, vol. 4. Norwood, N.J.: Ablex, 195–217.

Walker-Andrews, A.S. and Gibson, E.J. 1986: What develops in bimodal perception?. In L.P. Lipsitt and R. Rovee-Collier (eds), *Advances in Infancy Research*, vol. 4, Norwood, N.J.: Ablex, 171–81.

Wolff, P., Matsumiya, Y., Abrohms, I.F., van Velzer, C. and Lombroso, C.T. 1974: The effect of white noise on the somatosensory evoked responses in sleeping newborn infants. *Electroencephalography and Clinical Neurophysiology*, 37, 269–74.

Zellner, D.A. and Kautz, M.A. 1990: Color affects perceived odor intensity. *Journal of Experimental Psychology: Human Perception and Performance*, 16, 391–7.

14

Synaesthesia: Implications for Developmental Neurobiology

Henry Kennedy, Alexandre Batardiere, Colette Dehay and Pascal Barone

14.1 Introduction

Our understanding of information processing in the cerebral cortex has advanced considerably over the last two decades due to improved and combined anatomical and physiological investigations. It is now clearly established that the neocortex is composed of a vast number of separate areas and that each sensory modality has a constellation of areas clustered around a primary area. The primary area receives the major input from the thalamus and information is then relayed to the secondary, tertiary and higher order areas by means of cortico-cortical projections. In the visual system of primates including man, the primary visual area (V1) or area 17 is thought to project to as many as 20 to 30 separate visual areas, each dealing with different aspects of visual information (form, colour, movement and so on) (Zeki 1980; Felleman and Van Essen 1991). The functional anatomy of the primate visual system has been extensively studied and the principles of information flow in terms of parallel and serial architecture are just beginning to be understood (Bullier and Nowak 1995). Information from both the higher and lower visual areas is then projected to so-called association areas where it converges with inputs from other sensory modalities before being relayed to higher cognitive regions such as those dealing with language.

A least one important principle that emerges from this admittedly highly simplified scheme of the cortex is that information from different sensory modalities remains segregated at the early stages of cortical processing. However, early in development many connections are formed which do not survive into adulthood and are defined as transient connections. This raises the possibility that the developmental reduction in the number of connections could lead to changes in the overall schema of connectivity. The first indication that there is a qualitative change in connectivity came from work in the 1980s from Innocenti's laboratory in Lausanne and ours in Lyon (Dehay et al. 1984; Innocenti and Clarke 1984). This work came from a series of anatomical experiments in the cerebral cortex of young kittens. Retrograde tracers injected in area 17 of the adult cat are picked up by axon terminals and transported back to the cell soma. By charting the distribution of retrogradely labelled neurons it is possible to characterize the distribution of neurons that project to area 17. This shows that in the cortex, projections to area 17 of the adult originate entirely from the secondary and tertiary visual areas. However, it was shown that during early postnatal development the connectivity pattern in the kitten included a relatively strong projection from the primary auditory area. By repeating the experiments in progressively older animals we were able to demonstrate that the projection from the primary auditory area to area 17 was eliminated between 20 and 30 days after birth, and this projection can be referred to as a transient pathway.

The transient pathway linking auditory and visual cortex showed three important anatomical features (Dehay et al. 1988). First, the connection did not reflect a low degree of precision. By reconstructing the pattern of labelled neurons in the entire auditory cortex we were able to show that the transient projection originates from a restricted region and that the labelled zone was bounded by cortex which did not project to the visual cortex. Hence we concluded that the transient auditory to visual pathway is not part of a widespread and diffuse connectivity. Secondly, by injecting retrograde tracers in the auditory cortex we were able to verify whether the projection was reciprocal. Such injections in the auditory cortex led to little or no retrograde labelling in the visual cortex, meaning that the transient projections linking visual and auditory areas are unidirectional and therefore could serve only to relay activity from the auditory cortex to the visual areas. Thirdly, we wanted to know if the unidirectional transient auditory projection to the visual cortex could possibly activate the kitten visual cortex. If this was going to be the case, it would require that the axon terminals access the cortical grey matter. We investigated this issue by injecting anterograde tracers into the auditory cortex of kittens and tracing the axonal terminals to the visual cortex. This study showed that some labelled auditory axons penetrated the cortical grey matter where they could be traced up to the top of layer 2.

We shall briefly consider the significance of the transient cortical projection in the kitten in the following terms.

14.1.1 *The phylogenetics of cortical development*

The transient auditory to visual cortex projection in the kitten constitutes a connection between primary sensory areas which is not present in the adult of either carnivores or primates and therefore constitutes an altogether unexpected organization of cortical connections. However, in the adult rodent there are stable projections from auditory areas to the visual cortex (Miller and Vogt 1984). One possibility is that an early mammalian ancestor had stable projections linking auditory and visual cortex and that these connections have been lost in most present-day mammals except rodents. This would suggest that the immature transient projections to the visual cortex in the carnivore are the remnants of a phylogenetic ancient pathway. Finlay (Finlay et al. 1987) has suggested that the maintenance of such pathways during foetal development could lead to a greater developmental flexibility since it is theoretically possible to stabilize these projections.

14.1.2 *The functional properties of the kitten cortex*

By penetrating the grey matter of the visual cortex, transient fibres from the primary auditory area are in a position to play a number of roles during development of the visual cortex. Those transient axons that enter the grey matter may form synaptic contacts. Furthermore, there is increasing evidence to show that the formation of temporary synapses by developing axons is a general feature in the mammalian CNS, where they have been identified in a number of structures including the spinal cord, the visual cortex, the lateral geniculate and the cerebellum (Crepel et al. 1976; Shatz and Kirkwood 1984; Anderson et al. 1992). However, the absence of synapses would not prevent immature axons from relaying neural activity, since it has been shown that electrical activity in the chick spinal cord due to chemical transmission occurs *prior* to formation of synapse (Hamburger 1970). It has been concluded from this and other studies that growth cones may have synapse-like activity. These considerations suggest that electrophysiological studies would be able to decide whether these transient projections are functional.

The ubiquity of temporary connections in the CNS providing neural activity makes it highly probable that the transient auditory projection to the immature visual cortex actually does convey neural information of auditory origin. There would therefore be a developmental stage during which neurones of the visual cortex could be submitted to the influence of activity in other sensory modalities (some transient projections also originated from the somatosensory cortex). Thus the transient projections could provide the basis for a polysensory convergence that could, for example, be required for matching different sensory perception maps. Alternative roles can be envisaged. For instance, transient projections could modulate the maturation of corticogenesis in general, including the maturation of extrinsic or intrinsic connectivity of the target area. The influence could be either activity mediated or mediated by the release of substances which could have a trophic action. In the cat, transient auditory projections to the visual cortex are present during the first four weeks of life when the visual areas are undergoing profound developmental changes. It has been shown that the numbers of synapses increase rapidly up to the fifth postnatal week (Cragg 1975; Winfield 1981) and ocular dominance columns are not adult-like before five weeks of age (Levay et al. 1978). Further, neuronal migration is not achieved before the end of the second week (Shatz and Luskin 1986).

14.2 Transient Connectivity in Primates

If transient projections are fulfilling an important role in development, one would predict that they are to be found universally. The only other species where transient projections from the auditory to visual cortex have been reported is in the ferret (Dehay and Kennedy 1986) which, like the cat, is a carnivore. In our laboratory we have carried out large numbers of retrograde tracer injections in the visual cortices of monkey foetuses at closely spaced intervals throughout the period of pathway formation. These experiments were performed on cynomolgus macaque monkeys which are born 165 days after conception (E165). At birth the macaque is relatively mature and babies display sophisticated visually guided behaviour; this contrasts with kittens, which do not open their eyes until ten days after birth. This advanced degree of maturity at the time of birth makes it necessary to examine cortical development *in utero*. To do this requires some extensive surgical skills since it is necessary to open the uterus, expose the foetal head and inject tracers under strictly sterile conditions in the appropriate location of the cortex. Following injection the foetus is returned to the uterus for the appropriate survival period to allow retrograde transport before histological examination of the foetal tissue. These experiments have all been carried out in area V1 and the adjacent area, V2. These injections of tracers showed labelled neurons confined to those cortical regions which are known to project to areas V1 and V2 in the adult and no projections could be demonstrated from the auditory regions. These results suggest that transient projections to the primary visual areas is uniquely a feature of cortical development in the carnivore. However, it is possible that this apparent absence of transient projections in the monkey reflects differences in the cortical organization of the visual system of carnivores and primates. In primates, areas V1 and V2 appear to be highly specialized for dispatching visual information to a very large number of extrastriate areas, whereas in the cat thalamic afferents from the lateral geniculate nucleus innervate directly the major extrastriate areas.

As argued above, V1 and V2 in the monkey might not be homologous in function to V1 and V2 in cat (Payne 1993). In general, the organizational principles of extrastriate cortex in primate suggest that individual areas may be more specialized for a particular aspect of visual information than extrastriate areas in the carnivore. Hence, functions which are more highly distributed in carnivores might be expected to be localized in a single area in the primate.

These considerations lead to the possibility that in the primate transient projections to the visual cortex occur at later stages of cortical processing. Cortical pathways in the primate show a major split at the level of area V2 (Mishkin, Ungerleider and Macko 1983). Projections to area V4 and the temporal lobe are thought to be primarily concerned with colour and visual detail of objects, and a second pathway directed at V5 (or MT) is primarily concerned with movement and the location of objects in visual space (Van Essen and Gallant 1994).

14.3 Are Transient Auditory Projections Reserved to Particular Visual Areas in the Primate?

Injections of retrograde tracers have enabled us to determine the cortical areas which project to area V4 during foetal development (E120–140). Densely labelled neurons were observed in those visual areas which normally project to V4 in the adult (V2, V3, V5 and parietal and temporal visual areas). No labelled neurons were observed in non-visual areas and in particular none in auditory cortex. These results were all obtained with injections which were limited to the cortical grey matter, which is the outermost limit of the cortex where the cell bodies of the cortex reside. However, the results were very different when injections involved the underlying white matter. In two foetuses where the injection site was found to encroach on the underlying white matter, retrograde labelled neurons were found throughout the visual cortices which project to V4 as well as a population of labelled neurons in the auditory cortex. These transiently projecting neurons were for the most part located in supragranular layers and had a pyramidal morphology.

From these results we can conclude that the auditory cortex in the foetal macaque projects to area V4. The projection did not concern the grey matter, at least at the ages we examined. This means that the transient projection is largely confined to the white matter underlying the cortex. There are at least two reasons why white matter injections could lead to labelling in cortical areas while injections in the overlying grey matter do not. First, the white matter is primarily composed of axonal fibres, and injections in the white matter concern a much greater extent of cortex than injections of the same size which are limited to the grey matter. In other words, white-matter injections are bigger than grey-matter injections. Although, this might be expected to lead to an increase in labelling, this can not be the full answer since *no* labelled neurons were found after the grey-matter injections. Secondly, white-matter injections are more likely to label short-lived projections even if they do project to grey matter, since the transient connection will be in the white matter for a period during their approach and withdrawal to the grey matter. Once again, the absence of *any* labelled neurons after grey-matter injections plus the span of foetal ages investigated suggest that these projections do not penetrate the grey matter even for very short periods.

Once one has discarded the temporal and spatial objections outlined above, one is driven to the conclusion that the transient projections target specifically the white matter of area V4. These findings are of particular interest, because a number of recent studies have identified a potentially important developmental structure in the white matter known as the sub-plate.

The sub-plate is generated very early in corticogenesis (Allendoerffer and Shatz 1994). Cortical precursor cells undergo their last round of neurogenesis in the germinal zones lining the ventricles before undertaking a largely radial migration to the outer margin of the neuronal tube. Successive waves of neuroblasts migrate past the early-generated neurons, so the deeper layers are the first to be generated and the most superficial layer is the last. Once the neuroblast has finished its migration it begins to differentiate, and axonal and dendritic growth occurs. Hence the first-generated neurons are the first to arrive in the cortex and are the first to form connections. In this way the cortical sub-plate is relatively advanced at very early stages of development. Primates are characterized by a prolonged period of corticogenesis, so the sub-plate would be expected to constitute a particularly prominent structure (Kennedy and Dehay 1993; Kostovic and Rakic 1990).

Natural cell death is of widespread occurrence in the developing cortex (Finlay and Slattery 1983) and it has been claimed to occur at much higher levels in the sub-plate. Workers have gone so far as to claim that the entire sub-plate disappears, although this has recently been disputed, in rodents at least (Woo et al. 1991; Valverde et al. 1995). The sub-plate is a phylogenetic ancient structure which has been postulated to play an important role in cortical development. However, exactly what role remains elusive. Shatz's group has claimed that the sub-plate neurons project to the thalamus and could provide an early scaffolding for the growth of thalamocortical axons (Shatz, Chun and Lushkin 1988; McConnel, Gosh and Shatz 1989; Ghosh et al. 1990). This suggests that the sub-plate plays a role as a template for this pathway, although this position has been criticized recently (Bolz et al. 1993). Another possibility is O'Leary's suggestion that the sub-plate plays a role in the specification of cortical areas (see review of Lyon meeting in Sur and Cowey 1995; O'Leary, Schlaggar and Tuttle 1994), although here again we need to wait for more experimental details.

14.4 Restructuring of Feedforward and Feedback Projections During Primate Development

From the above considerations, the significance of the transient projection of the auditory cortex to the sub-plate of area V4 is difficult to ascertain largely due to our poor understanding of the developmental significance of the sub-plate. However, the injections in area V4 revealed the existence of another form of transient connectivity which is potentially much more important than the projection from auditory to visual cortex. To understand the significance of this transient pathway we need to consider briefly how the laminar distribution of projection neurons is thought to relate to feedforward and feedback pathways in the cortex.

In the adult, pathways in the visual cortex can be broadly subdivided into three different categories (figure 14.1). Rostral-directed projections originate from parent neurons in the supragranular layers and terminate in layer 4, while caudal-directed pathways originate in the infragranular layers and terminate outside of layer 4 (Rockland and Pandya 1979). These two patterns have been assimilated to feedforward and feedback connections (ibid.). Feedforward pathways are thought to link cortical areas in an ascending hierarchical sequence and feedback connections in a descending sequence (Maunsell and

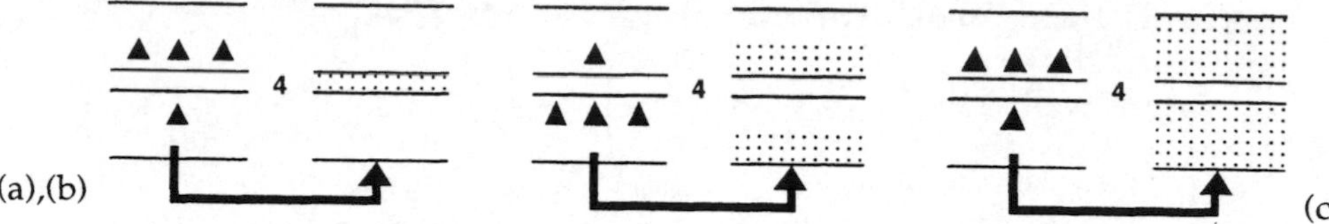

Figure 14.1 Schematic representation of the laminar distribution of cell bodies (triangles) and terminals (dots) in the three types of intrahemispheric connections between visual areas
(a) Feedforward (e.g. V1 → MT)
(b) Feedback (e.g. MT → V1)
(c) Lateral connection (e.g. V4 → MT)

Note: Ipsilateral connections fall into one of three types: feedforward pathways (a) arise principally from cells in supragranular layers and terminate in layer 4; feedback pathways (b) originate principally from cells located in infragranular layers and terminate in layers outside layer 4; lateral connections (i.e. between visual areas on the same hierarchical level) (c) arise principally from supragranular layers and terminate in all layers except layer 4.

Van Essen 1983). An intermediate category has also been identified which is characterized by a distribution of terminals throughout the full thickness of the cortex and which is thought of as a lateral pathway linking cortical ares on similar levels (ibid.).

In the adult, injections of retrograde traces in area V4 lead to labelled neurons in V2, V3, V5 and parietal and temporal areas. Using the laminar distribution we can determine the hierarchical organization of these cortical areas based on the scheme outlined by David Van Essen and others (figure 14.2). In the immature cortex the laminar distribution was quite different, at least in the feedback projections (i.e. projection from V5 and TEO). Here, whereas in the adult only 20–30 per cent of labelled neurons were located in the supragranular layers, this ranged from 70–90 per cent in the foetus.

Previously we had shown that there is a developmental redistribution of the projection neurons sending axons to area V1 (Kennedy, Bullier and Dehay 1989; Barone et al. 1995). The present results show similar findings for the feedback projections on to area V4. They also show that laminar reorganization does not affect feedforward projections. These results were totally unexpected since we had thought that the developmental reorganization of feedback projections to area V1 might be just one additional example of the uniqueness of this area. However, the present results suggest that this might be a universal feature of all feedback projections, in which case one might expect it

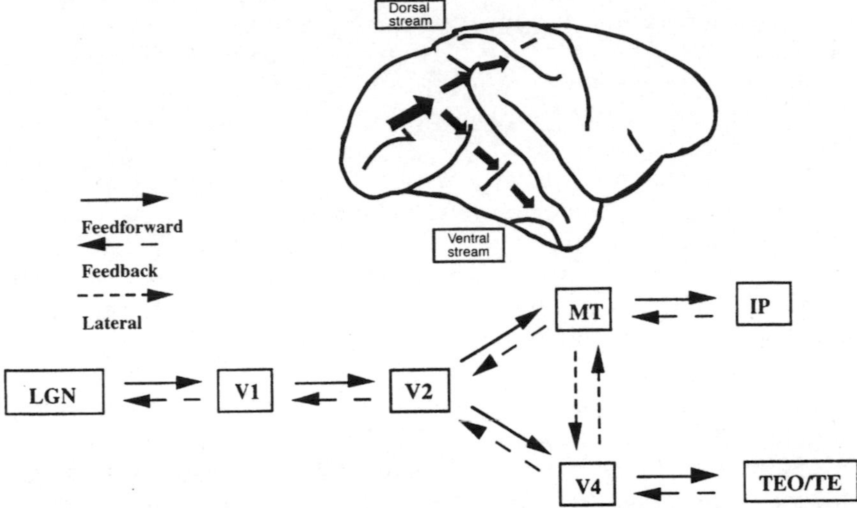

Figure 14.2 Schematic representation of the connections between visual areas V1, V2, V4, MT (medial temporal area), IP (intra-parietal area), TEO (occipito-temporal area) and TE (temporal area) in the macaque monkey

Note: The hierarchical relations of cortical visual areas are based on the laminar distribution of projecting neurons and terminations. Visual information from the lateral geniculate nucleus of the thalamus is directed to the primary visual area V1 and, subsequently, to the visual area V2 where it splits into two segregated pathways. A dorsal stream is directed towards area MT and the parietal cortex; a ventral stream is directed to area V4 and the inferotemporal cortex.

to occur in the feedback projections in the cortices of other sensory modalities.

If this is the case, then we have a developmental reorganization of incredible magnitude, quite unlike the transient pathways which have been described in the past. The sheer magnitude of the connectivity change could be of considerable importance for understanding primate development. At present we have not yet been able to consider all the possible implications. We do have evidence that developmental changes in the laminar distribution is a distinctively primate feature (the evidence in support of this is discussed in Barone et al. 1995). The functional significance needs to be considered with respect to what exactly is known about the physiology of feedback and feedforward pathways. Jean Bullier has been using single unit recording to tackle this issue (Bullier, Girard and Salin 1994). His results suggest that feedback projections do not provide an excitatory input but instead seem to exert a modulatory influence on the centre–surround interaction. It could be that the absence of an excitatory input is characteristic of the infragranular neurons (which predominate in the feedback projection in the adult). Since supragranular neurons predominate in the feedback projection of the foetus, this could mean that the excitatory contribution of the feedback projections is altogether higher in the foetus compared to the adult.

Assuming that it is the early feedback projections in the foetus that are providing an excitatory input, the extent of rostral cortex which is providing excitatory input to caudal cortex is much greater in the immature cortex than in the adult. This would amount to a partial inversion of the normal flow of excitation and lead to an increase in the multimodal activity in secondary and perhaps even primary areas in the young animal.

One possible consequence of this is provided by the recent findings of Bates who has been looking at the cortical localization of language in children and adults (in Thal et al. 1991). Her results show that during development there is a restriction of cortex dealing with language so that the cortical processes dealing with this function are considerably more distributed in the infant than in the adult. This would suggest just the sort of progressive restriction of connectivity that we find in the redistribution of projection neurons in feedback projections.

For the neurobiologists, the recent work of Baron-Cohen's group (Baron-Cohen, Wyke and Binnie 1987; Baron-Cohen et al. 1993) situates synaesthesia as an inescapable fact that needs to be taken into account when we come to consider the functions of the higher regions of the CNS. Recent findings with positron emission tomography (PET) supports a neocortical origin (Paulesu et al. 1995). In a sense synaesthesia represents a breakdown in modularity which constitutes a definite challenge to our understanding of cognitive function. If neurobiology can accommodate such a challenge by providing a description of pathways which could underline this phenomenon, then we would have gone some way to achieving the sort of multidisciplinarity so often sought after in the blurbs of popular science books and in the formula for requesting grant funding.

Do our preliminary results have any bearing on this? Well, they do, in so far as they suggest a developmental theory of the condition. Accordingly, for instance, there could be variability in the extent of remodelling of feedback connections so that certain adult individuals retain a juvenile connectivity. The well-documented stabilization of transient connections would be an appropriate model for generating such adult variability. Alternatively, the multimodal cortical functions set up in childhood could lead to permanent memory traces which in certain individuals will be revoked in adulthood.

A developmental theory of synaesthesia must make some attempt at explaining the finality of the mechanism that leads to the adult condition. Bates has speculated on the possible advantage of a more extensive connectivity in the early stages of language acquisition (Bates 1994). It comes down to the infant's necessity to name objects and to bring about a convergence of the senses in an effort to facilitate that process. It could be that early stages of consciousness are based on different strategies of modularity which require sensory convergence at relatively low levels of cortical processing. Interestingly, our results on the remodelling of cortical connections suggest that if this is a basis for early multimodal function, it is characteristic of primates and therefore of the emergence of prolonged and complex learning at the neocortical level.

14.5 Conclusion

In a very general sense, any early developmental increase in the extent of connectivity could contribute to synaesthesia. However, this is even more true of feedback projections. In our introduction we pointed out that sensory interactions in the adult cortex occur at some distance from the entrance of sensory input to the cortex. As we have seen, the direct transient connections between visual and auditory areas in the immature cortex could be one means of ensuring sensory interaction. Another and far more plausible method would be partially to reverse the normal flow of excitation in the cortex from caudal–rostral to rostral–caudal. The contingent of supragranular layer projections in the feedback projections of the foetus could provide the anatomical substrate for such a reversal.

References

Allendoerfer, K.L. and Shatz, C.J. 1994: The subplate, a transient neocortical structure: its role in the development of connections between thalamus and cortex. *Annual Review of Neuroscieuce*, 17, 185–218.

Anderson, J.C., Dehay, C., Friedlander, M.S., Martin, K.A.C. and Nelson, J.C. 1992: Synaptic connections of physiologically identified geniculocortical axons in kitten area 17. *Proceedings of the Royal Society of London, Series B*, 250(1329), 187–94.

Baron-Cohen, S., Wyke, M. and Binnie, C. 1987: Hearing words and seeing colours: an experimental investigation of a case of synaesthesia. *Perception*, 16, 761–7.

Baron-Cohen, S., Harrison, J., Goldstein, L.H. and Wyke, M. 1993: Coloured speech perception: is synaesthesia what happens when modularity breaks down? *Perception*, 22, 419–26.

Barone, P., Dehay, C., Berland, M., Bullier, J. and Kennedy, H. 1995: Developmental remodelling of primate visual cortical pahtways. *Cerebral Cortex*, 5, 22–38.

Bates, E. 1994: Modularity, domain specificity and the development of language. *Discussions in Neuroscience*, 10(1–2), 136–49.

Bolz, J, Götz, M., Hübener, M. and Novak, N. 1993: Reconstructing cortical connections in a dish. *TINS*, 16(8), 310–15.

Bullier, J. and Nowak, L.G. 1995: Parallel versus serial processing: new vistas on the distributed organization of the visual system. *Current Opinion in Neurobiology*, 5, 497–503.

Bullier, J., Girard, P. and Salin, P.-A. 1994: The role of area 17 in the transfer of information to exstrastriate visual cortex. In P. Peters and S. Rockland (eds), *Cerebral Cortex*, vol. 10, New York: Plenum Press, 301–30.

Cragg, B.G. 1975: The development of synapses in the visual system of the cat. *Journal of Comparative Neurology*, 160, 147–66.

Crepel, L.F., Mariani, J. and Delhaye-Bouchaud, N. 1976: Evidence for a multiple innervation of purkinje cells by climbing fibers in the immature rat cerebellum. *Journal of Neuroscience*, 7, 567–78.

Dehay, C. and Kennedy, H. 1986: Connexions corticales transitoires chez le furet. 1er Colloque des Neurosciences Françaises, Bordeaux.

Dehay, C., Bullier, J. and Kennedy, H. 1984: Transient projections from the frontoparietal and temporal cortex to areas 17, 18 and 19 in the kitten. *Experimental Brain Research*, 57, 208–12.

Dehay C., Kennedy, H. and Bullier, J. 1988: Characterization of transient cortical projections from auditory, somatosensory, and motor cortices to visual areas 17, 18, and 19 in the kitten. *Journal of Comparative Neurology*, 272, 68–89.

Felleman, D.J. and Van Essen, D.C. 1991: Distributed hierarchical processing in the primate cerebral cortex. *Cerebral Cortex*, 1, 1–47.

Finlay, B.L. and Slattery, M. 1983: Local difference in the amount of early cell death in neocortex predict adult local specializations. *Science*, 219, 1349–51.

Finlay, B.L. Wickler, K.C. and Sengelaub, D.R. 1987: Regressive events in brain development and scenarios for vertebrate brain evolution. *Brain Behaviour and Evolution*, 30, 102–17.

Ghosh, A., Antonini, A., McConnell, S.K. and Shatz, C.J. 1990: Requirement for subplate neurons in the formation of thalamocortical connections. *Nature*, 347, 179–81.

Hamburger, V. 1970: Embryonic mobility in vertebrates. In G. Quarton et al. (eds), *The Neurosciences: second study programme*, New York: Rockfeller University Press, 141–51.

Innocenti, G. and Clarke, S. 1984: Bilateral transitory projections to visual areas from auditory cortex in kittens. *Developmental Brain Research*, 14, 143–8.

Kennedy, H. and Dehay, C. 1993: The importance of developmental timing in cortical specification. *Perspectives in Developmental Neurobiology*, 1, 93–9.

Kennedy, H., Bullier, J. and Dehay, C. 1989: Transient projection from the superior temporal sulcus to area 17 in the newborn macaque monkey. *Proceedings of the National Academy of Science of the USA*, 86, 8093–7.

Levay, S., Stryker, M.P. and Shatz, C.J. 1978: Ocular dominance columns and their development in layer IV of cat's visual cortex: a quantitative study. *Journal of Comparative Neurology*, 179, 223–44.

Maunsell, J.H.R. and Van Essen, D.C. 1983: The connections of the middle temporal visual area (MT) and their relationship to a cortical hierarchy in the macaque monkey. *Journal of Neuroscience*, 3(12), 2563–86.

McConnel, S.K., Ghosh, A. and Shatz, C.J. 1989: Subplate neurons pioneer the first axon pathway from the cerebral cortex. *Science*, 245, 978–81.

Miller, M.W. and Vogt, B.A. 1984: Direct connections of rat visual cortex with sensory, motor, and association cortices. *Journal of Comparative Neurology*, 226, 184–202.

Mishkin, M., Ungerleider, L.G. and Macko, K.A. 1983: Object vision and spatial vision: two cortical pathways. *TINS*, 6, 414–17.

Kostovic, I. and Rakic, P. 1990: Developmental history of the transient subplate zone in the visual cortex of the macaque monkey and human brain. *Journal of Comparative Neurology*, 297, 441–70.

O'Leary, D.D.M., Schlaggar, B.L. and Tuttle, R. 1994: Specification of neocortical areas and thalamocortical connections. *Annual Review of Neuroscience*, 17, 419–39.

Paulesu, E., Harrison, J., Baron-Cohen, S., Watson, J.D.G., Goldstein, L., Heather, J., Frackowiak, R.S.J. and Frith, C.D. 1995: The anatomy of coloured hearing: a positron tomography activation study of colour–word synaesthesia. *Brain*, 118, 661–76.

Payne, B.R. 1993: Evidence for visual cortical area homologues in cat and macaque monkey. *Cerebral Cortex*, 3, 1–25.

Rockland, K.S. and Pandya, D.N. 1979: Laminar origins and terminations of cortical connections to the occipital lobe in the rhesus monkey. *Brain Research*, 179, 3–20.

Shatz, C.J. and Kirkwood, P.A. 1984: Prenatal development of functional connections in the cat's retinogeniculate pathway. *Journal of Neuroscience*, 4, 1378–97.

Shatz, C.J. and Lushkin, M.B. 1986: The relationship between the geniculocortical afferents and their cortical target cells during development of the cat's primary visual cortex. *Journal of Neuroscience*, 6, 3655–68.

Shatz, C.J., Chun, J.J.M. and Lushkin, M.B. 1988: The role of the subplate in the development of the mammalian telencephalon. In A. Peters and E.G. Jones (eds), *Cerebral Cortex*, vol. 7, New York: Plenum Press, 35–8.

Sur, M. and Cowey, A. 1995: Cerebral cortex: function and development. *Neuron*, 15(3), 497–505.

Thal, D., Marchman, V., Stiles, J., Aram, D., Trauner, D., Nass, R. and Bates, E. 1991: Early lexical development in children with focal brain injury. *Brain and Language*, 40(4), 491–527.

Valverde, F., Lopez-Mascaraque, L., Santacana, M. and De Carlos, J.A. 1995: Persistence of early-generated neurons in the rodent subplate: assessment of cell death in neocortex during the early postnatal period. *Journal of Neuroscience*, 15(7), 5014–24.

Van Essen, D.C. and Gallant, J.L. 1994: Neural mechanisms of form and motion processing in the primate visual system. *Neuron*, 13, 1–10.

Winfield, D.A. 1981: The postnatal development of synapses in the visual cortex of the cat and the effects of eyelid closure. *Brain Research*, 206, 166–71.

Woo, T.U., Beale, J.M. and Finlay, B.L. 1991: Dual fate of subplate neurons in a rodent. *Cerebral Cortex*, 1, 433–43.

Zeki, S.M. 1980: The representation of colours in the cerebral cortex. *Nature*, 284, 412–18.

Part V

Clinical and Personal Perspectives

15

Synaesthesia: Possible Mechanisms

Edmund M.R. Critchley

The word synaesthesia suggests a coming together of different forms of sensation whereby a stimulus presented in one mode seems to call up imagery of another mode as readily as its own (Vernon 1937); in certain circumstances, more than two forms of imagery may be aroused by just one form of sensation.

The level of the nervous system at which synaesthesia arises remains a matter of conjecture. Three possibilities are:

1 as *cross-talk* or anastomotic branching between sensory systems, each of which can be presented as a flow diagram:
External object → Peripheral sensor → Transmission → Recognition → Perception
2 as *release phenomena* akin to hallucinations, illusions, central pain syndromes and even delusions;
3 as *interplay* between higher cerebral function: emotions, perceptions, memory and language.

All these three mechanisms are recognized anatomical and physiological occurrences and, at a subconscious level, it is not yet possible to declare dogmatically that one mechanism predominates or that other mechanisms do not interact. Each mechanism will be examined separately for a better understanding before any attempt is made to integrate them into a plausible schema.

15.1 Cross-talk Between Sensations

Definitions of sensation (or of imagery) tend to be tautological: a physical condition, experience, impression or perception resulting from stimulation of one of the senses. Even Dr Johnson could do no better than to say: 'True, Sir: but sensation is sensation.' The peripheral sensors are selective and limited in their capacities. The ear is perhaps least so. Noises, sound waves, within the human voice range and beyond, are transmitted virtually unchanged; but high-pitched sounds (dog whistles, the transmissions along telegraph wires, the rustle of mice in grass, and the sonar signals of bats) are not heard by adults. The eyes can determine the shape and colour of objects, and can even see shadows, but are oblivious to the infrared and ultraviolet parts of the spectrum. To the four traditional modalities of taste we can add '*umari*' and astringency but other tastes are wholly dependent on smell. The skin (somaesthetic sensation) can tell touch, pressure and temperature but cannot transmit sensations from geomagnetism, static electricity, x-rays or ultraviolet light.

By virtue of the fact that the central transmission from the skin involves peripheral nerves, then neurones ascending in the spinal cord to the limbic system and brain, touch rather than any other form of sensation permits a clearer and more detailed look at the various stages of transmission from end-organ to brain. There are, in the non-hairy parts of the skin, four major dissociable sensory categories – warmth, cold, touch and pain – represented by nerve endings, each of which react preferentially to one of these modalities. In addition the pattern of discharges furnishes further information. 'Specificity' and 'pattern' theories were regarded as two separate and contradictory hypotheses of transmission but it is more probable that both influence the nature of the end-organ discharge. Fibres also vary in the speed of transmission. Any single spot on the trunk is innervated by nerve fibres running into many neighbouring posterior roots; thus, as part of the process of full, normal sensibility, the stimulus–response is enhanced by an overlap of fibres from neighbouring dorsal roots providing at spinal level a background of activity termed polysynaptic facilitation.

Factors potentially relevant to the occurrence of synaesthesia, observed in the peripheral nerves and also seen in the spinal cord neurones, include variations in fibre size. Thus diseases with loss of large fibres (for example, Friedreich's ataxia and the polyneuropathy of renal failure) or of small fibres (thallium neuropathy and Fabry's disease) or localized damage to peripheral nerves, can influence which fibres will conduct and the speed of transmission. In combination with additional factors such as the influence of descending activity from higher parts of the nervous system, they was alter the 'gating' or modulation of the incoming sensory data. Damage to peripheral nerves can result in electric shorting, particularly between fibres with defective sheaths: demyelinated fibres. Not only does this occur experimentally; it also occurs to produce tingling in peripheral nerves, L'Hermitte's phenomenon of showers of electric impulses running from the neck to the back, arms or legs, and flashes of light in optic nerves affected by retrobulbar neuritis. Such 'ephaptic cross-talk' could result in a variety of stimuli being *mislocated* or *misidentified*. The presence of increased activity from efferent fibres in the same pathways can enhance peripheral cross-talk. (This used to be ascribed to increased sympathetic activity.) Furthermore, the shorting between high- and low-threshold sensory channels may contribute to the problem.

Ephapse, a term derived from the Greek to describe a *touching*, is applied to any neural site where two or more nerve cell processes, such as axons or dendrites, impinge on one another, making lateral contact without forming a synapse. At these sites there may be increased neural excitability, with either an alteration of membrane permeability, or with chemical, or electrical change. Peripheral nerve injury may instigate a series of anatomical and neurochemical adjustments. A disrupted central nerve axon may regrow, sprouting from the damaged end. The newly formed intraspinal terminal arborizations may invade new territories within a dorsal horn and at the same time fail to produce their normal neuropeptides such as substance P or calcitonin gene-related peptide. In their place different substances – neuropeptine *y*, gelanin or vasoactive intestinal peptide – may alter the milieu, provoking dramatic and prolonged responses within second-order neurones with increased production of the endogenous opioid, dymorphin (Wall and Melzack 1994).

Yet another phenomenon relevant to the way sensory inputs may be altered is *facilitation* or *inhibition* by other afferent fibres arising from the periphery; by neurochemicals such as the neuropeptides (mentioned above), and from downward fibre activity originating from higher neural centres such as the cortex or brainstem reticular formation. The consequent gating or modulation occurs at many sites including the dorsal root ganglia, substantia gelatinosa and central grey matter of the spinal cord. Slow changes in potential may spread electrotonically, producing depolarization and partially or intermittently blocking afferent impulses. Other influences acting upon the dorsal roots include on-going activity which precedes any new stimulus, descending facilitatory and inhibitory effects from the brain and segmental interneurones, local spread of activity within the substantia gelatinosa and Lissauer's tract, and a flux in the relative balance of activity between different fibre systems. Modulation is aided by the presence of opioid receptors and by small closed loops or chains of interneurones.

Within the spinal cord there is a *convergence of input* from the viscera, the skin, deep structures such as joints and muscles, and from the sympathetic nervous system. The site of a nociceptive stimulus giving rise to pain may then be misidentified or referred, thus pain derived from one part of the body is experienced in a comparatively remote area. Examples of referred pain include from the heart to the neck, jaw or arm in angina; from a rupture of the spleen to the shoulder tip, from migraine to the teeth. The explanation of referred pain lies in the diffuse nature of the localization of visceral pain entering this sensory pool from autonomic nervous system afferents, and reference is therefore made to a presumed body-schema based on the embryonic division of the body into dermatomes.

Anatomical or *spinal synaesthesia* was a term current at the turn of the century (Jones 1907). Synaesthesia has a special and distinctive meaning with respect to spinal injury or amputation of limbs. Abnormal spread of sensation can occur and a variety of terms are applied. Synchiria is the term used when a stimulus such as a pin-prick applied to the unaffected side of the body produces an unpleasant feeling bilaterally; allaesthesia or allochiria, when the stimulus is felt only over the opposite affected side; and synaesthesialgia, for a form of causalgia when a unilateral stimulus to the affected side causes pain in the unaffected side. As an extension of these definitions, synaesthesia is used where a stimulus to a normal area above the level of injury *elicits two sensations: one well localized and the other on one or both sides of the damaged area.*

In its most florid form as spinal shock, the term *diaschisis* can have little to do with spread of sensation but the damage caused may affect the manner of sensory modulation. Diaschisis consists of a suspension of activity which usually arises suddenly, affecting a widely radiating field of function. Transitory depression of function in the lower parts of the nervous system can develop when the influences from higher centres cease to be exerted, either due to their destruction or to interruption of the pathways from the higher to the lower centres (Monakow 1914). If it occurs at cortical level following a focal lesion to the brain, there may be anatomical spread along the course of the association fibres from the side of the lesion terminating in primarily uninjured grey matter affecting one or both cerebral hemispheres. The onset and regression of symptoms due to loss of irritability and cessation of function do not correspond with the usual physiological paths of innervation. Alterations may involve blood flow, cerebral oedema, inflammation or metabolism, e.g. with increases in dopamine, reduced ATP or changes in glucose. Restoration of function may be patchy, with the recovery of physiological processes, reappearance of synaptic activity and a gradual, but not necessarily complete, compensation.

The myelin sheathes of fibres provide insulation and therefore reduce the potentiality for ephaptic cross-talk between neurones. Myelination begins *in utero* but may not be completed until adult life in the association areas subserving higher intellectual function, for example, in the parietal cortex. Delayed myelination is a possible explanation of developmental dyslexia and could well explain why synaesthesia is more common in childhood than in adult life. Synaesthesia due to the build-up of reverberating circuits and diffusion between nerve fibres may well occur in the higher levels of the central nervous system of children before the major fibre tracts are insulated from each other by the appearance of myelin sheaths.

In childhood the functional development of descending inhibition from the brainstem may be lacking and many neurotransmitter and signalling molecules do not reach adult levels for a considerable time. The electroencephalogram of children is less stable than in adult life. Children are more inclined to dream, to have epilepsy and to experience difficulty in distinguishing reality from unreality, especially when somnolent.

Werner (1948) postulated that synaesthesia occurred within a primitive, undifferentiated and undeveloped state of perceptual experience which permits the linkage together of the separate realms of sensation. He went on to suggest that the facility for linking the various sensory inputs is lacking or in abeyance in the highly differentiated and objectified forms of experience of most adults.

If synaesthesia arises physiologically in the immature nervous system it is possible to presume that it can occur in the adult nervous system either as the persistence of crude sensations which the body cannot analyse – e.g. flashes of light induced by pressure on the eyeballs – or where there has been damage to part of the nervous system.

15.2 Release Phenomena

Livingston's (1943) postulate, of a multisynaptic afferent system of short spino-spinal fibres capable of setting up reverberating circuits if interfered with, has been advanced by Gerard (1951), who showed that damage, at any level of the nervous system, to nerves in synaptic connection with each other can disrupt their firing sequences. With larger neurones, small Renshaw cells normally receive small branches of the main axon and fire back upon the mother neurone to prevent further discharge. But repetitive firing may become synchronous. Synchronously firing, neurone pools may recruit additional units, move along the grey matter, and become reinforced and sustained by impulses different from and feebler than those needed to initiate them. Volleys of excessive, abnormally patterned discharges could then reach the higher centres.

Sensations seeking to reach consciousness have to overcome the modulating influence of the gate, pre-synaptic and post-synaptic inhibition, and the downflow of inhibitory impulses from higher centres. They must also compete against other sensations, some of which will convey a totally different message, but others, not necessarily within the same sensory mode, may convey an allied message. In order to overcome the varied negative influences, selected impulses from each or all the sensory organs may pass through neuronal cell assemblies (Freeman 1990; Smythies 1994). Once these neuronal circuits have built up sufficient pressure, they may fire spontaneously to alert the nervous system to the causal stimulus.

Not only do neuronal cell assemblies (NCAs) have the potential to perform basic physiological functions, but they may also on occasion be responsible for rogue firing. Examples abound: spontaneous thalamic pain may be so induced; rogue firing may cause neuralgic pains; in epilepsy, sensations of fear or pleasure can be released; dreams, after-images and many hallucinatory experiences are readily explained; in schizophrenia, the boundaries of reality are fragmented. With hallucinatory drugs a similar confusion prevails so that release phenomena more readily occur. The definitions of illusions as misinterpretations of the form of external stimuli and of hallucinations as perceptions in the absence of an external stimulus virtually beg the explanation of release phenomena. How do delusions – false beliefs impervious to reason – arise and impinge on awareness, often dictating the individual's actions? There may be no proof that synaesthesia results from the rogue behaviour of certain neural networks but there are plenty of analogies to support the suggestion.

Release phenomena have been shown to occur in hypnagogic states and when dreaming. Bursts of electroencephalographic activity originate in the pons and then proceed to the occipital cortex via the lateral geniculate nucleus. These PGO (pons geniculate occipital) spikes provide electrochemical stimulation to the visual cortex which may give rise to visual images (Harrison and Kennard 1994). Complex visual hallucinations in the elderly with eye disease (White 1980) or without (Charles Bonnet syndrome) (Damas-Mora, Skelton-Robinson and Jenner 1982) appear suddenly, briefly and without emotional overtones, usually in a discrete part of the visual field superimposed in clear consciousness on the normal scene.

Allied phenomena which may appear in a similar way are: flying or floating dreams; Lilliputian visions; musical hallucinations; and autoscopic phenomena. These phenomena may arise from cortical irritation or the release of sub-cortical activity (Berrios and Brook 1982) Autoscopic phenomena may appear in epileptic and migrainous subjects before, instead of or after an attack. The subject commonly perceives his double with more than one sense – visual, auditory, kinaesthetic, emotional – and the whole experience lasts usually a few seconds at a time (Lukianowicz 1958). Some normal individuals see flashes of light, recognizable as sharp activity on the electroencephalogram, if aroused from a dreamy state by a sharp noise. Such sound-induced hypnagogic photisms are called *Schrekblitz* and *Weckblitz*. Synaesthetic seizures may occur (Jacome and Gummit 1979). Their patient had seizures characterized by sudden pain over the right side of the face; simultaneously, he heard the word 'five' in both ears and saw the number '5' on a grey background before both eyes. These episodes occurred about ten times a month.

15.3 The Interplay of Higher Centres

So far we have considered possible pathophysiological features which may explain synaesthesia in synaesthetes, in the immature and in disease. The mechanisms already described may also account for a small number of synaesthetic incidents in normal people. It is, however, my contention that the majority of synaesthetic experiences are generated at a mental level between the primary sensory cortex and association areas, memory and the limbic system. Everyone attempts to harmonize their surroundings, bringing together sensory and emotional data, past experiences and associations, merging the inflow of sensory information into something which awakens the thought processes. Such convergence need not be at a conscious level but may arise between recognition and perception.

The reality of such interplay at a subconscious level has been demonstrated by PET (positron emission tomography) studies in synaesthetes (Paulesu et al. 1995). In normal subjects word stimulation, as expected, activated the classical language areas of the perisylvian region, but with synaesthetes a number of additional visual association areas, including the posterior inferior temporal cortex and the parieto-occipital junctions, were also activated. Other areas activated in synaesthetes included the right prefrontal cortex, insula and superior temporal gyrus. More remarkable, perhaps, was the fact that conscious visual synaesthetic experience could occur without activation of the primary visual cortex.

Even more than *déjà vu*, synaesthesia is a phenomenon which may at times be experienced by most people. In fact, our culture makes considerable play of attempting to achieve a congress of sensations in order to heighten the emotional response. We actively seek this congress. In *nouvelle cuisine*, food is placed decoratively on a plate to heighten its appeal. We close our eyes sometimes when listening to music so that the hypnagogic-like patterns may change, dance and shine, reflecting the music.

In other situations a combination of sensations may be planned, not only to increase the emotional feeling (usually of horror or of pleasure) but in such a way as to achieve the possibility of a synaesthetic effect. Thus in going to a concert we may dress particularly well in expectation, and on arrival we expect to be enthralled with the decor, the gold paint of which may reflect the silvery tones of the orchestra. Synaesthetic effects when subtly achieved do appeal to the vast majority of people, though not necessarily to the same degree in every person. Walt Disney's film *Fantasia* is an example, as are Mondrian's paintings. There are a number of factors which enhance the emotional reaction to a sensory percept: the awakening of a previous experience of memory, the degree of alertness to other stimuli such as a sense of awe on a religious occasion, the pre-existing emotional mood, and an element of suggestibility. If in the heightened tension an additional sensory mode is evoked as an unexpected splashing over of sensory impressions, a sharper, more poignant emotional response may be aroused.

Most synaesthetic experiences for the average person appear to arise at a higher mental level than the original sensation as part of the added interplay of memory, thought and emotional moods. The stimulus evoking a synaesthetic addition may arise within the original sensory mode. Thus a taste may gain appeal from a soft chewy centre; or in looking at a Kandinsky composition the impression of movement generates a further impression of noise, hence a synaesthetic reaction. The generation of literary phrases, metaphor and analogy – synaesthetic descriptions such as loud, perfumed colours; the red smell of danger; darkness, winged and stinking – may arise subconsciously, but are more usually generated at a conscious level as the apotheosis of thought.

References

Berrios, G.E. and Brook, P. 1982: The Charles Bonnet syndrome and the problem of visual perceptual disorders in the elderly. *Age and Ageing*, 11, 17–23.

Cytowic, R.E. 1989: *Synesthesia: a union of the senses.* New York: Springer Verlag.

Damas-Mora, J., Skelton-Robinson, M. and Jenner, F.A. 1982: The Charles Bonnet syndrome in perspective. *Psychological Medicine*, 12, 251–61.

Dimond, S.J., Farrington, L. and Johnson, P. 1976: Differing emotional responses from right and left hemispheres. *Nature*, 261, 690–2.

Freeman, W.J. 1990: The physiology of perception. *Scientific American*, 264(2), 78–87.

Gerard, R.W. 1951: A new theory of caualgic pain. *Anesthesiology*, 12, 1–10.

Harrison, J. and Kennard, C. 1994: The neurological boundaries of visual reality. In E.M.R. Critchley (ed.), *The Neurological Boundaries of Reality*, London: Farrand Press, 101–10.

Horowitz, M.J. 1964: The imagery of visual hallucinations. *Journal of Nervous and Mental Disease*, 138, 513–23.

Jacome, D.E. and Grummit, R.J. 1979: Synaesthetic seizures. *Neurology*, 29, 1050–3.

Jones, E. 1907: Spinal synaesthesia. *Brain*.

Kobal, G. and Hummel, T. 1991: Olfactory evoked potentials in humans. In T.V. Getchall, R.L. Doty, J. Bartostuk and J.B. Snow (eds), *Smell and Taste in Health and Disease*, New York: Raven Press, 269–70.

Livingston, W.K. 1943: *Pain Mechanisms*. New York: Macmillan.

Lukianowicz, N. 1958: Autoscopic phenomena. *AMA Archives of Neurology and Psychiatry*, 80, 199–220.

Lukianowicz, N. 1967: Body image disturbances in psychiatric disorders. *British Journal of Psychiatry*, 113, 31–47.

Melzack, R. 1989: Phantom limbs, the self and the brain. D.O. Hebb Memorial Lecture. *Canadian Psychology*, 30, 1–16.

Melzack, R. and Wall, P.D. 1965: Pain mechanisms: a new theory. *Science*, 150, 971–9.

Monakow, V. von 1914: *Die Lokalisation im Grosshirn und der Abbau der Funktion Durch Kortikale Herde*. Wiesbaden: J.F. Bergman.

Papez, J.W. 1937: A proposed mechanism of emotion. *Archives of Neurological Psychiatry* (Chicago), 38, 725–80.

Paulesu, E., Harrison, J., Baron-Cohen, S., Watson, J.D.G., Goldstein, L., Heather, J., Frackowiak R.S.J., Frith, C.D. 1995: The physiology of coloured hearing: a PET activation study of colour–word synaesthesia. *Brain*, 118, 661–76.

Sicuteri, F. 1982: Natural opioids in migraine. In M. Critchley, A.P. Friedman, S. Gorini and F. Sicuteri (eds), *Headache: physiopathological and clinical concepts*, Advances in Neurology, vol. 33. New York: Raven Press, 65–74.

Smythies, J.R. 1994: On the nature of consciousness and the unconscious from the point of view of neuroscience and neurophilosophy. In E.M.R. Critchley (ed.), *The Neurological Boundaries of Reality*, London: Farrand Press, 43–60.

Vernon, M.D. 1937: *Visual Perception*. Cambridge: Cambridge University Press.

Wall, P.D. and Melzack, R. 1994: *Textbook of Pain*, 3rd edn. Edinburgh: Churchill Livingstone.

Wells, F. 1918–19: Symbolism and synaesthesia. *American Journal of Insanity*, 75, 481–8.

Werner, H. 1948: *Comparative Psychology of Mental Development*. New York: International University Press.

White, N.J. 1980: Complex visual hallucinations in partial blindness due to eye disease. *British Journal of Psychiatry*, 136, 284–6.

16

Two Synaesthetes Talking Colour

Alison Motluk

As a synaesthete, I inhabit a world slightly different from that of the people around me – a world of extra colours, shapes and sensations. Mine is a universe of black '1's and pink 'Wednesdays', numbers that climb skywards and a rollercoaster-shaped year.

I grew up not questioning that some numbers or letters are inherently 'stronger' than others: they are, after all, endowed with bolder colours. I simply accept that certain of the alphabet's letters dominate others. These strong letters quite naturally suffuse a word with their colour, and people and places whose names start with or are made up of them seem intrinsically more commanding. For me, the proud emerald green of the city name Edinburgh triumphs over the simpering yellow of London; Kathryn is dark and woody, while Catherine is like dirty beach sand.

Devices such as these give order to my world, yet for many years I was not even conscious of them. That letters and numbers should have colours and shapes, strengths and weaknesses, and therefore be the subject of affection or disdain, seems completely normal. The astonishing realization for synaesthetes is not that these characters are imbued with colours but rather that a world could exist in which they were colour-free, neutral, characterless. It would be like finding out one day that, while you have been savouring the smells of freshly baked bread, of brandy, of chocolate, all your life, your friends have only been able to taste them. You can't believe it. You try but fail to explain how scent influences you – it is harmless, you say, yet so meaningful.

Like most synaesthetes, I grew up assuming that everyone saw numbers and letters and words in colour, as I did. In my late teens, I abruptly learned that this was not the case. I was discussing a short story with my high school English teacher, trying to explain to her why the main character's name could not be changed. It had to be a 'strong, red name'. I remember saying, appealing to reason. She was intrigued, and asked me to elaborate, but warned me that 'other people don't think that way'. It was a relief to discover almost a decade later that this was not quite true either. In the summer of 1992, I chanced upon a newspaper article about the strange condition. It had a name – and I was not the only one who had it.

There are others out there, I thought with excitement, who understand the glorious cherry red of an 'S' or the buffed black of an 'R' – and how ugly was the powdery pale blue of the letter 'P'. But, no – after thinking that everybody has it, then that nobody has it, then that some people have it, my fourth discovery was that whatever it is that we have may be similar, but it is certainly not the same. For although we share the general phenomenon, we synaesthetes completely disagree on almost every colour, texture, shape and attribute that is embodied in a given letter, number or word.

The newspaper article I saw that summer reported the investigations of a small coterie of scientists in England. They had become interested in synaesthesia after an elderly painter, Elizabeth Stewart-Jones, wrote a letter to the British Psychological Society, claiming that she had throughout her life perceived words and letters in colour. Ms Stewart-Jones, more than anyone, is responsible for setting alight scientific interest in synaesthesia. She remains in this country something of a *synaesthete extraordinaire*: each word in her vocabulary seems to have a distinct fabric of its own, often irrespective of the colours of the component letters. It is hard to say how rare this form of synaesthesia is. But at age 85, her descriptions of the colours of her words remain precise and consistent.

In the summer of 1995, I had the pleasure of meeting Elizabeth Stewart-Jones at her home in Wales. We spent a weekend discussing her lifelong condition – how the colours continue to express themselves and how synaesthesia has affected her life and her painting. During our discussions, I could not stop myself from evaluating her descriptions and experiences in the light of my own. As far as possible, though, I have tried to record Elizabeth's own lively words in describing her synaesthesia, leaving my comments and conjectures to be woven around them. Two pictures of synaesthesia emerge – hers the more precise, detailed and distinctive; mine the more common and constrained.

Elizabeth was in her seventies when she finally came around to the idea that she might be a bit unusual and should ask a question or two about her colour associations. 'I had never thought anything about it,' she confesses. She has, she says, been a synaesthete all her life. She still has a vivid early memory of picturing her infant brother's name in colour. 'I was only two,' she says decisively. 'I remember thinking of my little brother, and saw quite clearly the colour of his name, the peculiar dark red of his name. That was the first time, I suppose, that I remembered consciously picking up the colour of a name.' There are other childhood recollections – of being flustered when learning to read because the word 'cow' was grey and not brown, as she felt it ought to be, or of being distracted by the brass blobs of a striking clock as a teacher's brownish voice tried to get her attention.

Still, decades passed and Elizabeth said nothing. 'It just never struck me as anything peculiar. I just thought that was the way people *would* think,' she says. Even today, she confesses, she keeps seven differently coloured toothbrushes: one for each day of the week. 'Peculiar?' she asks, smiling.

It was her cousin who finally persuaded her to write to the BPS. In 1988, they had shared a small London gallery for an exhibition of their paintings. Beside his rather traditional watercolours. Elizabeth had hung some of her innovative 'abstract portraits'. 'Instead of doing ordinary, straightforward portraits,' she explains, 'I was painting the colour of people's names.' These were vaguely squarish splotches of colour with titles like *The Thatcher Family* and *Harold Nicolson and Vita Sackville-West*.

Her first large abstract portrait was her most elaborate. A Welsh art competition had called for works on the theme of 'Origins', which brought to Elizabeth's mind the biblical phrase: 'In the beginning was the word'. 'I flipped through the Bible and there in Matthew's gospel were the forebears of Christ. They're rather a decorative crowd. Abraham begat Isaac begat Jacob ... forty-two times.' Forty-two splotches of colour, with 'the word' represented at the top by a dark greyish smear, which fades into the paler grey of 'spirit' whisking down the right side. It hangs in her sitting room, faded but still exotic.

I ask to see her collection. We climb up to the two-room studio at the back of the house and I find spread around me, on walls and propped on shelves and cabinets, a menagerie of framed coloured patches. From amidst the colour, she plucks a classical portrait and holds it up for me to inspect. 'I keep this traditional head handy, because it shows I'm a serious painter,' she says. 'This was a model in my last year of Chelsea School of Art, way back in the '30s. I did for a good many years simply do traditional portraits before I started using my colour range.'

We turn, and in front of us is an abstract portrait of the composer Brahms juxtaposed with Rachmaninov. 'I put people together if I think they look well together,' says Elizabeth, surveying this work. She means if the colours and textures of their names, as she perceives them, look well together. They are both more or less the same shade of plummy purplish-red. Brahms is not as dark as Rachmaninov. His shape is rounder. Rachmaninov is straight-edged, pointy. And she's right: they look very nice together indeed. Except for the fact that, for me, the colours, the shapes and the textures are all wrong. The name 'Brahms' should be a flat dark postal-service blue, with only hints from the black R and the red A. 'Rachmaninov' is quite a stark black name. I say nothing.

'I don't make the colours up, you see,' she says. I know this is true. Synaesthetes are simply confronted by the colours that words or letters conjure; we do not consciously dream them up. 'I never change the colours for the sake of making a picture,' she says. 'The colours have to be what they are, or I don't do it.'

Close by is a portrait with a bland patch of grey, and beside it a much darker greyish-blue. They are almost square and set against a common backdrop. 'Here are John and Norma Major,' she announces. '"John" is a blend of greys and some blue. Different "Johns" do vary quite a bit but that's "John Major".' Decidedly grey, really – rather like the hue of his *Spitting Image*, I have to confess. 'And Norma is this shade of dark blue grey,' she continues. 'And I've just put a touch of a light sort of reddish colour which picks up the "a" in the end of her name. This is a rather curious "Major" colour, a browny-pink, which they both look quite well on, I think.'

We move on to her four grandchildren. 'That's "Meredith". I don't know why it's that colour. M is dark. But not black. But it's quite dark here. And there is the R at the beginning of "Meredith". And these sort of heather colours. I don't quite know why "Meredith" has those colours in it but it does. Rather sort of heathery red and green. That's the whole effect in my mind.'

If there is such a thing as coloured word-envy, I have it now. These are not, I realize with some defeat, very much like the rather simple colours I attach to letters and words. Mine are all smoother, with a touch of shine here, velvet there, but overall rather flat and ordinary. 'Meredith' for me, for instance, is a kind of flat grass green. But for Elizabeth it is a virtual tartan of colour; deep greens and purples intertwine and rise from the canvas. I can't help thinking how lovely a 'Meredith' wool jumper would be.

'That's "Joscelyn",' she says, pointing to another grandchild's name. 'Which is in clear blue greyish colours with these dark black, not exactly stripes but bits running through it. I like the look of that name very much. And "Emily" is this lovely strong sort of what I think of as pansy-mauvy purple. And "Pelham" I had great trouble with, because I still haven't got the right shade of yellow.'

For many synaesthetes, the colour of a word can be understood by looking at the colours of the individual letters in it. The first letter is often the most influential, dominating the colour of the word. For me, then, 'rain' is black. 'Run', 'right' and 'religion' are all black as well, because the letter R is so strikingly black. Indeed, I cannot think of a single word beginning with R that is not black, and all black words seem to be R-words. Even the word 'red', some think curiously, is a black word, while 'black' is, because of its B, blue. The black R does show up subtly further into a word; it is all that distinguishes 'friction' from 'fiction'.

One of my earliest memories of synaesthesia is how disappointed I was to learn that the name for the bit of hanging porch on a high-rise building was 'balcony' and not 'valcony', as I had thought. In one swoop, the splendid rich purple that so befits the elegance of a balcony was replaced by a darker, less romantic blue. I protested that it couldn't be right – but spelling, I soon learned, is spelling, and no amount of coloured logic can change it.

Elizabeth's vocabulary is sometimes letter-based as well. 'Some letters don't affect the word at all,' she says, 'but on the whole, some dominant ones – Ps and Ls are both very dominantly yellow – are apt to influence words. V and R are dominantly dark sort of spinach green, Ms and Ns are almost blue-blacks. A is pretty dominantly a certain shade of red.'

We speak for a moment about the colour of the name of her childhood friend, 'Auriol'. It's a soft dark pink followed by soft green-grey, says Elizabeth. 'Oriel', on the other hand, the name of a small London gallery where she is exhibiting, sounds the same, but is coloured differently, she admits. It is blackish and dark green.

Where Elizabeth differs from many of us is that the colours triggered often diverge from this pattern. 'If you asked me the colour of "horse", I'd rather think of an actual brown horse,' she explains. 'H as a letter is dark red. But it doesn't affect a word like "horse".' Well, I point out, it does for me. 'Horse' is orangey, much like the letter H. The word 'milk' is green because M is green; 'water' is a yellow word, 'bread' blue, 'olive' white, and 'snow' red.

'The sun,' proclaims Elizabeth, 'is bound to be sun-coloured.'

Not so: my 'sun' is red. Elizabeth muses that, as it happens, her S is yellow and U another shade of yellow, so the word's yellowness would not be surprising. 'N is quite dark but it doesn't affect the colour of "sun".'

For me, the difference between the homonyms 'sun' and 'son' is basically the difference between an ochre U and a white O. 'Son' is still red, just slightly less yellow-tinted. For Elizabeth, the colours are similar, but the concepts vastly different. Of son: 'One notices the O in the middle and one notices the dark N at the end. Yes, that is different – although it starts with a shade of yellow, it does soften off into a grey and blackish.'

Numbers present another interesting dilemma. In its word form, a number may differ in colour from that in its digit form. For me, for instance, the word 'three' is a dull brown. This can all be explained by the brown T, which remains relatively unaffected by the orange H, black R and green Es. The number '3', however, is pale pink.

'Three as spelt out . . . ,' says Elizabeth. 'If you're writing the whole word then it's got this dark green mixed in with it. It's quite a mixed word, with grey and brown in it. But the number itself, the figure, is quite a light reddish pink.'

Elizabeth's synaesthesia is also exceptional because of the intricacies of the colours and patterns woven into her words. Her descriptions of her grandchildren's names serve as examples. Consider these words too. 'Sweden' is 'yellowish with touches of brown green'. 'Joy' is 'tones of clear pale blue grey'; 'thought' 'dark grey with an indication of white (not the colour white so much as a touch of no colour) and a tinge of dark blue grey and a touch of black'; 'thankfulness' a 'darkish red and a touch of dark purplish brown'.

Overall, I am disturbed by the colours Elizabeth assigns to letters and words. She confesses she feels the same about my choices. '"Fear"? Orange for you? Oh, is it! How odd. No. That has no connection.' The colours perceived by other synaesthetes have so little connection, in fact, that, like unwanted radio signals, they are immediately jammed from my mind. As soon as Elizabeth describes her colour for a word, I replace it in my mind with my own.

Still, I am amused by our different catalogues of colour. With 26 letters, scores of numbers, names of months and days all to be tinted, how is it that I have excluded some very beautiful shades from my repertoire? For example, Elizabeth sees the words 'James', 'Friday', 'six' and 'Nicholas' in variations of the same strong clean pinky-orangey red; yet I never see this shade. For me, no word, number of letter is coloured by it.

Those colour disagreements make our commonalities all the more sweet. For Elizabeth, both I and O can be pale, almost colourless. They are both very distinctly white for me. (For her, they swing back and forth from white to black, however.) Number 1 for her is black; for me also. Most peculiar, though, is our identical way of describing U as yellow ochre, the colour of a particular shade of oil paint. I remember more than a decade ago, during my brief flirtation with oil painting, recognizing the colour of U in a tube of dirty-yellow-coloured paint. Even more intriguing, Elizabeth and I are not alone in seeing the colours of I, O and U as we do. Across time and culture, many synaesthetes have reportedly perceived them this way.

We muse as well about other languages. Elizabeth says that French words are more apt to be dark, in blues and blacks and purples. Italian words show up more in brick-yellows. I made an odd observation a few years ago, when two friends I had met in Russia, and whose names I'd first learned in Russian, transplanted themselves to Canada, where I started to see their names transliterated into English. The name 'Sergei' in English is a red name, because of the red S. In Russian, where the first letter looks like a C, the same name is silvery-brown. Ditto for 'Sveta' – red in English and pale brown with a touch of blue as spelt in Russian.

The peculiarities of synaesthesia go on and on. Not only are our alphabets and numbers endowed with colour, but they are often positioned on grids or patterns. 'Letters come down from the top, numbers go up,' says Elizabeth, drawing a pattern in the air. By contrast, my letters stretch in an earth-hugging arch away from me; numbers go up in a straight line.

Elizabeth's numbers, it turns out, do more than just go up: they are fixed in an elaborate zigzag. 'From black 1, it swings up to the left to a grey 2 and then goes up from 3, which is this sort of raspberry colour. Up through 4 and 5, yellow five, and 6, 7 and 8. Then the 9 swings in a little bit, brown, to get to 10, which is a certain reddish colour . . . Then up gradually through the different colours to 20, where you swing right across to the right to 30, which is sort of plummish red. Then from there up to the dark rather metallic sort of blackish blue of 40, up through the yellows of 50.' And so on.

Time also adheres to a pattern. The year, the week, the day may each have shapes, and the synaesthete may slide or climb along the configuration in time, or perch at a favourite point to view the months or hours as they pass. Elizabeth's week is elliptical in shape and proceeds clockwise.

'I'm generally looking at it from Saturday, which is quite a long strip, a yellowish colour. On my left is Sunday, which is a much greener yellow, and turns the corner at the end of the elliptical shape. It then swings round to the blue-black Monday, and then there's Tuesday, which is sort of raspberry pink. Wednesday's very dark blue, and Thursday's a much paler brighter blue. By now, you're at the right-hand end of the elliptical shape. Friday's quite a clear strong tomato colour, rather more orange than tomato. And then that swings round the right-hand end of the elliptical shape, because it's lying flat, and turns into the yellow, sort of banana yellow of Saturday.'

The year is clockwise and circular for Elizabeth. Each month, not surprisingly, has its own distinct colour. She moves through the months in an anti-clockwise circle. My year is quite different – like a perpetual, but forward-moving roller-coaster. The ride begins at the New Year. Early in January, I feel myself sweeping down a steep decline, quickly past February and March, through April, and into the more moderate curve of early summer. The main summer months, July and August, are flat along the bottom; I do not start to climb again until September. Up, slowly, steeply up, till I reach the pinnacle of December again.

We are still in Elizabeth's studio. One of my favourite paintings has to be the one with a blanket of plummy red Brahms interrupted by little clouds of whitish grey. Elizabeth calls it *And she coughed all through the Brahms*. 'I remember it happening quite well,' she says. 'I was at a concert and the colour of the cough just broke into the colour of the music and I found that aggravating. So I jotted it down into a picture.'

It is a peculiar picture because it shows how Elizabeth associates Brahms's music more with the man's name than with the actual pieces he composed. She had in the past tried to paint the actual sounds of a piece of music, but was overwhelmed by the cacophony of colour. 'I remember when I was about sixteen thinking I would try and paint the colour of a Beethoven symphony that I was listening to. But it was far too confusing because the colour of the word "Beethoven" overlay the music. And anyhow, the details of the music are far too intricate, I found, to make any clear, straightforward colour of it. So I never tried again to paint music.'

Her sense of what colour a certain piece of music is may be less precise than her sense of the colours of words, letters and numbers, but she does nevertheless have some music-to-colour associations. I have none. She can generalize: 'Instrumental music is in the brown range because of the colour of the wooden instruments. Piano is blues and greys. But isn't that partly because of the keyboard?' she ponders.

And it is not quite true that she never again tried to paint music. She did a particularly beautiful painting called *Everyone Sang*. In it, the colours of men's deep voices gradually give way to those of women. 'I think women's voices are always blue,' says Elizabeth. 'Men's voices are in the browns, the basses and baritones. Tenor's a different, a lighter tone of brown. Basses are darker browns. So, a choirboy, a very high choirboy is practically white. Bound to be. But a contralto woman will be quite thick and blue. Different shade of blue. But I should have thought that everybody was bound to see it like that.'

Colour clearly extends beyond her vocabulary into the world of sounds. 'Any sound is a colour, you see,' she says. 'If a doorbell rings, it's instantly a colour. Or if there's a bang on the floor, or something, it's a colour. Or if a dog barks – anything, it just automatically is coloured.'

Are you glad you have synaesthesia, or does it just complicate your life? This must be one of the most common questions asked. It is rather like asking whether someone is glad to have the sense of smell. Does it add to your life or confuse you? On the whole, most of us cannot really imagine life without it; we even feel a bit sorry for those who do not have it. But we take it entirely for granted.

'I suppose I find it quite a help if I'm trying to think of somebody's name or a telephone number, or something,' says Elizabeth. 'Just occasionally, if I think I'm doing something at a certain time on a certain day, I might get the colours confused and get the colour of the day and then the colour of the time back to front. So I have to be a bit careful. That can be a little bit of a muddle. Occasionally. But not very often.'

Index